The Practitioner's
Guide to Mediation

The Practitioner's Guide to Mediation

A Client-Centered Approach

Stephen K. Erickson
and
Marilyn S. McKnight

John Wiley & Sons, Inc.

New York • Chichester • Weinheim • Brisbane • Singapore • Toronto

ISBN 0-471-35368-X

Contents

The Practitioner's Guide to Mediation

CHAPTER 1

What Is Mediation?

INTRODUCTION

THIS BOOK is written for professionals who provide help to couples and children in the midst of divorce. The professionals who provide this help include therapists, psychologists, school social workers, family law attorneys, tax accountants, corporate attorneys, juvenile court workers, custody investigators, marriage counselors, clergy, and judges. This book is also for anyone who experiences the devastating impact of divorce on families and wants to do something about it. To benefit from this book, you should have an open mind and a willingness to entertain new ways of thinking.

This book is also written for professionals who want to control the emotional and financial costs of conflict in their workplaces, their organizations, or their lives. The chapter on employment and other applications of the mediation process not only provides a detailed glimpse inside the working mind of a mediator but should also stimulate new thinking inside the mind of the reader. If you are an employee or manager considering mediation to resolve an employment dispute, you will want to choose a mediator who can effectively provide the type of help needed in order to prevent the conflict from becoming destructive. This book will give you the information you need to select the right mediator as well as to select the right mediation process. Finally, if you are considering becoming a mediator, this book is must reading before you choose a training program.

Chapter 1 encourages you to think of mediation not as something new, but rather as a new way of thinking. It provides a blueprint for becoming a mediator and discusses the almost endless opportunities for someone considering mediation as an addition to their existing professional practice or as a stand-alone profession.

Chapter 2 lays out the steps and the conceptual framework for a client-centered model of mediation, followed by a detailed description, in Chapter 3, of what goes on inside the mediation room and of the mediator's role in managing the people and the conflict. Because client-centered mediation is a distinct form of mediation that differs from labor mediation or other types of law-focused approaches to mediation, it is important to understand these differences to benefit from the tremendous power of this model of mediation.

Because divorce mediation was essentially the starting point for the mediation movement in the early 1970s, Chapter 4 takes a closer look at divorce, family, and custody mediation. Divorce mediation confronts one of the most difficult conflicts that exist on earth, the breakdown and ending of the intimate, complex marriage relationship. Understanding the reasons for divorce mediation's emergence, why it caught hold, and why it is such a growing field permits some exciting forecasting about the future of other mediation applications as well as the future of the legal adversarial system.

Chapter 5 describes other applications of client-centered mediation. Walk with the mediator into a workplace conflict mediation, and to a school closing dispute that brings out the entire town to see how the power of a client-centered model of mediation can promote healing and resolution of these problems.

Chapters 6 and 7 explain how to get trained as a mediator and how to build a mediation practice. Both chapters help sort out the many choices faced by the professional who sees the benefit of learning and applying mediation skills. Chapter 8 closes with some dos and don'ts about ethics, accountability and practical pitfalls, and a look at the potential impact of mediation on society in the future.

As you begin to read this book it is important to know how it has been structured. Because it is written by two authors, it is written in the first person plural, *we*, and possessive, *our*. *We* and *our* refer to both authors as mediation practitioners. It is also written to you, the reader. It addresses you directly, and also speaks about people, couples, spouses, children, and other mediators by referring to them in the third person, either singular, plural, or possessive, or as participant(s) or party (parties). Erickson Mediation Institute is the authors' mediation practice or business and is referred to as the institute.

We believe you will appreciate what follows. We have included as much actual dialogue as is possible from our cases. Although the people discussed are real, the names and details of the cases are changed to avoid identifying our clients, and the events and dialogue described all actually happened. We hope that through the experiences of the people described and through our attempt to define this new way of thinking, you will be encouraged and motivated to embark on the journey toward becoming a mediator.

MEDIATION IS NOT NEW; IT IS A NEW WAY OF THINKING

Mediation is not really new. It is as old as the new testament and perhaps older. The Greek word for mediate means to stand between. People have always known that standing between two people in conflict can be helpful. What *is* new is that mediation has been rediscovered as a replacement for many of the present methods of addressing adversarial conflict. The mediation method encourages cooperating with and helping your adversary. This new way of thinking is gaining a foothold, not only in conflict resolution theory, but also in business.

Tim McGuire, the editor of the *Minneapolis Star Tribune* describes why his newspaper decided to cooperate with another newspaper that it perceived as a competitor:

> One of the most intriguing books I've read in recent years is *New Rules for the New Economy*, by the executive Editor of *Wired* magazine, Kevin Kelly. Kelly pokes holes in scores of traditional business principles in a way that is bound to leave business people who are products of the industrial age scratching their heads. Perhaps the most challenging of Kelly's contentions is that we should embrace our competitors. (McGuire, 1999)

Embracing or helping one's competitors is at the heart of this new way of thinking that is called mediation. Indeed, embracing competitors was at the heart of Reconstruction after the Civil War and it was the principle behind the Marshall Plan after World War II.

Bill Ury (1993) illustrates this concept in his book, *Getting Past No* with the following story:

> During the American Civil War, Abraham Lincoln made a speech in which he referred sympathetically to the Southern Rebels. An elderly lady, a staunch Unionist, upbraided him for speaking kindly of his enemies when he ought to be thinking of destroying them. His reply was classic: "Why madam," Lincoln answered, "do I not destroy my enemies when I make them my friends?" (p. 171)

The concept of helping instead of destroying an adversary is what forms the basis of the present increased interest in mediation and the study of co-operation. It also forms the core of this book. Only since the mid-1970s have we begun to study earnestly and experiment with more constructive ways to resolve conflict. By looking closer at mediation and all its forms, we have discovered that when people in conflict participate in a cooperative journey guided by a mediator, they begin to experience a healing and transforming of their relationships. The transforming is an empowering event for most people. The participants will have worked through perceived personal or strategic weaknesses to own a good solution for themselves. This generates authentic personal growth and strength for the participants. As they take this journey, they are changed by their interaction with each other and with the mediator. This change is made possible by what we call new thinking, but it requires shedding some old baggage. Specifically, it requires us to adopt the radical and unpopular notion that nothing works until we accept the fact that we must help our adversary.

BLUEPRINT FOR BECOMING A MEDIATOR

Our main goal in this book is to provide a detailed blueprint for how the behavioral science practitioner, the lawyer as well as other professionals, can expand their professional practice by either adding mediation services to an existing practice or by moving into mediation as a full-time career. Therapists, counselors, and lawyers are the most common group of professionals to become mediators. At this time, because there are no regulations limiting the field to only those professions, many successful mediators come from other backgrounds. In fact, accountants who have traditionally given only accounting advice are now becoming trained as mediators in order to provide more comprehensive services when they advise boards or other multiple parties who often experience conflict. Managers find that having mediation training on their resumes enhances their possibilities for promotions and, perhaps, most exciting of all, schools have embraced mediation by formal programs that train children to become peer mediators. It is just as important for professionals who do not wish to become mediators to be knowledgeable about mediation in order to best serve their clients' interests by making competent referrals to skilled mediators. Law schools are teaching their students that the use of mediation will become an integral part of the future practice of law. Practicing lawyers increasingly find that more and more clients are asking them about mediation. Therapists are finding that their counseling skills are a good platform for learning divorce mediation skills and serving a new group of clients. Other professionals, such as accountants and educators, who serve divorcing families are interested in becoming mediators. Even if one never intends to practice as a mediator, understanding and applying the mediation concepts in this book will forever change the thinking of the practicing attorney, therapist, or other professional when serving divorcing families. Finally, for the consumer of legal, therapeutic, or mediation services, this book is written in a manner that does not require advanced degrees to understand. In many ways, traditional academic learning is no guarantee of achieving an understanding about mediation. In some cases it may be a hindrance.

Before considering mediation as part of your practice, it is important to have a clear understanding of not only the process of mediation but also its tremendous potential for changing the way people interact. What really is mediation? Why is it needed? Who can become a mediator? How can you incorporate mediation into your practice? Are there any pitfalls? These are just some of the questions that will be discussed in this book.

This book also sets forth a conceptual framework for client-centered mediation by examining, in detail, the role of the mediator and the skills used by a mediator in the mediation room.

MEDIATION'S BRIGHT FUTURE

We believe that mediation will continue to be a strong alternative to conventional legal proceedings and the need for competent mediators will continue to grow. Several reasons for this optimism exist.

LITIGATION DOES NOT WORK

The public has lost confidence in the integrity of the court system, because litigation is not serving its needs. Not only is there a growing backlash against litigation, but also against the entire lawyer-managed system of conflict resolution. For many people, their first encounter with the legal system is through a divorce struggle or by knowing someone going through divorce. Many come to realize that the litigation system is responsible for breeding much of the ill will and fall-out that contaminates postdivorce families and postdivorce functioning. There are many trends that point to a rapid change in attitude on the part of the public. All family courts are reporting a dramatic increase in the number of *pro se* (unrepresented) litigants. More and more state courts are mandating mediation before clients can enter into a legal adversarial divorce. Family mediators also report an increase in the number of clients who actively seek divorce mediation assistance through yellow-page ads, Internet searches, and referrals from clergy and therapists. Although a certain number of people are ordered into mediation by the family court, a growing number of couples have heard about mediation and seek it on their own. An interesting trend reported by many mediators is that a small but growing number of couples use mediation to strengthen and preserve their marriage relationship particularly when financial or other issues not typically addressed in a therapeutic setting are at the core of the couple's relationship dysfunction. In the future, mediation may serve the ongoing marriage in much the same way therapy and counseling now attempt to strengthen the marriage relationship.

Adding strength to the observation that the public is tiring of litigation and lawyer-managed conflict resolution procedures is the growing use of mediation in workplace, business, and community disputes. Practicing mediators report heightened interest in mediation on the part of human resource executives looking for ways to reduce the time and cost of workplace litigation. Many companies are adding a clause to their employee manuals requiring attempts at mediation before grievance procedures or formal hearing procedures can be commenced. We seem to be entering a period of experimentation with many types of mediation applications. In the far northern town of Grand Rapids, Minnesota, a mediator is present in court every Thursday to mediate harassment cases. In the U.S. Postal System each day, in quiet back rooms of post offices around the country, law suits involving Equal Employment Opportunity Commission claims are being mediated under the Postal Services REDRESS program (Resolve Employment Disputes Reach Equitable Solutions Swiftly) instead of being litigated.

Large segments of the public are already searching for better ways to resolve their disputes and are looking to mediators instead of attorneys for these answers.

For those few people who are bold enough to become mediators, business is brisk. No longer is it necessary to implore people to try mediation. In fact, mediators who have Web sites report more people searching for mediation services. In our early years, we had to convince people to use mediation. Now, it is more common for people to interview several mediators; because they are already committed to using mediation, they are merely searching for the right one.

Traditional beliefs about using the court system are rapidly changing. In this changing world, there are fewer and fewer true adversaries. We are beginning to see that we are all linked in some way to each other. Although there is still some of the old Wild West mentality of staring the opponent down with a threatening lawsuit, more and more, people and corporations are finding that such tactics are costly and such tactics contaminate the business relationship. (Remember Tim McGuire's words about needing to embrace and cooperate with our adversaries.) Moreover, as we move toward a global economy, the court system in the United States will become increasingly viewed as antiquated and not capable of providing quick answers to the needs of parties. The Internet business philosophy basically is built on trust, and it is fascinating to see how e-commerce is transferring billions of dollars of goods without detailed legal contracts signed in triplicate.

Traditional beliefs about how divorce should occur are also rapidly changing, giving rise to the increased use of divorce and family mediation. Fault (i.e., who caused the marital breakdown) is no longer a factor to consider in most states. In almost all states, there is an increase in the number of couples experimenting with equal time sharing of the children. This trend, advised by professionals and supported by the divorcing public, is an indication that many want an end to the battle mentality of divorce. The traditional divorce, which awarded custody to mothers and made dads visitors to their own children, is no longer the status quo. Instead, couples are sharing their parenting responsibilities equally after the divorce and competition for physical and legal custody has become less important. How each parent can get assistance and support from the other parent is more important than who will have custody. Because both parents usually work full time to survive financially, they realize that they need to cooperate to cover all the emotional, physical, and financial needs of their children.

> **Mediation works better than the court system in high-conflict relationships because mediation addresses the underlying causes of conflict.**

In high-conflict spousal-abuse situations, the legal adversarial system has failed to address the underlying causes of abuse. The occurrence of spousal abuse seldom results in a termination of parental rights of the abusive spouse. After all the court battles are over, after all of the protective orders have expired, after professionals are no longer in the picture, both parents will still have a visitation order and a relationship with each other through their children. Client-centered divorce mediation does a better job of resolving the high-conflict spousal-abuse cases because it helps the couple build internal controls that address the underlying anger, chemical abuse, or control issues that create the conflict. External court orders do a poor job of addressing these issues. The adversarial system most often increases the level of conflict, further alienating the parents, and thereby harming the children. Client-centered mediation offers the opportunity for parents to learn the elements of cooperative behavior by helping them jointly agree to ground rules about their future conduct to ensure the protection of each. When the ground rules are established by the couple in the safety of the mediation room, these rules are more likely to be followed. Mediation for spousal-abuse couples has proved safe when the necessary protocols are followed, such as continuing a protection order, asking that attorneys be present at some of the mediation sessions, and taking agreed-upon precautions when danger signs begin to surface.

In any high-conflict relationship dispute, client-centered mediation does a better job of addressing the underlying causes of the conflict. The

Postal Service's REDRESS program found that "Half of all respondents, including most managers, report the process changed the way they dealt with conflict, and a significant majority (74% of all respondents and 92% of supervisors) report mediation to be better than the traditional EEO process" (Anderson & Bingham, 1997).

> **Mediation is not bound by the rules or restrictions of any existing professions.**

Mediation is emerging as a separate and distinct profession. It has not been appropriated by the legal profession as a subspecialty of the practice of law (and, therefore, it is not controlled by the judicial system) and it has not become a subspecialty of social work or psychology. Some universities and colleges are creating new majors and master's degrees in conflict resolution that are not part of any existing department. It will continue to incorporate the best aspects of the fields of behavioral science, law, and, also, just plain common sense. As with any emerging field, the opportunities are greatest for those who possess the foresight to climb aboard early.

CONSIDERING MEDIATION AS A PROFESSIONAL PRACTICE

There are two groups of people from other professions who clearly would make good mediators: mental health professionals and family law attorneys.

MENTAL HEALTH PROFESSIONALS

Therapists and other mental health practitioners make good mediators because

- They already serve couples and individuals in the midst of personal turmoil;
- They are comfortable working in the midst of conflict;
- They are knowledgeable about human behavior, and psychological theory;
- They can easily learn some of the legal information needed to practice

as divorce, civil, and employment mediators, or community dispute resolution facilitators;
- They see conflict not as a win-lose proposition but rather as an opportunity for healing and closure;
- They understand many of the intervention tools such as listening, reframing, and uncovering underlying needs and interests.

Mental health professionals, particularly marriage and family therapists accustomed to working with families, make ideal mediators because of their training and experience in working with people in conflict. When they enter the field of divorce mediation, they find they already possess many of the necessary skills to become divorce mediators. Children of divorced parents who experience adjustment difficulties usually are first seen by child psychologists or clinical social workers. Individual marriage partners may seek counseling for their own stress and find that the problems are rooted in the marriage relationship. Therapists also serve divorcing couples by assisting them in marriage closure and divorce adjustment. Specialists in child therapy evaluate the effects of divorce on children and make recommendations about postdivorce parenting. In these ways, mental health practitioners are already deeply involved in the divorce process of couples, individuals, and children.

The appealing aspect of divorce mediation for counselors, therapists, clinical social workers, or psychologists is that they are already experienced in addressing high conflict and, in general, have acquired skills that enable them to function well in a room filled with intense marital stress. In the past, though, few therapists have offered to help the divorcing couple resolve parenting, property, and support issues created by divorce, no doubt because these issues have always been considered to be solely the province of divorce attorneys. Because the issues of children, housing, money, and resolution of conflict are now being seen more as mental health-related issues than legal issues, they should be addressed by people who are skilled at reducing the conflict rather than by people skilled at using the adversarial rules of engagement. With the advent of divorce mediation, the therapist can now urge the couple to use mediation and can refer the couple to supportive *advisory* attorneys who represent the husband and wife instead of referring them to aggressive lawyers who manage the battle in the adversarial system.

Many therapists have found that adding mediation training to their therapy practice is a better way to serve the entire divorcing family. They can treat the entire family as their clients, including the children, who are not always present. They have learned that the role of a mediator is very different from the role of a therapist, something that is seldom addressed in clinical training. Although the two roles are complementary, they must clearly differentiate between the two if they plan to offer both. As later chapters spell out, mediation is distinct from the practice of law and distinct from the practice of therapy.

The mental health professional as mediator has a wealth of knowledge and training about family systems, human behavior, and psychological theory to bring to the practice of mediation. At the same time, the mental health professional has much to learn about mediator neutrality, impartiality, and client self-determination in mediation practice, as well as the laws impacting parenting, financial support, and property division. In the short history of the field, mediators with backgrounds in therapy, counseling, and psychology have made up a large segment of the practitioners who work as mediators.

Some therapists have told us months after a mediation training that they have to unlearn many of their therapy techniques in order to master mediation. Although they begin to gain a deeper respect for accepting what the clients believe is best for them, therapists will learn that they can still question a client about those choices and beliefs without giving a cue that, as mediators, they believe the client's choices are unhealthy or detrimental. Mediators do not have to become overly invested in ensuring that the clients make responsible choices for themselves as long as the model of mediation used encourages each spouse to be represented by an attorney. In fact, one of the most liberating things to unlearn is the myth that people cannot be trusted to make good decisions for themselves. When they are provided a safe and cooperative mediation environment in which to make those decisions, they usually are quite able to make informed lasting decisions that meet their needs.

In order for therapists to become divorce mediators, they need to first consider their own feelings and biases about divorce. Therapists must adopt a different way of thinking and learn the power of being neutral even when they may know what is best for the children. If they have practiced as custody evaluators in contested divorces, they might feel a need to advise parents about what is best for their children. Becoming a mediator requires learning the difference between telling someone something they *should* do and reframing *advice* as an idea or option for the parents to consider. Learning to operate from the mediator's perspective when you are a therapist is a new exercise in control and mental gymnastics. It is like leaving the perfect gift at the door in hopes it will be discovered and used, and if it isn't, allowing it to go unused.

In divorce mediation, the practitioner directs the process and leads the couple through the steps necessary to reach agreement about parenting, support, and property division. The couple comes to mediation with the goal of getting a divorce. If divorce is counter to your own beliefs, especially when you believe the couple could perhaps survive their differences and stay married, you need to decide if you can help them mediate their divorce.

Moreover, it is not appropriate to ask or consider traditional therapist questions such as assessing their *appropriateness* for divorce, or their *appropriateness* to enter mediation. These are decisions to be made by the couple, not the mediator. A mediator's own personal doubts about whether the couple should divorce or whether they should be in mediation are not pertinent. Even in the most violent situations, such as nonreciprocal spousal abuse, mediators must overcome their own concerns about clients' *appropriateness* for mediation when, after in-depth screening and imposition of safety protocols, the couple chooses to mediate. This is counter to the beliefs of some battered-women's organizations and courts that still insist mediation is absolutely not appropriate for any couple when there has been a history of nonreciprocal abuse.

A therapist learning to become a divorce mediator sometimes questions clients' readiness for divorce. Such a question only gets mediators in trouble. Usually when couples begin a divorce process, one spouse is always more interested in proceeding with the divorce than the other. This difference in readiness is explained more fully in Chapter 3. The following discussion distinguishes between the readiness to divorce and the readiness to mediate. Chapter 3 illustrates that spouse A is the partner, who during the period of the marital breakdown, was the first to consider divorce and did so for quite some time. Then, perhaps after a period of months or years, spouse A makes a personal, private decision to divorce long before letting spouse B know of the decision. This common scenario sets up a situation in which, at the time of divorce, spouse A has had more time to think about and adjust to the decision to divorce. Meanwhile, spouse B may believe that things were getting better because spouse A was emotionally detached, no longer engaged in arguments or fights with spouse B. Spouse B interpreted this as, "Maybe things are getting better in our marriage." Obviously, when these two people enter the mediation consultation, they are in conflict. Spouse A does not understand why spouse B is so angry. Spouse B does not understand why spouse A wants to get a divorce. A therapist as mediator may feel that spouse B is not ready to mediate a divorce because spouse B is so distraught, angry, or deeply hurt. Spouse B may insist that they are not *ready to divorce*. The problem with this assessment approach is that spouse A is not waiting for spouse B to be emotionally *ready* for divorce. Spouse A can always have an attorney serve spouse B with litigation papers and neither the attorney nor the process server will ask, "Is the other emotionally *ready* for this divorce?" Spouse B, although in denial, does actually know about the problems in the marriage, and may even have heard spouse A say he or she is getting a divorce! Therefore, when both husband and wife show up for a divorce mediation consultation, the therapist as mediator needs to assume that spouse B is aware that the divorce is moving forward. Perhaps a more realistic view of the entire problem of readiness for any divorce process is to assume that couples are always more ready to engage in a more humane process such as mediation, rather than in an adversarial process that can be devastating to the family.

As previously noted, the therapist learning to mediate possesses a wealth of knowledge and experience that is consistent with the practice of mediation. They also have developed the important people skills from their experience of interacting with clients professionally. Thus, for mental health professionals entering the field, mediation is really a natural progression in career development. Therapists already understand and know how to assist couples and individuals in resolving their dysfunctional behavior. The therapist as a mediator understands basic skills such as eye contact, clarification, reframing, interested curiosity, respect, and rapport building, to name a few. Add the concept of neutrality, learning information about family finance, budgeting, and net worth, and the therapist has a very good start at becoming an excellent mediator. Going a step further and learning more about mediating the things of the dissolution, such as assets, liabilities, budgets, and support, allows the therapist to build upon skills already possessed.

In summary, a mental health practitioner is ideally suited to become a divorce mediator. However, some traits or typical ways of acting as a therapist are not helpful to the process of becoming a mediator. Therapists must be willing to unlearn the following tendencies:

- Advising what is best for clients;
- Being too directive;
- Delving too far into past history;
- Assessing who is appropriate and who is not appropriate for divorce or for divorce mediation;
- Making a diagnostic assessment of each spouse's pathology;
- Trying to save marriages.

At the same time, mental health professionals must be willing to learn the following traits or tendencies that are unique to the role of mediator:

- Appreciating the value of being neutral;
- Being nonjudgmental and nondirective;
- Functioning with multiple parties in the room;
- Sharing observations about the conflict;
- Guiding without pushing;
- Helping each spouse step into the shoes of the other;
- Helping the couple create mutual respect for the needs of the other;
- Managing the process in the midst of high conflict.

FAMILY LAW ATTORNEYS

Many family law attorneys make good divorce mediators and are quite able to make the transition from advocacy to mediation because:

- The attorney knows and understands divorce laws and the limitations of those laws;
- The attorney has seen first hand the destructive aspects of court litigation and wants to do something to change the system of divorce;
- The attorney has a capacity to focus on the numbers and the details of divorce as well as an ability to anticipate future problems due to experience in resolving postdivorce problems;

- The attorney knows and can see both sides of the issues. This can make it easier to respect client self-determination and to act as a neutral for both sides;
- The attorney understands the concepts of questioning and bargaining.

The lawyer who legally represents a husband or wife in a divorce is familiar with the laws of the state, with how to draft and present a legal case in court, and can generally understand the various types of settlement options that are used to resolve typical divorce questions. However, this skill is only a small piece of the overall divorce puzzle. Most family law attorneys bring other helpful skills to the task of learning divorce mediation. The family law attorney has seen both sides of divorce, from the wife's perspective and from the husband's perspective, often making it easier to learn neutrality. Many lawyers attending mediation training programs have also seen the destructive impact of the adversarial process on families. Lawyers practicing family law seem to be in one of two camps: Either they are caught in the competitive game of winning the fight, believing that strong advocacy is the proper way to resolve divorce disputes; or they recognize the havoc this adversarial process creates for families, particularly children, and they seek mediation as a new profession or as a way to humanize their law practice.

Lawyers who look to mediation as a new profession or as an addition to their legal practice are generally deeply concerned about the negative impact of adversarial divorce on parents and children. Such lawyers will see mediation as a better method of settling marriage dissolution issues and they are usually open to learning client-centered mediation. A few lawyers view mediation only as a new revenue producer. These lawyers will often bypass training or adopt a very authoritative advisory process that evaluates the couple's situation, tells them what the courts are likely to do, then advises them on how they should settle. We call this directive approach a *lawyerized* model of mediation akin to one lawyer legally representing both parties in a divorce. An even greater problem with this lawyerized model of mediation is that it seldom addresses the underlying conflicts and often does not result in lasting settlements.

Family law attorneys are experienced in developing client budgets and creating support arrangements with minute details of how they will be implemented. They have knowledge about the various ways of valuing the marital estate, dividing the assets and liabilities, and proposing buyouts of spousal maintenance. Because family law attorneys are expected to protect individual clients in divorce and postdivorce issues, they are usually well acquainted with the settlement options available to them. Their expertise serves them well as mediators because they do not have to relearn this information in mediation training. They also can anticipate future problems because they have litigated issues not anticipated by spouses in divorce.

The lawyer most successful with client-centered divorce mediation is often the one who recognizes that there are always two sides to the story; each spouse has his or her own perspective. This lawyer also knows that by listening for areas of mutual interests in the clients' stories, they will find options that create their own mutually beneficial solutions. By assisting husbands and wives to find their own solutions by confronting the underlying conflict, each spouse will create solutions that are fair and equitable. The same lawyer may have an undergraduate degree in one of the behavioral sciences and understands that issues are really more complex than dealing with simple facts and legal truths. Such a lawyer understands clients' deep feelings of guilt, loss, fear, and desire for fairness. Some family lawyers have attended our initial divorce mediation training course and have concluded that it would not be possible to return to the practice of law. Not every lawyer who learns about client-centered divorce mediation has this revelation, but there is usually some transformation the attorney undergoes to become a successful client-centered mediator. The mediation process requires a new and different way of thinking and of practicing law.

The family lawyer also enters the divorce mediation profession understanding concepts of questioning and bargaining. Because lawyers learn how to ask questions in their legal training, they can also understand the power of asking open-ended questions in mediation. Instead of using the legal tactics of positional bargaining, they need to learn to focus on interests as the basis of the negotiation process in mediation. For many who understand the elements of the battle, it is easy to turn 180 degrees from the battlefield and help couples find peaceful settlement.

There are certain traits that a family lawyer needs to unlearn in order to be a good client-centered mediator. For the lawyer entering the divorce mediation field, the most important roadblock to overcome will be the tendency to be directive or to make judgments about each client's behaviors or motivations. The lawyer needs to learn to listen for clients' agreements, not their mistakes or weaknesses; to listen for opportunities for growth, not the shortcomings or misbehaviors to attack; and to see conflict as an opportunity for clients to grow and learn, not to see conflict as negative. The lawyer needs to discard the adversarial philosophy that justice emerges out of the good fight and that winning at the expense of the other creates acceptable solutions. In order to become a client-centered mediator, the lawyer must abandon the notion that the building blocks of settlement are blame and fault leading to winners and losers emerging from the competition of good, zealous advocacy.

In summary, lawyers must unlearn or discard the following tendencies they may have acquired over decades of practicing law:

- Believing that the law is the only standard of fairness that can be applied;
- Viewing everything as either right or wrong;
- Believing that clients are not capable of making informed, correct decisions;
- Believing that justice emerges out of the good fight;
- Assuming that most people are incapable of taking care of themselves, even after they have been given the opportunity to consult counsel and know the cost of the decision they are making.

Lawyers who invest the time and effort in learning to become client-centered mediators will learn the following:

- To make different use of their skills in framing and presenting questions;
- To learn and appreciate some of the skills employed by the behavioral science professionals such as reframing, empathy, and creating empowerment;
- To see the power of neutrality as opposed to advocacy;
- To trust the innate intelligence of each client;
- To see people change on their own and not as a result of some court directive.

NOT ALL MEDIATORS PRACTICE CLIENT-CENTERED MEDIATION

Mediation is a method of resolving conflicts outside of the traditional litigation model of conflict resolution. Most conceptual frameworks of mediation agree that a neutral professional assists parties in narrowing issues, considering options, and choosing solutions to resolve their differences. Beyond this, however, there are distinct differences. The client-centered model originated in the early 1970s as a reaction to the excesses of the legal system. Another model that has more recently emerged from the legal profession is described as a law-focused approach where the mediator is directive and evaluative. This model focuses on the law as the standard by which agreements are made, not client creativity or choice. Being directive means that the mediator directs and controls the agenda, the process, and the conversation. The law-focused mediator has a prescribed method of addressing all of the issues in an evaluative way by measuring the strengths or weaknesses of the case from a legal perspective and advising the clients to use only those options that fit within the scope of the law. Law-focused settlements closely resemble what a court-ordered outcome might be. This approach is practiced almost exclusively by attorneys and is based upon their experience as a predictor of court outcomes. Client-centered mediators object to this as being called mediation. This law-centered approach resembles what is called settlement conferencing, which is a facilitated process used in courts to expedite the settlement of cases. Aspiring mediators need to be aware that they may encounter this approach and be very disappointed that it is not what they understood mediation to be. We do not use this model of mediation because it fails to address and resolve the underlying issues of conflict, and misses the opportunity to create a lasting foundation for agreement.

The following is an example of the difference between a client-centered model and a law-focused model. To better illustrate these two distinctly different models of mediation, here is the couple's explanation of what they want to accomplish in their divorce.

Mary and John are attending their first session in mediation. They tell the mediator that they want to share the parenting of the children. The children will reside in the house with Mary. However, after school each day they will go to John's house until 6:00 P.M. on Mondays and Thursdays, and until 8:00 P.M. on Tuesdays to best accommodate both of their weeknight obligations and the children's activities. They will alternate weekends beginning Friday after school until 6:00 P.M. on Sunday. This way both parents remain involved in their children's lives and have one home-based overnight on weeknights.

On their own Mary and John have decided to share the children's expenses by following a budget of the children's essential financial needs, and each will pay for the needs from the checking account. The checkbook and register will be exchanged with the children, and once a month each will deposit a child support check into the checking account. The amount each pays will be calculated according to a pro rata percentage of their gross incomes. They will meet periodically to review the children's expenses, the budgets, and settle any differences. They will make adjustments as the children's needs change or as the children get older. For any unbudgeted or large-ticket items they first have to agree on the item and the expense before assuming the other will share in the expense.

The client-centered process would unfold as follows:

The mediator begins by asking if Mary has any other thoughts about the plan. Mary says that John often speaks for her without knowing whether she agrees, which really upsets her. Although she believes that the children need an ongoing significant relationship with each of them, she is not sure how the children will react to the schedule. The mediator then asks John what he thinks. John is upset and suggest that Mary was reneging on their agreement. The mediator asks John to say more about this. John says that he always feels on the defensive when discussing the divorce and parenting with Mary, because he knows that she can run circles around him when it comes to knowing what the children need and how to care for them. The mediator asks John if he would talk about Mary's parenting. He says that she is the best mother any child could ever have, and he is scared to death to have to compete with that fact in the divorce. The mediator asks Mary what she thinks of what John has just said. She tearfully responds that she didn't know he felt that way about her as a mother. She states that she always felt that John minimized her role as a mother as being unimportant, and his remarks really made her feel appreciated. She also says that she knows that the children are very important to John, but is afraid he won't know how to take care of them, especially in a warm, understanding way. For John's plan to work, Mary wants to be able to help him with the children, but believes that he would be offended by that. John is blown away by Mary's words. He desperately wants her help, but doesn't know she will be willing to help him. The mediator seems to back away from them while they turn to each other and begin to discuss what they each need to do to make the plan work. After some heartfelt discussion, they agree upon a plan that will begin with a transition period in which they will interact frequently with each other about the children. With the mediator's assistance, they go on to develop a schedule for this transition period, and a half-time schedule to be implemented after the transition. The mediator asks them if they also need a holiday schedule, and they agree. Developing a holiday schedule is difficult because neither wants to think about not being with the children on a holiday. They go on to mediate the financial support arrangements with the mediator offering them information about ways other parents have designed theirs. They then create a method of sharing the children's expenses that will work best for each of them and is fair from each of their perspectives.

In a law-focused process, the laws restrict the scope of the discussions and strictly limit the options to those that meet the minimal criterions provided by law. The law-centered facilitator is very powerful and directs the course of the discussions. This professional also advises about the law. The clients may be represented by their attorneys in mediation, and when that is the case, the attorneys frequently do most of the negotiating for the parties. The goal of a law-focused process is to settle as much as possible while adhering strictly to the law of the particular state.

This concept suggests that conflict is best settled by lawyers acting as facilitators. They usually advise both parties about the best way to settle by predicting what a court might decide. The clients are relatively silent. They can offer information and ask questions, but they take advice from the lawyer/facilitator about the best outcome. For example, the law-focused neutral would respond to Mary and John as follows:

Upon hearing their plan, the mediator explains that what they have actually decided is a primary residence for the children with Mary, which makes Mary the sole physical custodian of the children. John will not have physical custody and legally will not be making the day-to-day decisions about the children's care. John will become the visiting parent. Although John certainly could have the children on scheduled afternoons, this would be a deviation from the normal court-ordered custody arrangement, which gives John visitation with the children every other weekend Friday through Sunday, and Wednesday evenings.

In addition to Mary having sole physical custody of the children, John will be required to pay her child support according to a formula that calculates a percentage of John's income to be paid to Mary every month. The mediator explains that they could of course deviate from the guidelines; however, it would be difficult to justify their plan, because it doesn't have a payment of child support made by the noncustodial parent to the custodial parent. Moreover, this checkbook idea is something the court would not order.

Both Mary and John are confused by this, and say that they understood that in mediation they could be creative in their divorce decisions. The mediator replies that indeed they could; however, their creative ideas would have to conform in some way with the laws of the state. The mediator then suggests that perhaps the mediation would work better for them if they brought their attorneys to the next session.

This law-focused process uses a cookie-cutter or one-size-fits-all approach. Because the neutral attorney basically directs the settlement toward what would most closely resemble a court decision, Mary and John probably would not be able to use their creative parenting plan unless the mediator could justify it within the parameters of the law. Their unique method of meeting the children's financial needs is innovative, but it is not likely to be supported by the law-focused facilitator particularly because that professional believed that Mary needed greater assurance that John would actually pay child support. In fact, the mediator would further advise that the child support payment should be withheld from John's paycheck and paid to Mary through the county's Child Support and Collections program.

The two conceptual frameworks are very different. Yet, each will assist Mary and John in making their divorce decisions outside of court. A neutral attorney can offer these services as an alternative to the adversarial process and save the couple some time and money. The couple might actually appreciate this service as a means of getting things settled quickly with little acrimony. When gathering all of the data about divorce mediation training, you need to reach your own comfort level with the distinctions between these different approaches. Decide which conceptual framework fits your own understanding of what mediation is. In our opinion, the law-focused approach is an ADR (Alternative Dispute Resolution) process, but it is not mediation.

CONCLUSION

It is possible to combine some of the best, most useful aspects of the fields of behavioral sciences and law and integrate them with a new set of skills in the field of professional mediation. In fact, that is the foundation of client-centered mediation.

The process of becoming a mediator is not easy. The job of teaching peace has always fallen on those who are willing to make sacrifices and who are willing to swim upstream. In some quarters, you will not be welcome. We have inherited an ancient legal decision-making system that is deeply entrenched and based upon an adversarial model. In addition, you will find that humanity has a tendency toward violence and confrontation. Your job is to change that tendency and offer new thinking, cooperation, and peace.

CHAPTER 2

The Client-Centered
Mediation Model

INTRODUCTION

A LTHOUGH THERE are different models of mediation, this book emphasizes client-centered mediation. Client-centered mediation is closely tied to the work of the divorce mediators of the 1970s, who were the first to create a new mediation concept and apply it beyond labor negotiations to the intense and often bitter conflict of divorce and child custody battles. Their model differed from labor mediation by having mediation conducted with the clients meeting together (face to face), rather than by caucusing between the clients in separate rooms, and with the mediator acting in a less directive, noncoercive manner.

In client-centered mediation, a professional mediator works with both parties in the same room to help them find their own solutions to the issues raised by divorce or other conflicts. Instead of asserting personal biases or opinions about what a necessary or fair solution is, the client-centered mediator creates a structured environment for the parties so that, once they have agreed to the rules of mediation, it is likely they will achieve resolution. This process is based upon the client's sense of what is right, what is fair, and what will work for them.

In client-centered mediation, the negotiations follow a path based upon cooperative principles, rather than competitive principles. Client-centered mediation is based on the belief that clients know best and that state divorce laws, used as principles of fairness, provide only minimal guidelines and are not always the best way to create mutual, fair settlements. Clients tend to become reasonable and fair when they are given a safe environment in which to communicate and are encouraged to recognize and meet the needs of the other spouse as well as their own. They may start out having very different ideas about fairness, but the process of client-centered mediation motivates them to be more fair with each other than if they were in an adversarial environment.

Client-centered mediation also encourages parties to realize that they can only obtain good results for themselves when they also assist the other to reach fair, just results. This principle of mutual connectedness is at the core of client-centered mediation. It is explained by the mediator in such a way that clients come to understand it is to their advantage to figure out ways to meet the needs of the person with whom they are negotiating. Meeting the needs of the other and achieving fairness is far easier when it is not necessary to spend many thousands of dollars on the transaction cost of adversarial conflict resolution procedures.

CLIENT-CENTERED DIVORCE MEDIATION

To many readers, this may sound like a naive and risky way to achieve fairness, particularly if you are a professional who has experienced divorcing people needing protection, advocacy, counseling, or anything except allowing them to decide on their own what is fair. The mediator takes a very active role in helping the couple determine future separate financial needs, future separate parenting plans, and future use of property, based on how they intend to divide that property. Client-centered mediation does not use the mediator as a substitute therapist or attorney. The couple will be asked to obtain legal representation and encouraged, if they are financially able, to engage in marriage closure therapy.

Client-centered divorce mediation is respectful of each client and seeks to empower clients to reach agreements that transform their relationship, preserve their integrity, and focus on their best interests. Divorcing parents are empowered to make agreements that take into consideration that they will be parents forever, that preserve the assets of the marriage, and that it is in their best interests to find solutions, rather than fighting continuously about what is right or wrong. In fact, contrary to the vagaries of an adversarial process, in client-centered mediation, couples more easily see that good solutions are those that allow both of them to carry the burdens of divorce somewhat equivalently.

Clients may seek to impress the mediator with their ability to be fair, which creates a desire in the other partner to give this impression as well. This dynamic may begin as face-saving measures by both partners, but can be used by a skilled mediator to create a positive energy or environment for agreement in the mediation room.

A FUTURE-ORIENTED APPROACH

Client-centered mediation uses an innovative approach to resolving problems that is healthier, easier for clients to use, and results in lower financial and emotional costs. One of the core principals of client-centered mediation is its future-oriented approach—it asks future-oriented questions that require a mutual effort to answer. For example, when a divorce involves a custody dispute, a standard legal question is, "Who is the better parent based upon their past behavior with the children?" The parent who is found to be better is awarded physical custody (based upon applying a series of best-interest tests—such as which parent was more nurturing in the past, who changed more diapers, or who had more contact in recent months—whereas the less fit parent is labeled a noncustodial visiting parent). This whole process is demeaning to parents and creates more conflict while generating large fees for divorce attorneys who litigate custody disputes. In a client-centered mediation process, the mediator asks the question, "What future parenting plan can both of you agree to so you can have a constructive parenting relationship that best meets your children's needs, even though you will be living separately?" This question focuses on the future and does not require parents to debate about past behavior or compete for custody. It offers the opportunity for mutual and cooperative discussion and the possibility of achieving their shared goal of joint parenting. Client-centered mediation uses as a tool innovative questions to make it easier for conflicted parties to collaborate and agree to a fair resolution of the conflict.

Another example of the power of the different future-focused question occurs in farmer-lender debt mediations. In the legal system, the traditional approach has simply been to ask, "Were the payments made on time and if not, is everything in order so the bank can foreclose on the property?" In the early 1980s, when we began to experiment with mediating between financially distressed farmers and their frustrated lenders, we urged them to move beyond the strictly legal wrangling of whether or not there was some arcane legal defense to the foreclosure and instead focus on the future to see if the loans could be restructured to the mutual benefit of both the farmer and the lender. If they could not restructure the loans, at least the lender and the farmer could work out a voluntary liquidation plan mutually beneficial to both. Invariably, at the first mediation session, there was always the tendency for participants to fall back into the past to blame each other for the present problem. At one of these farm mediations in a remote North Dakota town in 1985, it went something like this:

MEDIATOR: I appreciate your concern about explaining the history and legal issues of this problem. Perhaps you could focus on the entire farm operation and let the numbers tell what needs to be done, not the attorneys who are absent today.

BANKER: Well, we wouldn't be here today if this farm operation had been better managed. Albert here is a poor manager. We shouldn't really be here today. He had plenty of time to avoid this situation. He . . . .

ALBERT *[Interrupting]*: What do you mean bad manager? Look at these beans. I brought a clump to show you *[pulling a bunch of stunted soy beans from a grocery bag]*. If you know anything about farming you would see that they have barely had a chance to grow. Every time a rain cloud goes over, it drops on Minnesota farmers, not here. And another thing about me being a bad manager, you knew very well that I was holding back four car loads of durham wheat last summer. I kept you informed every inch of the way. In fact, you even agreed that it was a good idea. It wasn't my fault the bottom fell out of the futures market. You knew when that happened, and another thing. . . .

MEDIATOR *[Interrupting]*: Could I please say something? I didn't get up at 4 A.M. and drive two hundred miles just so I could hear all of you argue about whether Albert is a good or bad manager. I came up here to help you decide how to settle your differences. So the first question I have is, Is this farm operation viable in the future? Let's take a look at the farm plan. If it is viable, or can be made viable, then you may wish to consider some options about restructuring some loans. If it is not viable, then perhaps you need to bury the horse now without it costing any of you anything further. Even if you decide you have to liquidate the farm operation, you can cooperate in such a way that both of you can get as much as possible at the auction.

Just as the mediator in divorce mediation asks a different future-focused question that requires the people to get out of the past and realize their shared goals, the mediator in a farm mediation can do the same.

Similarly, in employment mediation, the first question is often future oriented, "Are the two of you interested in improving your relationship at work, or do you wish to discuss the terms of ending the employment relationship?" If they decide to improve their work relationship the next question might be, "What do you want to do to change the employment relationship in order for you to become comfortable and productive at work?" The legal adversarial question usually focuses on the past and asks, "What are the legal elements of a workplace law that have been breached and by whom?"

In a boundary dispute, after hearing each side's story, the mediator may encourage a future focus by not asking whether the disputed easement meets the legal test of an easement of use or an easement of convenience. Instead, the mediator offers to help the parties determine what they need to do differently in order to live peacefully side by side in the future. In another case the participants in conflict decided to join together and share the cost of building a new road near the swamp instead of waiting for re-hearings in the state supreme court. In all of these situations, the mediator helps the parties achieve a resolution of the past by offering them the possibility of building a new future without the problems of the past. This task is usually much more successful than trying to determine who was a faulty parent, a poor farm manager, or an easement violator in the past.

CHARACTERISTICS OF CLIENT-CENTERED MEDIATION

Other processes of mediation are either centered on the law, on meeting the court's needs for evaluation and case management, or on the mediator's understanding of fairness instead of the client's understanding of fairness. Not to be confused with Carl Rogers' theory of person-centered therapy, client-centered mediation places the clients at the center of the process. Their beliefs, attitudes, wishes, hopes, and desires are the most important consideration. We chose the term for two reasons: (1) it focuses on the people in the room, rather than on the law of the state or on the past causes of the conflict, and (2) it differentiates the model from other processes that employ a form of mediated settlement conferencing and legal evaluation that are more akin to using a judge to force a settlement prior to trial. Client-centered mediation is truly in keeping with the new thinking discussed later in this chapter. It assumes that once participants begin divorce mediation, they are striving to reach the shared goals of cooperative parenting, building separate financial futures, and obtaining a fair, though not necessarily equal, division of property. In nondivorce disputes, they might be striving to reach the shared goals of restructuring the farm finances to make the operation viable; to reform the workplace environment so it is not hostile, harassing, or destructive; or to reach the shared goal of keeping a school open, as in the case discussed in Chapter 5.

Client-centered mediation is a radical departure from the traditional steps taken when resolving a conflict through litigation. For example, it would be impossible to create a popular movie like *Kramer vs. Kramer* or *The Firm* if the people in these movies followed a client-centered approach, because in client-centered mediation there are no rewards for adversarial behavior, nor are there advocates encouraging such behavior in order to prevail. It becomes very difficult in a client-centered process for participants to act as adversaries or competitors because almost every aspect of the process is designed to encourage cooperative responses by each side. The following are important characteristics of client-centered mediation as practiced by mediators who embrace these new ways of thinking.

OPPORTUNITY VERSUS CONTEST

A client-centered mediator asks mutual, future-focused questions to help people in conflict begin to realize they have shared goals. This tends to change the situation from a contest, in which one person wins and the other loses, to a shared journey of looking for joint answers to shared issues. The questions are designed to encourage a mutual response. The questions asked by an attorney or judge in the legal system are more often related to the contest, rather than future planning. The questions asked by the mediators are just as different from the legal system's questions as night is from day. A client-centered mediator does not think about different sides; instead the mediator thinks in terms of shared goals. For example, in the typical custody battle, instead of asking for help from psychologists to evaluate and determine who is more fit to have custody of the minor children, the parents in a mediation process can ask a thera-

pist to help them jointly resolve their complaints about the other's parenting behaviors. In a fence-line dispute between two neighbors that ended
in a fight, instead of seeking who is at fault, the client-centered mediator
asks, Would you each talk about your perspective of what happened?

In the usual adversarial divorce, clients are often told by their attorneys that the other spouse is not to be trusted, is at fault for things not
working, and is to be seen as the enemy. In client-centered mediation,
participants are encouraged to see that they have conflict, not a contest.
Contests require winners and losers; conflicts require constructive communication and decision making. Mediators can turn contests into mutually resolved outcomes by offering an environment that encourages
cooperation. By influencing the communication patterns, the attitudes,
and the bargaining process, the mediator can change the battle from a
contest into a journey that helps participants achieve their shared goals.
As any contest is a tug of war between two or more sides, mediation is a
conversation that results in changed people.

In client-centered mediation, the mediator will ask clients to identify
shared goals. If they have been in intense and bitter conflict for some period of time, the mediator may need to ask a series of small questions that
leads them toward a realization of shared goals. In divorce mediation
with parents who have minor children, the client-centered mediator asks,
"Is it important that the children have a meaningful relationship with
each of you?" which is usually answered affirmatively. The mediator can
also ask a leading question such as "Bob, you aren't trying to terminate
her parental rights are you?" Bob will never answer this question in the
affirmative. This is another small positive building block because Bob acknowledges the importance of the goal of shared parenting.

Similarly, a couple might be locked in battle over the issue of spousal support. Instead of blaming one spouse for this problem, the client-centered
mediator helps them identify shared goals by asking if they both agree that
one of them is partially or completely dependent upon the marriage relationship for their support. If they agree to this, the mediator then asks them
if they are interested in building a plan that allows the more dependent
spouse to gain an increased measure of financial self-sufficiency. Some couples wish to unhook completely. If this is the case, the mediator will help
them look at options such as lump-sum buyouts of the spousal support
obligation. Once they realize they have the shared goals of each helping to
solve the problems of less money and more expenses after a divorce, most

adopt a standard of fairness calling for each of them to share some of the burdens of the divorce.

This peaceful resolution by the parties is in sharp contrast to what happens if the case goes to court. There, attorneys may argue that one caused the problem by asking the other to stay home and not work, or the attorney may charge that one spouse is lazy and unwilling to work or that the higher-income spouse is lying about income, or if the spouse was telling the truth, accuses the spouse of not wishing to be fair about support.

In a sexual harassment mediation the mediator asks each side to tell their story. As the story unfolds, each person listens to the other without interrupting. After discussion and clarification of each person's concerns, the mediator is respectful to each, asking what each needs to resolve the issues. This future-focused question offers the opportunity for both people to move from blame and fault of the past to think of what will repair the damage. This often results in the person who was harassed asking for such things as an apology, payments for lost income, costs of counseling, a recommendation for a new job, attorney's fees, or recognition from the harasser of the pain or harm inflicted. Usually, the harassed person also wants the other to go to counseling to work on the problem of harassing behavior so no one else will have to experience the same. Interestingly enough, the person who harassed is usually agreeable to these requests. When these cases are submitted to the contest of the court system to assess blame and damages, the important needs of the parties are not met, and the goal is only to win. Sadly, everyone loses.

Old Thinking

Unfortunately, many current mediation programs perpetuate old thinking. Some processes that are called mediation are competitive settlement conferences cloaked in the term *mediation*. Some court systems addressing custody issues go so far as to use the term *mediator* to describe custody investigators who evaluate which parent is more fit to have custody of the minor children. Calling a custody investigator a mediator is old thinking. Not only does it violate the principle of self-determination that is at the center of client-centered mediation, it also turns the mediator from a neutral into a judge. This contaminates the cooperative process. Moreover, old thinking still uses the concept of asking who should have custody, which is an adversarial question. New thinking focuses on how parents will raise their children in the future.

Old thinking holds that the parties are in a contest and one wins while the other loses. It is impossible to openly embrace your adversary if you are told that a mediator will help you decide a contest and that if you cannot decide for yourself, the mediator will recommend to the court who should win the contest. In a truly cooperative process, the mediator will suggest that the goal is not to determine winners and losers, but to build a resolution that meets their shared goals. From this, it is easy to see that one of the first principles of establishing a cooperative process is to ask a future-oriented question that offers participants the opportunity to realize their shared goals, rather than questions about custody, which require participants to battle over who is fit and who is unfit.

NEW THINKING

New-thinking processes ask questions in a very different fashion. As pointed out earlier in custody mediation, for example, the new question is, "*What are the future parenting arrangements the two of you can agree to that allow each of you to build a parenting plan that will work best for you and the children in the future?*" This question does not encourage participants to engage in a battle over who is the better or worse parent. The client-centered question moves the parents into a new way of thinking about their future relationship with the children and with each other. Unfortunately, this is not the type of question asked by the family courts in most states.

Old-thinking law-focused approaches use the same old adversarial questions and try to find a settlement in the context of a battle. New thinking changes the entire game that is being played so that participants in conflict can create their own solutions. There are many other strategies that client-centered mediators use to help people in conflict. The following illustrates in more detail how client-centered mediators can make an impact on the course of the conflict by creating a cooperative environment.

Creating a Cooperative Environment

The client-centered mediator influences the participants' communication by encouraging the use of nonlegal, positive words that focus on the practical parenting tasks at hand rather than negatively loaded legal words, allowing them to work together more easily. Client-centered divorce mediators, for example, do not use words like *custody* and *visitation* because those words are generally used to create a lower-level visitor parent and a higher-level primary parent. Determining custody in such a way serves the courts' need to attach labels more than it serves the parents or needs of the children. When finding one parent more fit to have custody, the court must award certain perks, such as the house, child support, more parenting time or authority over the children at the expense of the other parent.

Words are important. In client-centered divorce mediation, parents are simply called parents. The mediator asks participants to set a goal of creating a parenting plan for the future that allows both of them to be the kind of parents they wish to be, even though the children may spend more time at one house than the other or one parent may have more responsibility in certain areas than the other. By changing the labels from *custody* to *parenting*, and by asking a different question, the mediator helps participants in conflict over their children see that they have shared goals in building a future parenting arrangement as opposed to having a contest over who has been most unfit in the past in order to obtain the status of primary or custodial parent.

Open and Honest Communication

In client-centered mediation, there is no need to engage in the type of deceptive and dishonest communication that so often occurs in the adversarial game of trying to catch the opponent in a misstatement or admission. Open and honest communication is more likely when the mediator changes the game being played, thereby eliminating the chance that participants' words and statements could be used against them if the conflict later ends up in court. By establishing strict confidentiality of the discussions, the mediator can assure participants that their words and statements will not be used against them if mediation reaches impasse. When a person does not have to worry about their words being taken out of context or used against them later in a competitive battle, they are more likely to speak freely, openly, and honestly. This is accomplished in several ways:

- Clients are asked to sign an agreement to begin mediation that is a contract between the mediator and everyone involved. The mediator promises not to testify in court, should the mediation reach impasse, and the clients promise not to call the mediator as a witness in any subsequent proceeding. Because over 90 percent of clients we have worked with at the institute have been successful in mediation, the likelihood of even thinking that the mediator's testimony could be helpful at a future trial is remote.

- Common-law legal traditions have always held that settlement negotiations are off the record and anything said in furtherance of a settlement may not be used at trial. For example, it would be improper for an attorney to produce a settlement letter from the other side and read it to the jury as evidence of a willingness to settle their case for far less than they are asking for in the trial. Common sense dictates that few disputes would settle if words and statements in these discussions could be used against them in court.

- Most state divorce courts have by now established court rules that keep the mediation process confidential, private, and not subject to inquiry in the unlikely event participants end up in court after having first started mediation. However, a few courts have adopted a perverted approach to mediation that requires the mediator to make a recommendation for settlement to the court if the mediation fails. This evaluative mediation approach is in the minority. Yet it is an example of the way some courts contaminate the integrity of mediation for the sake of efficiency and cost cutting.

- Much of the information exchanged in mediation can be easily documented. Financial information, workplace time cards, and any other records or information necessary to informed decision making can be tracked, traced, and verified, which is particularly beneficial to those situations in which trust has been broken and needs to be rebuilt.

The only narrow exceptions to the confidentiality of the mediation process relate to those circumstances where people in mediation threaten harm to themselves or others, or report instances of child abuse. Except for these rare exceptions, the mediation process is confidential and encourages the parties to speak freely and honestly in an effort to resolve their conflict.

Persuasive versus Threatening Communication

Anyone who has ever been the subject of a threat knows how upsetting it can be. Most recipients of threats dig their heels in and fight back. A threat is a type of communication pattern that often contains an if-then sequence resulting in a negative consequence for the recipient if they don't act or refrain from some act. Such coercive patterns tend to shut communication down and make it difficult to proceed with the mediation. A client-centered mediator will actively manage the sessions in such a way that coercive and threatening communication seldom occurs. The mediator accomplishes this goal by using one or several of the following three techniques:

1. If a threat is made, the mediator intervenes and asks the recipient of the threat to describe whether or not the statement feels threatening. If the recipient says yes, the mediator asks the originator of the threat to speak persuasively rather than coercively. The mediator could begin a discussion of how threats are really assertions that something bad will happen, and that it is possible to be persuasive by making an assertion that something good will happen as a result of requested behaviors or actions taking place. For example, a parent might say, "If you allow me to have more time with the children, I will be more willing to pay for extra child expenses." The mediator has given the originator of the threat an opportunity to restate the threat as a need or concern.

2. The mediator also tries to eliminate the need for people to make threats by assuring participants that their worst fears will not come true. People who use threatening communication generally feel as though they are up against the wall without any power or options. By assuring people that bad things will not happen to them, the mediator can reduce their need to make threats against each other. For example, client-centered divorce mediators might say, "Bill, are you able to say to Susan that you will not try to harm her relationship with the children and will not try to take the children away from her?" or "Susan, are you able to assure Bill that you will not try to do anything to interfere with his relationship with the children and will not try to take the children from him?"

3. The mediator also tries to probe underneath the threatening statement to see whether it is possible to resolve the underlying need that motivated the threat. Suppose a person in the room says, "If you don't back off from your outrageous demands for support, then maybe it would be better if I had the kids and you paid me to take care of them." This usually indicates that the person making the threat is uncomfortable with the discussion about how the responsibility for sharing the costs of raising the children will be decided. By returning to a discussion about the child support, the mediator can usually help the person eliminate the need to make

this threat. The mediator might respond with, "*Bob, it sounds like you believe the child support amounts discussed so far are unfair.*"

Discouraging Blame and Fault Finding

Perhaps the most destructive aspect of the adversarial system is its constant focus on blame and fault. Blaming and fault-finding statements are critical to the success of an adversarial process where the goal is to show that the other party is at fault, unfit, or not entitled to something they want. When a mediator is attempting to create a cooperative environment, it is essential that the mediator assist people to communicate without the contaminating impact of blame and fault. In most cases, such blaming and fault finding only serve to create a toxic environment in which little can be accomplished. Indeed, if the mediator is not able to move the discussions from blame and fault, clients will usually not return to mediation. To reduce blame they use a number of techniques:

- *Changing the focus of the discussions from past blame to future shared needs and shared goals.* A focus on the future more easily moves people away from blame and fault. All blame and fault finding focus on some event that happened in the past. Such statements declare that something bad happened in the past and it was the other person's fault. Blame and fault-finding statements are essentially of no use to a cooperative process, unless they are acknowledged by participants and they choose to move beyond them. Instead of asking participants to deny history, a mediator offers a future focus so they can make decisions that will keep the past mistakes from reoccurring.
- *Asking future-focused questions.* We first wrote about this principle with regard to divorce mediation in Chapter 6 of Folberg & Milne (1988). Justice Byron Johnson of the Idaho Supreme Court also cited this principle of asking different questions to elicit shared goals in a concurring opinion in the case of *Stockwell v. Stockwell*, 775P. 2nd 611 (Idaho 1989). In that case, the court urged a couple to quit their adversarial custody battle and begin a mediation process. Quoting extensively from our chapter, Justice Johnson writes:

  The adversarial system asks, "Who will be awarded custody of the minor children?" The result is that the parent who is not awarded custody is then labeled a noncustodial, visiting parent. In many ways, this question is much like the law school professor's example of an inappropriate leading question, the most famous of which is, "When did you stop beating your wife?" Just as the wife beating question assumes an answer by the way it is asked, the usual custody question assumes that it is necessary to determine two levels of "ownership" of the minor children. This is absurd, because the question of ownership need not even be asked; the focus should be establishing the parenting obligations that must be practiced in the future by the parties. A more appropriate question to ask the divorcing couple is, "What future parenting arrangements can you agree to, so that each of you can continue to be involved, loving parents?" This version of the custody question creates a different focus and a very different outcome. First, the question is mutual, and answering it requires cooperation. Asking "Who shall have custody?" creates a competitive focus and is likely to produce an adversarial or fighting response, but asking participants to agree to create certain parenting arrangements requires collaborative discussions and mutual planning. Second, the question is future oriented. Mediation pushes participants to look more to the future because it can be controlled and changed. When the mediator asks a future-oriented mutual question, participants find it easier to work through the difficult task of being two parents living in different houses.

- *Asking the participants if they will agree to a communication ground rule.* This ground rule suggests that whenever either party makes a blaming or fault-finding statement, they agree to follow such complaints with a positive, constructive statement about what must be done differently in the future to prevent their complaint from occurring again. Frequently, a mediator will say to a participant, "I understand you are concerned about what happened in the past, what do you want to be done differently in the future so the complaint goes away?"
- *Discouraging participants from shifting responsibility for some problem.* Blame and fault statements say, "I am not responsible for the mess we are in, you are!" Instead, the mediator seizes the blame or fault statement as an opportunity for the participants to discuss future responsibilities to resolve what underlies the blaming statement.

Encouraging Neutral Language

An adversarial, competitive model of conflict resolution uses inflammatory words such as *plaintiff* and *defendant* to identify who brought an action and who it was brought against. Words such as these only serve to heighten the sense of battle.

Divorce courts have promoted the use of words like custody and visitation in connection with the ending of the marriage partnership. If you think about our language, the only other use of the word *custody* is in connection with prisoners. The only other use of the word *visitation* is at funeral homes. Courts have consistently created a labyrinth of terms that are confusing and tend to incite conflict because the system is based upon competition as the vehicle to solve all divorce decisions. How would you like to be labeled a noncustodial visiting parent? Or, would you rather like to be labeled a nonresidential parent, whatever that may mean? Perhaps you would like to be labeled a nonpsychological parent? Words like *primary custody, dual custody, split custody, residential parent, custodial parent, sole custodial parent, legal custody, physical custody* and finally, the best of the lot as is used in Texas, the *managing conservator* and the *possessory conservator,* are all reminiscent of the Middle Ages when the Church invented words that only the elite clergy could understand.

Unfortunately, these labels and phrases are very important in court because a lawyer tells the client it is necessary to fight hard to be designated with the label that gives the client the most power, the most benefits, or the most perks in the future. Nothing at all in the courtroom approach says anything about embracing your adversary, or being willing to help your adversary. Instead, the words are used to designate gradations of power based upon who won or lost the contest. This traditional approach has been destructive because, as Deutsch (1973) observed in his statement about shared goals, competition creates a destructive process in which only one person swims while the other sinks. A client-centered approach to mediation changes the definition of the problem by asking mutual, future-focused questions to create cooperation. Cooperation results when embracing your adversary. This is what is meant by new thinking.

Mediators can exert influence in the room by suggesting different word changes because neutral labels remove the fight and create options for participants to choose shared goals. In client-centered mediation, people use regular, ordinary, everyday words like building a *parenting plan* and creating an *exchange schedule* for the children. Here are some helpful substitute words that make the mediation process more cooperative. In divorce mediation,

- *Custody* becomes *parenting;*
- *Custody proceeding* becomes *building a parenting plan;*
- *Visitation* is changed simply to *be with;*
- *Custodial parent* changed to the *on-duty parent according to a parenting schedule;*
- *Visitation schedule* becomes *parenting* or *exchange schedule;*
- *Primary residential home* or *secondary home*, are all simply *mom's home* and *dad's home* in the eyes of a child;
- *Legal custody* is the *how* of parental decision making;
- *Physical custody* is the *when* of parenting;
- *Sole physical custody* makes sense only when used if one parent dies or has their parental rights terminated, leaving only the surviving parent to be an only or sole parent;
- *Changing custody* becomes *revising the parenting exchange schedule;*
- *Supervised visitation* becomes *helping the parents to overcome some parenting problems and to assure the safety of the children by using a mutually agreed upon person or persons to be present with a parent and the children until the problem is resolved;*
- *Custody investigation* becomes *engaging a neutral mental health professional* to advise the parents about their concerns and conflict over what is best for the children, not investigating or evaluating who was better or worse in the past as a parent.

For civil and other types of mediation, the substitute words are:

- *Foreclosure* becomes *loan workout;*
- *Plaintiff* or *defendant* becomes *participant* or *party;*
- *Grievance procedure* becomes *employment* or *workplace dispute;*
- *Perpetrator, victim,* or *abuser,* becomes *participant* or *party;*
- *Problems* become *issues;*
- *Petitioner* or *respondent* becomes *participant* or *party;*
- *Illegal conduct* becomes *dispute;* and
- *Position* becomes *an option.*

Client-centered mediators encourage people in conflict to use neutral words that remove the negative charge and battle syndrome carried in the words. When neutral, noninflammatory words are used, people are challenged to think more constructively, and to understand how words can hinder positive communication. Using these new words facilitates a change in people's thinking from the contest mentality to respect and cooperation.

Influencing Attitudes

Skilled client-centered mediators help participants change their attitudes, thereby making it more likely that they will achieve a cooperative outcome. Client-centered mediators intervene to influence people's thinking so that new thinking will occur. These interventions on the part of the mediator are not meant to be directive or controlling; they are meant to help generate the creative thinking process that Deutsch (1973) explains as being necessary for the cooperative resolution of conflict:

> There are three key psychological elements in this process: (1) the arousal of an appropriate level of motivation to solve the problem; (2) the development of the conditions that permit the reformulation of the problem once an impasse has been reached; and (3) the concurrent availability of diverse ideas that can be flexibly combined into novel and varied patterns. (p. 360)

Client-centered mediators influence and foster attitudes of trust rather than suspicion, of future possibilities as opposed to past mistakes, of mutual interests as opposed to individualistic attitudes, of positive as opposed to negative thoughts, and finally, of assertive as opposed to aggressive behaviors.

Rebuilding some trust through making and following small agreements requires a great deal of attention because of issues of power and control between the two parties. For example, mediation assists participants who have experienced nonreciprocal abuse in their marriages by encouraging each party to become more assertive, not aggressive, in the controlled environment of the mediation room. The client-centered mediator is trained to screen for and recognize abuse signals when working with divorcing clients. By being nonjudgmental yet serious about abuse, the mediator will offer special protocols for participants to follow in order to keep the mediation room a safe environment. When they follow through on these protocols, they begin to rebuild the trust that will be necessary for them to operate as parents after the divorce.

Creating an Environment of Trust

Deutsch (1973) observed in his research that as mistrust and suspicion increased, the parties grew increasingly competitive. An essential element of a cooperative process is that the clients begin to trust each other. This is accomplished in three ways:

1. Client-centered mediators conduct an orientation session, explaining that even though it is desirable for participants to have some measure of trust as they begin mediation, significant trust in each other and the process is not really possible at this point. In divorce mediation, for example, most couples experience some terrible affront to their self-esteem when their marriage is crumbling. They may think that they can never trust the other again. In addition, they have never been through mediation before, much less a client-centered process. If they decide to begin mediation, they are offered the opportunity to make small, manageable agreements having a high likelihood of success that will start to form the basis for a more trusting relationship.

2. The divorce mediator helps couples distinguish between different levels of trust, suggesting that if they are going to exchange children in the future, it is not necessary to have the deep, abiding level of trust that was present in the early years of the marriage. They may only need a more businesslike trust, for example, *"I will pick up the children at 4:00 P.M. on Friday. You can count on me to be there at that time and I will count on you to have them ready for me."*

3. The mediator offers participants joint tasks to complete so that they each have the opportunity to carry out their promises. As the mediation progresses over a period of 3 to 12 two-hour sessions, depending upon the level of conflict or complexity of the issues, participants begin to see that progress is being made and that both are following through on commitments made at previous sessions.

Creating Mutual Attitudes

For parties who have children, helping them to see that they are connected as parents is very important in creating a mutual attitude. However, even participants in mediation who do not have children or those who will not be exchanging spousal support find that they are connected to each other and that it is necessary for them to cooperate in order to get through the unhooking process of divorce.

A mutual attitude means that both parties can better achieve their goals of being treated fairly if each treats the other fairly. A mutual attitude does not encourage one or the other to try to win or lose. Most importantly, a mutual attitude links people in such a way that they either sink together or they swim together. This mutual attitude is achieved in the following three ways:

1. At an initial mediation consultation, clients will be encouraged to negotiate in very different ways than they would in the adversarial court system. The mediator suggests that they not turn each issue into a contest, but, instead, look at each issue as requiring joint decision making.

2. Mediators point out how people are connected. There are many opportunities within a mediation session to point out instances in which each may get what he or she needs only when they also help the other obtain their needs. For example, one parent will have difficulty being a parent if the other constantly attempts to turn the children against them by making negative remarks about that parent. The divorce mediator may suggest that negative comments about the other parent may come back to haunt the parent making such statements.

3. As pointed out earlier, different questions are also useful in the task of creating a mutual attitude. The mediator asks, "How will the two of you share the costs of raising the children in the future?" rather than, "How much does your lawyer think you should be paying for child support?" The mediator asks, "What kind of plan can you agree upon that will help increase the financial self sufficiency of the dependent spouse?" rather than, "How much spousal support do you think the court will require you to pay and for how long?" The mediator implies that participants have mutual goals by the way the question is framed. The questions are future focused and ask what the couple wants to do, not what the court or lawyer would do. This reliance on participants' choices, rather than the court's or the lawyers' choices, is a critical distinction between client-centered mediation and law-centered mediation or other more directive forms of using a neutral party to assist in the negotiations.

Being Future Focused

When conflict is managed competitively, the parties look to past events for answers based on who was right and who was wrong. The goal is often to determine who is entitled to some benefit or who is at fault. This wastes an enormous amount of time and is one of the greatest drawbacks of an adversarial system of conflict resolution. Client-centered mediators create a future focus when establishing a cooperative setting. This is accomplished in the following two ways:

1. Unlike the traditional labor-mediation process, the client-centered mediator does not ask for an opening statement. Formal opening statements tend to exaggerate the pain of the past or are used to stake out extreme positional demands. In a client-centered process, the past is not rehashed in order to determine who caused the problems, it is only mentioned as much as is necessary to allow people to let go of the past or to help them determine what must be done differently to make the future more acceptable (Etheridge, 1994, p. 5). People focus on the past when they are asked to make opening statements. If they are, instead, asked to tell their story, without making positional demands, their view of the past can be acknowledged by the mediator and they become more hopeful that things can be better in the future.

2. Questions about future goals offer clients an opportunity to talk about those goals. Questions about the past focus people on the past. More often than not, it is the past wrongs and past harm that people want to focus on. However, when the mediator asks people to build new agreements about their relationship in the future, it becomes easier to continue talking about the future. Client-centered mediators ask questions in such a way that the future goals can become linked.

This future focus has positive results for the mediator offering a cooperative environment for participants. A past focus tends to create disputes about whose version of the past is correct, whereas centering the discussion around the future will help people let go of the past as they concentrate on building a new future.

Creating Assertiveness

Many people think that mediating is for wimps. In fact, we have heard it said: "Real men don't mediate, they litigate." The attorneys who seem to have difficulty with a client-centered mediation process are generally those who do not appreciate the difference between assertiveness and aggressiveness. As stated earlier, because people have a difficult time embracing their adversary if they are being attacked, the first step in helping people act assertively is to keep the mediation room a safe environment.

Client-centered mediators understand that when discussions are safe and productive, people can more easily be assertive and take care of themselves. When people are not assertive, they either want someone else to take care of them, or they are busy attacking or defending. Here are four ways a client-centered mediator will encourage assertiveness in the mediation room:

1. The mediator invites people to be assertive by asking them to state very clearly what they need. If they have trouble stating what they need, either because they are so emotionally distraught or they are confused and frightened about the future, the mediator will take participants through a series of steps that make it easier for them to understand what it is they want and need. For example, at the institute we ask divorcing couples to complete budgets of their monthly expenses. This helps them think about their future living expense needs and sets the framework for discussions about building separate financial futures and deciding whether any exchange of support is necessary.

2. Client-centered mediators also assist the more aggressive person by influencing that person to communicate more constructively. The mediator takes responsibility for ensuring that one person does not verbally victimize the other while in the mediation room. If someone becomes overly aggressive, the mediator intervenes to halt the behavior. This may be accomplished by asking the other spouse how it feels when the aggressive spouse leans over and points a finger in his or her face while making a threatening remark. The mediator asks the aggressive participant to agree not to do so. Client-centered mediators are scrupulous about keeping an emotionally safe environment. Some mediators, unfortunately, believe that it is appropriate to let participants have at it until they get it out of their system. This loud wrangling, when it becomes intense, unrelenting, and harsh, may be very destructive to the other person, if not both people. For this reason, client-centered mediators believe that participants will be more

likely to act cooperatively and assertively if they are in a setting in which the mediator eliminates destructive behavior such as blame, fault, intimidation, and threats.

3. To encourage assertiveness, the mediator discourages either person from taking control of the session. Sometimes this has been seen as a power imbalance that the mediator attempts to correct by balancing the power between the parties. Our own experience tells us that it is not a question of who has more power. It is a matter of both parties being offered the opportunity to be assertive. One person cannot be assertive if it appears that the other is dominating the conversation and the process. Therefore, client-centered mediators attempt to keep the conversation balanced by respectfully intervening to ask the more quiet participant questions like, "What are your thoughts, Bill?" or by saying, "What do you have to say about this, Mary?"

4. Client-centered mediators prevent anyone from dominating the process by ensuring that one person does not do all of the proposing while the other always responds. For example, in divorce mediation, when one person has prepared a detailed settlement proposal, the mediator can delay discussion of the proposal until the other person has had the opportunity to understand the underlying facts upon which the proposal is based. Most client-centered mediators delay the final negotiating process about support and property division until budgets have been accepted and agreement has been reached on the disclosure and valuation of all property assets.

Mediators do not balance power, but they help clients create a better use for their power. Unlike a competitive system of conflict resolution based on score keeping, evaluating, and winning, a client-centered mediation process uses new thinking that says keeping score is not at all necessary. Although it is not necessary to determine who has more power, it is necessary to help both of them tap into the innate power they already possess. When participants are able to do this, they become more confident when addressing and planning for the future. This is what is meant by writers who emphasize empowerment or who define mediation as a self-empowering process. Client-centered mediators do not assess who has more power; instead, they are sensitive to the common misuses of power. They are intent on providing both people with new understandings by helping them become empowered.

Thinking Positively

Most people get divorced to make things better, not worse. However, when they employ a mediator, they are at an impasse because they are unable to make agreements by themselves. They are hopeful that the mediator will help them build a settlement agreement, but they also have doubts. Learning to think positively helps them overcome these doubts.

In any serious conflict, people who consider mediation are frustrated and most likely at the end of their tolerance level. Their negative attitudes become magnified by their constant fixation on the harm they perceive that has occurred to them and to their dreams. They are usually skeptical of any process that tells them they will have to solve it themselves. In order to create the environment for even choosing mediation, most mediators will conduct a brief initial consultation about the process. At this early stage, it is necessary to help them believe that the conflict is able to be resolved and they are capable of resolving it. Deutsch (1973) has referred to the three steps of the creative thinking process with the first being an arousal of the belief that the problem can indeed be resolved. This is what we call helping people to think positively.

An adversarial system fosters negative attitudes because it assumes that one side is out to defeat the other. A natural outgrowth of the contest mentality is the motivation for one to prevail over the other. A cooperative process encourages a positive attitude. If participants are expected to respect (or, at least, not destroy) the other, they are more able to move out of the contest mode. When those positive attitudes are lacking or doubtful, the client-centered mediator helps build positive thoughts, attitudes, and hope. This is done in the following three ways:

1. Client-centered mediators are somewhat like cheerleaders, cheering participants on to a successful conclusion, reminding them that if they do not hang in there and do it themselves, somebody else will do it for them—probably not as well and at a significantly greater cost. For example, mediators express appreciation for clients' good work, and encourage them to continue by pointing out that there is no third party, such as a judge, who knows their issues as well as they do. They are the best experts about their conflict, their relationship, and their issues.

2. Client-centered mediators focus essentially on what may work, instead of on what does not work. This is the opposite of what goes

on at a court trial, especially in cross examination, where the purpose is to tear down the theory of the other side's case. Focusing on what will work presents a challenge to the mediator, because it is often easier to talk about what won't work. As the mediator inquires about their ideas for the future, if one or both of them lapses back into the terrible things of the past that have not worked, the mediator will gently bring them back to the present and the future. This can be done simply by asking them to say what it is they think will work. By continually focusing on the things that may work in the future, people move away from the negative into the positive. They become more hopeful, more creative.

3. Client-centered mediators reinforce hope and change by appreciating whenever one or both of them acknowledges and recognizes the good effort of the other. For example, when a divorcing spouse says, "Well, I really think he is a good father. . ., but. . .," the mediator may intervene at this point and say, "Bob, in all the months the two of you have been fighting about custody, have you ever heard her say, 'you are a good father?'" Of course, Bob will say, "No, I've never heard her give me any kind of a compliment; all I have heard her say is she wants to restrict my time with the children." By dwelling on these positive remarks as an opportunity for each of them to acknowledge the other, however weakly the appreciation may be stated, the mediator helps participants recognize each other's humanity and, thus, helps them move closer to cooperation. In the foregoing statement, an attorney bent on winning a custody trial will disregard the good part of the statement and instead focus on whatever comes after the *but*. . . . For client-centered mediation to be successful, the mediator must be a good listener willing to intervene at those times it appears a party is being positive, or is about to acknowledge something positive about the other.

Bargaining from Interests

Client-centered mediators influence the way clients bargain and negotiate with each other. To understand the difference between positions and interests, think of it in this way:

Two business partners are fighting each other for control of the company. They are locked into bitter litigation and the conflict is so great that it has been necessary for the attorneys to obtain a court-appointed receiver to temporarily run the business. Because they are court ordered to participate in mediation, they start in mediation by stating their opening positions. Each wants control of the company and will not consider any option other than being the person to prevail in the ownership battle. They have a bevy of accountants who disagree about the value of the company, making buyout discussions even more difficult. They present each other with offers to buy out the other, and when one makes a low-ball offer for the other partner's interest, the other says, "If that is the fire-sale price you think the company is worth, then I will buy it from you at that price." As they continue to try to reach agreement, each attaches so many onerous conditions relating to noncompete clauses and time to pay off the purchase price that it appears they will never be able to reach agreement. They are stuck in positional bargaining.

In the real world, a case that started out similar to this was resolved when the mediator offered the observation that it appeared their true interests were in completely unhooking from each other in the shortest period of time. One of the ways they could achieve their interests for control of the company and at the same time unhook from each other was to consider a range of options. One of the options that was considered and later chosen was to divide the company. Fortunately, the company engaged in a national business effort that made it possible to divide the company along different state lines. As the option of dividing the business continued to be discussed, they realized that dividing the business into two entities allowed for each to retain control, while achieving their mutual interest of no longer working together as business partners.

In another case involving personal injury, the lawsuit had turned ugly after the first set of insurance company attorneys accused the injured man of faking his leg pain during a deposition. In a car accident that everyone agreed was not the fault of the injured young man, he lost his leg just below the knee. As with some amputations, he had nothing but problems related to infections and he experienced what is called phantom pain. He was in terrible shape and so angry that at the end of the mediation, when the insurance company finally agreed to pay him a large sum of money for his loss of limb and for related compensation (he was a high school math teacher and coach of the state championship tennis team), he confided to the mediator that he had planned to leave at the end of the first morning but was persuaded to stay. The mediator inquired about why he chose to stay. He said, "When you came back at the end of the first morning of mediation sessions and said, 'Great news, they have agreed to your $200,000 demand for pain and suffering, but we are still working on the other amounts related to your loss of wages, future medical costs, and the like,' I said to myself, 'Finally, perhaps, somebody is listening to me,' and I stopped unpacking my bags and decided to stay." What the young man didn't know is that in separate caucuses with the insurance company attorneys and claims representatives, they instructed the mediator to respond with an offer of $250,000 in response to the young man's attorney's demands for $800,000 and not a penny less. The mediator had been listening to the interests expressed by the young man in the room and the mediator asked the insurer if they would mind if the mediator characterized the $250,000 offer as "$200,000 for pain and suffering and $50,000 for lost wages, medical costs, and other." The insurance company attorneys responded with, "You can package it any way you want, but just let them know that $250,000 is our best offer and not a penny more." Eventually, the case settled in the $500,000 range, but it would not have settled if the mediator did not understand interest-based bargaining principles. That is, cases settle when people's interests are met, and this young man had to have someone acknowledge his pain before any settlement could be possible. True interests are the real needs that are beneath what people state as positional demands.

A father sits in the mediation room pounding the table and demanding that the mediator acknowledge his legal right to have custody of the minor children. He wants physical custody because his lawyer has told him this is the highest level of parenthood he can achieve without being declared a saint. He wants to be the best parent he can be and fears losing the children. He is now bargaining about his position that he should have custody. Positional bargaining is based on the concept of winning and losing. Father wants to win custody and it means the mother of his children will lose custody. On the other hand, if the mother wins this battle, he will lose custody. This is the classic contest played out in divorces with minor children. The mediator can point out that it is possible to view custody from a different perspective. Underlying his position is an interest that he be allowed to continue to be significantly involved in his children's lives. It is assumed that the mother also has this same interest. Interests can be met in hundreds of different ways. Positions can only be met in one way, that is, either you win custody or you lose custody. If his interest in remaining a significantly involved parent is raised, that is what the mediator will focus on. This is what is meant by interest-based bargaining. Mediators believe that if mutually shared interests can be found, every conflict can be resolved fairly for both sides.

As we said earlier in this chapter, the client-centered mediation process is about a completely and radically different, new way of thinking.

A therapist, an attorney, and a mediator are sitting together watching a college football game. The attorney, in frustration, complains that if only there weren't so many restrictions put on recruiting, like the number of scholarships that could be offered and the amount of benefits that could be given to football players, the home team would be able to attract better athletes and maybe win more often (like in the good old days when things were a bit less regulated). The therapist muses about the aggressive behavior of the linemen and wonders what kind of upbringing they had to turn them into such antagonistic ruffians. The mediator says, "I think they should go out and buy another football so each team would have one and then they wouldn't spend all day fighting over the same ball."

This example might seem absurd to some, but in many ways, this new form of thinking is so contrary to our normal thought patterns that many would-be mediators will never be able to change their thought processes unless they are willing to adopt the idea that embracing your adversary is at the core of the mediation concept. The mediator encourages interest-based bargaining instead of positional bargaining when the mediator offers the idea that children need two loving homes after a divorce and invites participants to build a plan that allows both of them to have a relationship with the children. Client-centered mediators have a strong belief that the size of the pie can always be expanded by cooperation. This is the secret of interest-based bargaining.

Fears, Values, Beliefs, and Concerns

Bill Ury and his colleagues (1988) describe interests as "needs, desires, concerns, fears—the things one cares about or wants. They underlie people's positions—the tangible items they *say* they want" (p. 5). If parents talk about their rights to custody of the children, they are probably talking more about their fear of losing the children, or their fears of becoming the noncustodial visiting parent. They may be talking about their concern that they want to remain a significant parent, not one who is relegated to the status of a mere visitor, legally entitled to visit the children every other weekend and on Wednesday evenings each week from 5:00 P.M. to 7:00 P.M. When a person starts talking about their legal rights, a client-centered mediator will dig underneath the rights statement to attempt to find out what the person is really concerned about or find out what the person really desires. The mediator will then have moved the issue from rights to interests. There are two other ways that mediators help participants engage in interest-based bargaining:

1. By focusing almost exclusively on what people need, the mediator moves beyond what people say are their legal rights. When the discussion resides in the area of rights, people usually start talking about wrongs and then the blame and fault finding intensifies.
2. By searching for the things that both of them need, the mediator can show shared goals. Occasionally, the mediator will offer ideas about universal needs that appeal to both of them, such as the need for both parents to continue to be significantly involved in the lives of their children, the need to have some measure of financial security about the future, or the need to be able to divide the property in a fair way that preserves most of the assets and serves each person's desire for housing, transportation, and fairness.

Self-defined Standards of Fairness

Perhaps the most innovative concept of client-centered mediation is that of encouraging participants to create their own standards or laws of fairness. For those accustomed to seeing the law as the ultimate standard of fairness, this idea that conflicting parties can be allowed to make their own law might sound like heresy. For the person still in old-style thinking, it is absolutely unfathomable. The first response is often, "You mean people are simply supposed to just throw out the law? How do you get fairness?" Actually, it is much easier to achieve fairness when participants step outside the rigid legal concepts and create their own customized fairness principles. Consider divorce. Because most state divorce laws are designed to serve the court's need for efficiency, case management, and uniformity, they are not responsive to the needs of families in conflict. The laws take a cookie-cutter approach to the complex problems of joint parenting, child support, spousal support, and property division.

One couple decided to deviate from the law based upon their own idea of fairness. The husband was agreeing to (1) give the house to his wife in addition to an equal division of the rest of the marital property, (2) pay her spousal maintenance at a high level for ten years when his attorney told him that he would not be ordered to pay any at all, and (3) pay child support for both of his boys though one was 17 and the other was 19, an adult. When the mediator inquired about this arrangement, the husband answered, "Well, I don't expect you to understand, but in the first 14 years of our 20 years of marriage, I was a drunk, a practicing alcoholic. My wife stayed with me and took care of me without ever complaining. She raised the boys and made ends meet on my income, which was diminished by the cost of my alcohol. She picked me up when I was too drunk to drive and she was always there for me. I owe my life to her. I do not want to be married any longer, and no matter what my attorney says, I am not crazy agreeing to this. My wife deserves all of this and more. I would not be successful in my business nor my life if it hadn't been for her. About the child support, I know my wife will provide a home for the boys while they attend the university, so why should child support end when they turn 18 when she is still supporting them? I am doing all of this not out of guilt, but out of gratitude, and because it is right.

When we say the laws were designed to serve the court, we mean just that. As such, the court's inquiry focuses on determining who is right and who is wrong, or who was a better or worse spouse in the past.

Most divorcing couples exposed to the concept of building parenting plans choose not to engage in a contest over which parent is most unfit. They opt to build parenting plans because common sense tells them it is better to cooperate about parenting their children than to fight about who should be awarded custody. Those who say participants should not work from their standards of fairness frequently are those who are skeptical of any possibility of cooperation or are still interested in keeping score. They might say, "Well, how are you going to judge which parenting plan is better if they have a fight over it?" Or, they will say, "It won't work because people cannot be taught to cooperate." Resistance to new thinking most often comes from those who have great difficulty accepting any other concept of fairness other than that which is designed by the legislature and ordained by the courts.

Participants find that in mediation they design fairness standards that serve them better than those dictated by state law. For example, in Minnesota, the state child-support guidelines do not consider the income of the custodial parent when calculating the amount to be paid by the noncustodial parent. In some cases, this can create an injustice because state law does not take into account disparities in income between the parents. In mediation, participants may consider the incomes of both and then adjust the child support upward or downward from the state child-support guidelines in order to better achieve fairness in their own particular case. Many participants find that if they rigidly followed the state law, it would result in unfairness. Consider the plight of one parent under the law:

The law calls me a noncustodial visiting parent. I get to have my three children four overnights out of every 30. I am told to pay 35 percent of my net income for child support, without regard to what the other parent makes. I am told that I cannot expect to participate in how that money is spent on behalf of my children because it is none of my business. I am told by the court system that I am not trusted to pay this amount each month and, therefore, it is the law that the money must be withheld from my wages by my employer. I am told that I get my kids two weeks in the summer and I will have alternating holidays. Is it any wonder that we have so many deadbeat parents? Oh, and if one parent wants to move out of state and take the kids along, that's okay in this state because that parent was declared the custodial parent because of a history of more caretaking time.

Sadly, refusing to pay child support is often the only way some discontented, noncustodial parents can express anger at being treated this way. The above comment was made by a mother who had worked 13 years full time as a dentist while her husband stayed home and raised the children. He was encouraged by his attorneys to take advantage of what the law would give him and not yield to his wife on anything. Fortunately, these participants decided to enter mediation and deviate from the standard cookie-cutter approach. In mediation, the husband decided to become employed outside the home rather than receive alimony. They agreed to follow an almost equal parenting schedule, exchanging the children weekly. For child support, they opted to each put money into a joint children's checkbook account (contributed to on a pro-rata share of their gross incomes as compared to their combined incomes) that was exchanged each time the children were exchanged. This is just one example of how divorcing parents can deviate from the standard law-focused approach.

CONCLUSION

Client-centered mediation is a radically new way of thinking. Client-centered mediation is not practiced by everyone who claims to mediate. However, most mediators who believe in the power and potential of mediation do follow most of the principles outlined in this chapter. Mediators who practice in a client-centered manner are arguably more successful than other mediators. They are also, perhaps, the most maligned, because their approach does not support the need for an adversarial system to settle divorce. Client-centered mediators do not promote adversarial practices and sometimes this is seen as a lack of respect toward the judicial system. This is threatening to those who are afraid the adversarial system will be disregarded and perhaps discredited by the success of mediation.

Those unwilling to adopt new thinking will find the conceptual framework of client-centered mediation difficult to comprehend. Those who are committed to an adversarial competitive process will find client-centered mediation threatening. The reason client-centered mediation creates excitement is because it restores faith in the basic good in people and touches them to their core. It continues to attract clients and new mediators because they are encouraged that a system that relies on the basic principles of fairness, trust, common sense, and the strength of an individual's capacity to make good choices has emerged. People these days are yearning for ways to effectively control their lives. Client-centered mediation presents a powerful tool for solving interpersonal conflicts, while reducing cost, stress, and time spent in the conflict.

CHAPTER 3

The Mediation Process
and the Mediator's Role

MEDIATION HAS become a common word used to describe the method of resolving legal disputes outside of the formal court system with the use of a neutral, third-party, professional mediator. It identifies approaches in dispute resolution that leave the ultimate decision-making authority in the hands of the conflicting parties rather than the law. When we opened our practice in 1977, few people knew about mediation, and those who did thought it only related to unions and bargaining units. Our telephone answering service called us either Family Medication Services or Family Meditation Services. Mediation is now recognized by most people as a structured negotiation led by a neutral, but few people understand its enormous value. In this chapter, we describe the divorce mediation process from beginning to end. Mediating other types of disputes follows a similar process. We also talk about the role of the mediator and address issues of mediator neutrality and power imbalance—two concerns frequently raised by critics of mediation.

OVERVIEW OF DIVORCE MEDIATION

Divorce mediation offers the way for a husband and wife to end their marriage with care and dignity. It is based on the philosophy that the husband and wife are each capable of participating in making the decisions in their own divorce; that a process based upon respect for each person and their family will empower them to achieve the best settlement possible for them; and that with the help of a skillful and compassionate mediator, they can rise above the chaos and conflict of the marriage breakdown and move toward a higher level of functioning as they negotiate to successfully unhook from each other and build separate lives.

Divorce mediation begins with an initial informational meeting held with clients to discuss mediation and how it works. If the couple chooses to proceed with mediation, they receive information necessary to begin mediation and are given financial forms to complete along with other information on how to be best prepared for the first working session. Although different mediation settlements require more time than others to achieve, 3 to 12 two-hour sessions is the average range of time needed to mediate most divorces. At the end of the mediation process, the couple receives a memorandum of their decisions and other documents necessary for the legal divorce to be concluded. They take the memorandum to their attorneys to have it converted into the settlement document for their signatures. Different jurisdictions have different names, such as Marital Termination Agreement or Settlement Agreement, for this document. In most jurisdictions, the attorneys will also prepare the court order putting the agreements into effect, often called Findings of Fact, Conclusions of Law, and Judgment and Decree. There may be other documents as well, usually related to division of retirement accounts and real estate. The terms of the divorce papers prepared by the attorney will follow agreements memorialized in the mediator's memorandum of agreement. If either attorney recommends changes to the mediated agreement, the parties are expected to return to mediation to rework any final disputes. Their attorneys may be present at any time in the mediation process, though they usually attend only the last sessions, if any. In many states the divorce occurs through an administrative process and the couple does not have to appear in court for the divorce to be finalized.

INITIAL CONSULTATION

Former Georgia District Court Judge and Emory University Professor Jack Etheridge suggests that before all else,

> A mediator's first role is to establish a mood and tone that leads the parties toward collaboration. In effect, the mediator directs the disputants away from

the war and toward the peace conference, encouraging them to stop posturing and to start thinking about resolution. Setting the tone of collaboration is an essential characteristic of the process. (Etheridge & Dooley, 1994, pp. 5-6)

We refer to this as rapport building. The first responsibility of a mediator is to build rapport with clients during the initial consultation (Etheridge & Dooley, 1994, p. 5). The mediator greets each respectfully and equally, shaking hands with each, asking each the same questions, making comments to both. The mediator offers the opportunity for conversation by being genuinely interested in their unique situation, clarifying their comments to fully understand their meaning, and appreciating them in spite of their distress and bad feelings toward each other. It is an offering of humanity and soulfulness. Surprisingly, clients will begin to respond in kind. Those who are burdened with great anger find it difficult to hold that anger in the presence of a mediator who cares deeply about them. The mediator invites their questions and welcomes challenges to the unorthodox thought that mediation is not only a viable method, but is also the preferred method to address their differences and conflicts.

The initial consultation is a face-to-face meeting between the couple and the mediator that usually lasts about an hour. Prior to beginning the consultation, the husband and wife each completes an intake questionnaire. The questionnaire contains some background questions about them, their addresses, phone numbers, work status and position, marriage date, separation date, names and ages of children, whether or not they have been in counseling, names of attorneys, and each person's area of greatest concern about the divorce. The intake questionnaire includes a self-report, about the level of domestic abuse present in the marriage relationship, which is completed separately by each spouse to be shown only to the mediator and never shared with the other spouse. This information is reviewed by the mediator before seeing the clients. If the information raises questions for the mediator about violence or abusive dynamics in their relationship, the mediator may choose to meet with them separately to discuss past abuse and safety issues. If the information does not indicate a history of physical or verbal abuse, the mediator will begin by seeing them together after reading their intake forms.

It is standard practice for mediators to talk about their credentials, experience, and personal approach to divorce mediation at this first meeting and to invite any questions about the mediator's background, competence, or potential conflicts of interest. The mediator will provide a general explanation of mediation and describe how it works in divorce. The mediator also explains the difference between mediation and the adversarial process as applied to the three major areas of decision making in the divorce: parenting children, financial support, and division of marital assets and liabilities. By emphasizing the clients' connectedness and mutual needs, the mediator demonstrates that the couple is not limited to the adversarial approach.

Because mediation is conducted in private between the mediator and the couple, it is governed by a contract (see Appendix A) between the three of them. The contract governing mediation will likely spell out:

- Confidentiality rules regarding communications made during the sessions,
- Exceptions to confidentiality for child abuse and threats to do harm to self or others,
- Agreement to fully disclose all information necessary to making informed decisions,
- The role of the mediator as administrator of the process, use of experts, and role of attorneys,
- Expectations of each client,
- Steps to be taken in the mediation process.

These rules, a fee statement (see Appendix B), and a detailed questionnaire (see Appendix C) are given to the clients to review and prepare before returning to the first mediation session. The mediator's goal in the initial consultation is to have an interactive discussion with them so they have the opportunity to have all of their questions answered and have sufficient information to make a choice about whether they will litigate, negotiate through their lawyers, or mediate their divorce.

WORKING MEDIATION SESSIONS

Working mediation sessions take place in two-hour blocks of time. Three to five sessions are commonly needed for more cooperative couples who have children, own their home, have their assets invested mostly in retirement accounts, and have incurred some credit card debt. More sessions are needed when there are issues of domestic violence, addiction, high conflict, large or complex marital estates, custody disputes, nonmarital property, or large debt. These issues often require the assistance of neutral experts such as accountants or actuaries.

The mediator is in charge of managing the sessions in accordance with the clients' needs and goals. Together with the clients, the mediator discusses which issues to begin with and how to proceed. The mediator often asks clients to establish some agreements about their communication in the mediation room, such as not allowing name calling, speaking one at a time without interrupting the other, keeping voices calm, and listening respectfully to each other. These informal rules are offered as they are needed during the process rather than laid out by the mediator in advance. When clients make an agreement about a rule, they will then be more likely to comply with it. In addition, the mediator models cooperative behaviors, such as speaking with a soft voice, giving each equivalent eye contact and attention, apologizing for making a mistake, not holding one's shortcomings against them, and respectfully addressing each of them. These are all ways that the mediator keeps order and emotional safety in the mediation room. The mediator is aware that the clients may have had trouble communicating recently and is always prepared to address these problems openly, honestly, and with positive regard for each client. At the end of each session, the mediator summarizes what has been accomplished, what needs to be accomplished next, and what each needs to do to be prepared for the next session. The mediator also sends each client a memo of these items to help them prepare for the next session. This provides continuity for the mediation process.

FINALIZING THE MEDIATION PROCESS

When all the issues have been addressed and decided by the clients, the mediator prepares a Memorandum of Agreement (see Appendix D) for the clients to review. This is a compilation of all of the session memos, flip-chart notes, and the settlement agreements organized into a memorandum which, when reviewed by their attorneys, becomes the basis of the divorce decree. The attorneys then draft all the legal papers according to their mediated agreements, each person signs all the documents necessary for finalizing the divorce, and they are filed with the court.

THE ROLE OF THE MEDIATOR

"So what does a mediator actually do?" is the most frequently asked question about the work of a mediator. It is a legitimate question. Helping others work through a divorce or other dispute sounds like an easy task. If it were, then why couldn't couples just ask a neighbor to help them resolve their differences? Because it is actually a complex and difficult role. A mediator's role involves a lot more than the skills and techniques listed later in this book. In many ways, the role of the mediator has as much to do with being as it does with doing. That is, the personality, humanity, and life experience of the mediator is an important part of the role. Acting as a mediator requires the ability to move with the flow of the conflict and the ability to understand each person's inner feelings and motivations without seeing them as right, wrong, good, or bad. In this chapter we describe the mediator's role as it relates to divorce mediation, but many of the same skills are needed for mediating other types of disputes as well.

Think of a mediator as someone who is invited into the intense conflict of couples during one of the most difficult times of their lives— their divorce. Couples choosing mediation are seeking the assistance of a neutral person to help them make sense out of the chaos of the marriage breakdown. They are distraught, fearful, angry, and hopeful, all at the same time. The countless coping books about divorce describe the normal dysfunction that divorce brings to each person. Deep hurt, pain, and fear accompany the feelings of loss. Husbands and wives experience a tearing of their core being and have only the other to fault for the misery they are experiencing. The mediator, aware of the depth of the conflict and pain of divorce, never takes sides, but strives to help them arrive at a place where they can begin to build new lives without erasing the past. Is the mediator a miracle worker? Not really. The mediator's task is to transport them from their chaos to a higher level of functioning where they can begin to work together to create the best outcome possible to close their marriage with dignity and care. Often, it begins with small manageable agreements that have a high likelihood of success. With some couples, it may only be possible to point out the fact that for the very first time in a long time, they have been able to agree upon something, even if that something is as small as agreeing to begin mediation.

CONNECTING EMOTIONALLY WITH CLIENTS

Rapport building or connecting with the soul of each client sets the stage for mediation to occur. Mediators may have difficulty connecting with a client who is very guarded and refuses to trust anyone, much less a mediator. When this person presents himself in mediation, the challenge is to find a way into the heart of this hurting person. Sometimes, the way to do this seems too obvious. Asking the person to talk about what has happened is a way to learn what has gotten them to a place where there is only anger and no communication or other constructive interaction. In therapeutic terms this is called meeting the person where they are. When that is done, the person usually begins slowly and guardedly to pour out their feelings. Sometimes there will be angry feelings, and a mediator must learn not to shrink from a client's anger but to view it as an opportunity to connect with the soul.

When a mediator achieves and maintains this connection, the husband and wife are more likely to be able to express themselves constructively. Once there is rapport between the mediator and each client, the clients begin to see each other differently because they have chosen to function at a higher level than the angry conflict of the marriage breakdown.

John and Julie were very stiff and guarded at the initial consultation. The mediator had great difficulty connecting with either of them. Julie seemed hard and cold toward John. John, a lawyer, dominated the conversation, trying to impress the mediator with his knowledge about family law (though he had never practiced it) and about mediation. No matter what attempts the mediator made to build rapport, they were each too self-absorbed to accept it.

The first mediation session was especially difficult because John was using positional bargaining techniques he had just learned from another lawyer friend. This was met with silence by Julie. Again, the mediator had little ability to connect with either of them, though they were each very respectful of the mediator.

Between sessions, John called with a frantic message, reporting that Julie had told him she was serving papers in order to keep him from changing some of the marital assets. The mediator had a phone conference with the two of them, and commented that both of their actions were certainly understandable from their own perspectives. A further observation by the mediator seemed to begin to break the ice. The mediator said it seemed that Julie acted out of her fear that John was going to cash some of their assets, and that John also acted out of fear that Julie was going to end up with everything. Then John admitted that perhaps he had entered mediation with the wrong understanding about how to act in mediation. He explained that he was bargaining for the most he could get because he believed everything would be settled in the middle of their two positions. The mediator suggested that this mediation was really more about ensuring that the other gets as good an outcome as oneself, and asked if they would like to mediate with this understanding in mind. Julie said she really wanted to be in mediation, but she needed assurances that John would cooperate with her instead of competing. John agreed, grateful that Julie wanted to continue.

At the next session, they both began to listen to each other with their hearts. They talked about what would really work best for the children. They worked on their budgets and came up with many options about how they would financially raise their children. The mediator listened, clarified, appreciated each of them, and helped them communicate with care for each other. By the end of the third session, the mediator and the clients were working together with great regard for each other. They were functioning on a higher level, and being creative in their discussions of what would work best for each of them.

The ancient Israelites viewed human beings as having a soul that was their life breath or their personality. Ancient man and woman had no concept of a personality broken into a number of parts. Instead, they viewed the soul as part of God and as a vehicle for connecting with God and each other during their lives on earth. In this way, the ancient view fits well with an ultimate understanding of the true role of the mediator. For a mediator who has achieved mastery of the craft, the first and most important task becomes connecting to the soul of each client. Mediation is based upon having a positive relationship between the mediator and each of the clients. Thus, we refer to the mediator's ability to do the soul dance with people in mediation.

MANAGING THE MEDIATION PROCESS

A mediator operates on several levels simultaneously. The mediator needs to connect with each person, while at the same time accomplishing the practical task of identifying the issues that need to be addressed in order for the divorce to occur. Once a couple and the mediator have attained a comfort with each other and have a good working relationship, they begin to work together on the issues of the divorce. Couples will share the goal of reaching a fair settlement, assisted by the mediator in achieving that goal.

ADDRESSING THE ISSUES

The mediator next helps them explore the broad topics, breaks them down into manageable components, and then assists them in gathering the information necessary to build options. The mediator also provides order to the discussion of each issue that is referred to as the decision-making process, which we suggest is only one aspect of the role of the mediator. The order of the decision-making process of each issue is as follows:

1. Identify the issue.
2. Create an understanding of the issue. (This is accomplished through education and information provided by both the mediator, the clients, and sometimes by neutral experts.)
3. For each property issue, place an actual value on the item, and discuss the value of each item.
4. Consider options for decision making about each issue.
5. Analyze the consequences of the options for each spouse and for their children.
6. Discuss their standard of fairness about each issue.
7. Make a decision based on their standard of fairness.
8. Draft and review each agreement.
9. Submit their agreements for review, drafting, and implementation by their attorneys.

This is the skeleton outline of the decision-making process for the couple. The mediator assists the couple in building the content of each step by discussing the issues in the context of their history, conflict, children, and all that they have built together to this point. The task here is to put meaning on all the issues needed for each of them to build separate futures. In the next section, we explain how mediators rely on certain tools, skills, and techniques to assist them in this process.

MEDIATOR TOOLS, SKILLS, AND TECHNIQUES

Although the mediator works with a couple through each issue in a divorce, the mediator is also modeling basic communication skills of listening, clarifying, questioning, reframing, and empathizing. The most important skills center on asking questions. This technique opens conversation, creates possibilities, and offers opportunities.

Asking questions correctly opens the discussion and provides couples the opportunity to go beyond their old ways of thinking about a particular topic. In divorce, for example, consider the consequences of asking the following mutual questions:

- How do the two of you plan to raise your children in the future living in two separate homes?
- What kind of a relationship will each of you have with the children after the divorce?
- If you each desire to have a close significant relationship with the children in the future, how will you accomplish it?
- How much does it cost each month to raise your children?
- Is one of you financially dependent on the marriage relationship?
- When will the children live with each of you?
- Do you want to discuss how you will let go of what you hold against each other?
- How can you build a cooperative parenting plan when you are so angry with each other?
- What do you need the other to do differently?
- Is it your desire to share the parenting responsibilities as equally as possible?
- How will you share the parenting when you live so far apart in different school districts?

All these questions are open-ended and broaden the conversation about a particular topic that the clients have already introduced. They are designed to elicit a response other than yes or no. They are not leading questions designed to reach an outcome the mediator is seeking. Asking a question moves them out of their boxes from narrow, individualistic thinking into viewing these topics mutually. For more extensive discussion of asking questions, see Chapter 2. Asking appropriate questions is paramount to competent mediation practice. Consider the following case:

Dave and Hilary sought mediation to discuss some conflicts they were having since their divorce was finalized a few months earlier. They have two children: Caitlin, age eleven, and James, age six. The litigated divorce settlement gave Hilary sole physical custody of the children and visitation to Dave every other weekend from 5:00 P.M. Friday to 5:00 P.M. Sunday and Wednesday evenings from 5:00 to 7:00 P.M. In addition, Dave has 30 percent of his net income garnished from his paycheck and sent to Hilary through the County Child Support and Collections Department.

Since the child support order, Dave lost his job for a few months then began a new job. During the time of his unemployment he did not pay child support and is being sued for child support arrearages. Both Dave and Hilary see the other person as the problem. Hilary wants Dave to quit harassing her by calling her at work. He is insisting on being present at the children's medical and dental appointments, having full knowledge of their day care location and costs, and having assurance that the child support he pays is actually being spent on the children's needs. Although Hilary understands some of his requests and has no disagreement with them, she is frustrated with his constant monitoring of her and the children.

In addition to all of this, the visitation (which we refer to as parenting time in mediation) is going very poorly. Neither parent trusts the other and is fearful of saying or doing anything that will cause the other to file another complaint in court.

At this mediation session they wanted to talk about the problems with visitation. Hilary believes that Dave's parenting time needs to be cut back so the kids would not have any overnights with Dave. Dave wants his parenting time expanded to half time with the children. They each spoke as though the other was the scourge of mankind and was the worst parent for their children. They used hateful, contemptuous words to describe the other's behavior. The mediator asked them, "How do you think your children are handling this?" Both said they thought the children were doing fine in light of the circumstances of divorce. They went on continuing to blame the other for the parenting problems.

Finally the mediator intervened and said, "It is very hard for me to sit here and hear these awful things that you are saying about each other. It's a wonder to me that your children are surviving all of this. If they are continually exposed to this, I would fear that they will wither up and die inside from all the pain it brings them. Children know they are made up of half of each of their parents. Usually when children hear one of their parents disrespect the other, they begin to feel that half of who they are is bad, and their self images fall to their toes, and they become very distraught. Is it possible that this may be happening to your children and neither of you know it?"

Dave and Hilary, sobered by this comment, both quietly say it was possible. They each admitted that they were worried about the children, because the children were each having problems in school and at after-school care. In fact, Caitlin is in therapy, and both parents see her therapist from time to time.

The mediator follows this with, "So what do the two of you want to do so the children will be least harmed by all of this?"

The mediator's comment is hard hitting and heartfelt. It is not judgmental, but it reveals what happens to children amidst parental conflict. This comment was made for the purpose of shaking up the game board and offered the parents a different path toward resolving the differences they have with each other.

Unexpected comments made by the mediator are not for the purpose of surprise, but to uncover the underlying conflicts that drive destructive behavior. When this happens, the mediator may offer several ideas about how the clients can begin to resolve these underlying conflicts. In divorce a frequent suggestion is for them to consider how they might begin letting go of what they hold against each other. Usually the conflict is associated with some unresolved hurt and pain related to the marriage breakdown and decision to divorce. When this is the case, the mediator may suggest that they enter marriage-closure therapy together, so they have the opportunity to analyze how their marriage relationship ended in divorce. This is not a process for them to re-evaluate the divorce decision or to consider reconciliation. It is meant to help them understand what happened, to recall and appreciate the positives of their marriage relationship, and to begin to let go and forgive each other for what they hold against the other. As we all know, forgiveness frees the forgiver and changes how the forgiver perceives the other. If forgiveness is mutual, both will be rewarded by a significant improvement in their relationship as parents.

When we were teaching divorce mediation to a group of Hmong professionals, they did not understand the concept of holding resentments. We tried to explain it as allowing someone to live rent free in your mind.

After awhile one of them said, "That's like walking around with a hot coal on one's head!" Even though the hot coal colloquialism is not common in American culture, we all know that if one walked around with a hot coal on one's head, the coal would eventually destroy that person. This is exactly what mediators are trying to help divorcing couples understand about conflict and resentments. A good way to help them understand this is intervening by use of a metaphor. The comment can be an observation about the process or the conflict made by the mediator to help people understand the conflict, not to judge the parties or to direct the outcome.

MEDIATOR NEUTRALITY

One of the most frequently asked questions about mediation is, "How can you be neutral when there is a power imbalance between the parties?" This assumes three things: (1) that there is always some power imbalance when people are in conflict, (2) that a mediator would recognize this, and (3) the mediator would have to balance it. Think for a moment of the scale of justice. To balance the scale, the mediator would need to take something from one person and give it to the other. Unfortunately, mediation is not that simple. The following illustrates the mediator's neutrality dilemma:

The husband confronted the mediator just as the consultation was beginning, "Are you a born-again Christian believing in Jesus Christ as your one and only true Master and Savior?" The mediator responded by saying, "That's an interesting question. I would think you would be more interested in whether I am a good mediator. Let me ask your wife." Turning to the wife the mediator asked, "Is it important that I be a born-again Christian believing in Jesus Christ as my one and only true Master and Savior?" The wife immediately replied, "That is why we are getting divorced! He has joined a conservative religious church, and I didn't. He wanted someone from his church to mediate, and I refused. So we came to you because of your reputation as a mediator."

If the mediator indicated beliefs similar to the husband, the wife would have viewed the mediator as favoring her husband. If the mediator had not, the husband would have seen the mediator as in favor of the wife. To maintain neutrality, the mediator changed the question and inquired of the wife the importance of the husband's stance.

The ability to remain neutral is a primary characteristic of the client-centered mediator. The mediator is sometimes referred to as a neutral third party or neutral facilitator. In the literature of mediation, neutrality is emphasized as a primary aspect of the mediator's role. As you consider becoming a mediator, we suggest examining your own perspectives on neutrality. Certainly, as human beings, we are rarely neutral about anything. We believe that this is the same in mediation. We all bring our opinions, ideas, and biases to the mediation table, and they enter our thoughts as issues emerge from the clients. Mediators must always be aware of their own perspectives and recognize how they might impact the mediation process by raising them or by refraining from raising them. This may seem like a simple point, but it gets to the heart of neutrality and power, which is a core aspect of client-centered mediation.

BEING NEUTRAL ABOUT DIVORCE

It seems that we all have our own opinions about divorce. One out of every two first marriages in the United States ends in divorce, and the rate is even higher for second marriages. Aspiring divorce mediators need to discover and take responsibility for their own feelings and biases about divorce before entering this field. Many people attending our training sessions have disclosed that they really would prefer to mediate a reconciliation of the marriage relationship and prevent the divorce. A mediator who interjects this underlying motivation into a divorce mediation consultation may find one very agreeable client and one who is very distressed. It takes a lot of thoughtful preparation for a couple to actually seek a consultation with a divorce mediator. The mediator who makes the assumption that the couple should be reconciling discounts the couple by not respecting their wishes.

The mediator asked the couple at the beginning of the consultation, "Are the two of you getting a divorce?" Jake said yes, and Sonja looked at him stunned and said, "What? I thought we were coming here for counseling." She began to weep. Jake turned to her and said, "You know that I wanted to come to mediation to work out our divorce. Counseling has not worked, and I told you last week that I didn't see any other way to stay married." The mediator observed, "This must be very hard for both of you," and then asked them, "Is there any commitment that either of you are looking for from the other that would provide enough incentive for you to stay married?" Sonja said, "We've tried counseling, I know, but I never wanted to divorce. I don't know if there is anything more we can do. Maybe I'm just fooling myself wishing things would work for us." Jake agreed. The mediator then asked, "Do you want to continue with this consultation? I can explain how mediation works in divorce or a trial separation period, and I can answer your questions so you at least know what your options are as you go forward." Both agreed to continue.

Divorce mediators need to be clear with themselves and with their clients that they are comfortable mediating divorces. Mediators need to demonstrate respect for the decision to divorce, no matter what they believe about the propriety of divorce.

It is normal for people considering divorce to experience a period of deep ambivalence about whether to end the marriage. The decision to divorce or not belongs to the clients. It is inappropriate for a mediator to persuade people to stay married or to pursue a divorce. Because all no-fault jurisdictions allow a spouse to divorce over the objection of the other, the mediator may appear to favor the spouse wanting the divorce when the mediator explains the choices available to the person opposed to the divorce. Even though Sonja did not want the divorce, it is important for her to become fully informed about the choices she has, because the divorce may proceed against her wishes.

If you struggle with your own dislike of divorce, it may be helpful to view mediation as a service that assists divorcing couples to make things better for themselves and their children. Because most couples who begin a divorce process do eventually divorce, concentrating on what mediation can offer them is a better way to proceed with their divorce and their decision making. One great value of divorce mediation is its acceptance of a couple's choices. It helps them create their own best outcomes. The mediator who is able to set aside personal biases benefits the clients by assisting them to make things better, not worse.

As illustrated in the above example of Jake and Sonja, the mediator can demonstrate neutrality and avoid a discussion about whether or not the marriage should end by asking one of the following two questions:

1. "Are the two of you getting a divorce?"
2. "Are you each of the opinion that the marriage should end?"

These questions offer each person an opportunity to articulate their commitment to the divorce, without having to say *why* the divorce is occurring. Usually, one strongly agrees with this question while the other quietly agrees or is silent. The question keeps the mediator neutral and generates important information for the mediator. The mediator can ask the client who seems less committed to divorcing, another question like, "Are you then less inclined to proceed with the divorce?" This question may provide the client an opening to talk about feelings about the divorce. The divorce mediator, maintaining neutrality, may choose to comment on how difficult it must be for that person to proceed, and then acknowledge that it also may not be easy for the other person to have been the first to decide to divorce. As you can see, the mediator does not comment on the correctness of their decision to divorce but offers some understanding of what it must be like for each of them. This is not to say that mediators do not have feelings about the wisdom of some couples' decision to divorce. However, mediators understand that voicing such an opinion would only validate one person and alienate the other, thereby jeopardizing mediator neutrality. Mediators usually learn that as the couple's story unfolds, their personal biases about the decision to divorce are mistaken.

A mediator's neutrality is challenged not only at the beginning of mediation, but may be questioned at any time during mediation process. In training and supervision of mediators, we teach the phrase, "the mediator does not have a vested interest in the outcome." This means that the mediator does not gain anything based upon how or whether the divorce is settled. For example, it is not appropriate for a mediator to offer to mediate and agree to be paid only if the case settles. Although beginning mediators may see this as an innocent method of proving themselves, that kind of contingent fee arrangement places inappropriate pressure on the mediator to compel or coerce the husband and wife into a settlement. Ethical codes for mediators forbid contingent fee arrangements. Another example of an inappropriate influence on the process can result from referral arrangements that are overtly or covertly confidential, conditional upon the mediator's settlement rate. Even worse is a situation in which the mediator feels that he or she will be highly regarded by a referral source if the mediator influences the settlement in favor of a particular client. This does not serve anyone well, because the outcome will not be the best possible solution for the couple.

BUILDING BLOCKS FOR SETTLEMENT

A mediator actively engages in the discussions, building rapport, listening carefully, asking questions, clarifying statements, and creating understanding between a husband and wife who may have had little success understanding each other at least in the recent past, if not for quite some time. The mediator listens and watches for opportunities for one to understand the other better or to acknowledge the other's thoughts, ideas, and feelings.

Another phrase that mediators use is, "The best decisions are made when each is fully informed about the issue at hand." This does not suggest, however, that all information is necessarily hard data and facts. Although there must be full disclosure of data and facts, being informed also means understanding data, facts, motives, and behaviors. The best decisions are made when people are understood, appreciated, and respected. They are empowered to think more clearly, be more creative, and use the mediation process most constructively and cooperatively. By actively broadening the information base, managing the discussions, and seizing opportunities for the husband and wife to appreciate and understand each other better, the mediator increases their chances of creating good, lasting settlements. As an illustration:

Mary entered the mediation session silently, avoiding John's greeting and barely acknowledging the mediator. After they both sat down at the table the mediator asked Mary if something was wrong. Mary talked very carefully and intensely, "I do not think mediation can work when John is lying to the children." John was surprised and retorted that he never lies to the children much less anyone else, and in fact, this whole divorce is based on Mary's dishonesty. The mediator asked Mary what she meant by her assertion that John was lying. Mary very emotionally said, "John told the children that I do not love them anymore." The mediator asked John if he understood what she said. He coolly said yes, but that he didn't lie, "The kids asked me why I didn't live at home and I told them the truth. Aren't I supposed to tell them the truth?" The mediator asked, "Did you tell them that their mother doesn't love them anymore?" John replied, "Well she doesn't love us, otherwise she would not be going through with this divorce." Mary, crying, said, "I am divorcing you, not the kids." The mediator asked John if that was correct. He insisted, "This divorce is ruining our family. How can you do this to us?" The mediator then softly and compassionately asked John if he believed that Mary truly doesn't love the children. His tone dropped to a whisper, and he replied shakily, "I know she always loved the children. But I don't know how she can do this to our family." Mary quickly said, "I am divorcing you, because I do not love you anymore. I could not stay married to you when you insisted that I not go back to being a nurse when you have been unemployed for eight out of the last twelve months, believing some miracle would save us all. And when I finally said things were not working you blamed me for buying too many groceries! I do not know of any family with two preschool children who could exist on twenty dollars' worth of groceries a week. When I suggested that if you wouldn't let me work and that you should take any job you could get, you got angry and slapped me. So I had you removed from the house. Maybe we should tell the children *that* truth!" The mediator commented on how sad all of this must be for each of them, and asked what they wanted to do. John carefully disclosed that his brother had taken him to a therapist who told him he was severely depressed. He asked Mary if they could just put the divorce on hold for a month while he started on antidepressants. Mary, moved by this revelation, said, "I can do that for only one month, but I won't do it if you continue to deny that we are getting divorced. You also have to learn how to help the children and not lie to them anymore." The mediator asked if they both wanted to make some agreements about how they would relate to each other and the children during the next month. They both agreed, and continued mediation with that goal.

There are many ways a mediator could have managed this discussion. Of course, the mediator may have felt some inclination to judge John or Mary with each new revelation. However, the motivation to remain neutral, rather than to intervene with advice or make assumptions, allowed Mary and John to begin on a new path in their decision making. Other mediators may have said more or less, but by responding with compassion, the mediator offered them the opportunity to continue their conversation without being judged or faulted for their behavior. We sometimes suggest to new mediators that one of their best strategies is to "bite their tongue until it bleeds."

In divorce-mediation training there is a section on the importance of *emotional divorce.* Sometimes the emotional divorce process contaminates the mediation process, most often when each spouse is at a very different place in their adjustment to the decision to divorce. It can be more easily understood with the following illustration:

Spouse A	*Spouse B*
Considers Divorce	**In Denial About Marital Problems**
Spouse A considers divorce alone, not sharing it with anyone. Weighs pros and cons. Ambivalent feelings of guilt, fear, hope, depression, anger, joy, etc. This may go on a long time.	Not thinking about divorce. Unhappy with marriage relationship. Wishes things would get better. Feels there is too much dissonance in marriage. May be depressed about marriage relationship.
Decides to Divorce	**Still In Denial**
Spouse A privately concludes that the marriage will never work, and divorce is the only way for things to get better. Feels excited, guilty, fearful, hopeful, happier, etc. Disengages emotionally from Spouse B. Is psychologically moving forward, seeing the light at end of tunnel, etc.	Ignores signs of marriage problems. Is not aware of Spouse A's decision to divorce. Is emotionally more hopeful, because there is less dissonance. Thinks marriage relationship is getting better. Is getting along better with Spouse A.
Acts on Decision	**Forced to Consider Divorce**
Tells Spouse B. (May also act on the decision by moving out of the house, filing a divorce petition with the court, and having Spouse B served with papers.) Talks to lawyer, mediator, others. Is both hopeful and fearful about future. Anxious to move forward, to separate from Spouse B. Worried about divorce process. Fearful of divorce process.	Is shocked at Spouse A's decision to divorce. (May choose not to believe it if Spouse B does nothing else, like continues to reside in the house.) Didn't see it coming. Thought things were getting better, especially lately. Is angry, hurt, and fearful. Wants time to work on marriage. Talks to lawyer, friends, etc. Depressed, distraught about idea of divorce.

The divorce mediator can assist people who are at different stages in the emotional divorce process by empathizing with each and acknowledging that these differences are not unusual. Most clients identify with the illustration and take comfort knowing that they are not alone feeling the way they do. This may help them make some sense out of what has felt like absolute chaos. This is also an opportunity for each of them to better understand the dynamics of the emotional divorce process. It is especially beneficial for the mediator who wants to disengage from being in the middle of having each client try to convince the mediator to take their side in the divorce.

OFFERING IDEAS AND OPTIONS

Some mediators practice a more directive, evaluative mediation process and will answer this according to the conceptual framework of that process. The client-centered mediator will routinely offer ideas and help build options in mediation. Clients often ask experienced mediators what other divorcing couples have done when faced with this issue. A client-centered mediator might do the following:

"I don't think Jim or I know what to do about the house. It would be nice if one of us could keep it, especially for the children. But only Jim can afford it with his income. But that's so unfair! I can't even qualify for a mortgage to buy a house for myself. And then I lose out in every way, just because I don't earn enough money!" Jim replied, "My budget is just as tight as yours, and in addition, I have to pay you child support. How can I even think of home ownership?" Turning to the mediator he continues, "How do most people do this? You must have some ideas from your experience." The mediator says to both, "You're right, you two are not the first to grapple with these issues. If your first choice is for one of you to own the house, would it be helpful if you first look at the consequences of one of you owning it and then of the other of you owning it? Then if that doesn't work, you have narrowed the options to selling the house and, if you wish, looking at whether or not it is feasible for you to each purchase a home with your half of the proceeds from the sale of the house. Does that sound like a way you would like to pursue these questions?" They each agree to begin by looking at one and then the other keeping the house with the other purchasing or securing similar adequate housing.

The mediator who gives ideas and suggestions without advising them, remains neutral as long as the husband and wife are free to decline the mediator's suggestions. They are still in control of the decision making and even the process, but may be relieved to learn from their mediator that there are ways to find out the answers to their concerns. In contrast, a law-centered mediator replies as follows:

"Mary you stayed in the house with the children when you two separated, right? If you were in court today, the judge would probably award you the home until the youngest child reaches 18, at which time you would need to pay Jim his half of today's equity plus interest. Jim, you will pay child support to Mary, and she will make all of the house payments and pay for the children's needs. If the child support calculation, according to the guidelines, shows that you do not have enough money to live on, Mary, we may need to look at a spousal maintenance award since you have been married over twenty years, are financially dependent on the marriage relationship for support, and do not have sufficient income to support yourself. So let's first look at the budgets and the income to determine what the support arrangement might look like."

The second example shows the mediator making decisions based upon that mediator's beliefs about what a court would do. Some would say that this is not actually mediation. Mediation clients are generally aware that they may seek coaching from legal counsel at any time, which may include information regarding likely outcomes in court, and most mediators will encourage them to do so. They can then choose how much deference they wish to give those predictions.

GENDER NEUTRALITY

Some clients will view mediator gender as very important and will specifically request either a male or a female mediator. There may be various reasons for their request. A man may ask for a female mediator because he believes his wife would be more comfortable, or a man may ask for a male mediator because he believes his wife will be more respectful of a man than a woman. A woman may ask for a male who can be strong and can control her husband, or for a female because she believes a woman will understand her better. Whatever their reasons, the mediator needs to be aware of gender, its impact on the couple, and their expectations based on the mediator's gender.

Being aware, however, does not necessarily resolve the dilemma of mediator gender. Mediators need to understand the potential impact of their gender on the mediation process and be willing to discuss it at any time it becomes an issue for either party. For example, the mediator who believes that women, because of their gender, are innately weak, cannot be neutral. If the mediator believes that women are at a great disadvantage in mediation because their husbands have all the power, the mediator cannot be neutral. Likewise, the mediator who believes that women should remain in the family home and be the primary parent for the children after a divorce may actually be doing the husband, wife, and their children an injustice by taking away their choice. In addition, following a law-centered approach might unwittingly impair mediator neutrality since many laws are gender biased. Being aware of gender issues does not mean the mediator is neutral or free of gender bias. It is the beginning point to address gender issues in mediation.

There is always a gender imbalance at the mediation table when working with divorcing couples. We suggest that each new mediator think through how their gender may affect the couple and if a mediator has deep personal wounds related to one gender or the other, typically because of childhood issues, it is important for them to do some inner work of their own. Mediators must be gender aware as they meet each divorcing couple. The husband and wife are both sensitive to issues of gender and will often notice any obvious gender bias.

This first became clear to us when we were teaching divorce mediation to a group of professionals in Chicago in 1982. Someone asked us what issue we addressed first when mediating a divorce. Simultaneously we answered, with Steve saying *the children* and Marilyn saying *the marital estate.* We looked at each other, dumbfounded at our different answers. We surmised that we each started with the subject area in which we might be perceived as being least knowledgeable from a gender perspective. The couple might assume that a male mediator would not be as capable of mediating the children's issues as a woman mediator would, and a woman mediator would not be as capable of mediating the issues of the marital assets and liabilities. After that, we both began to ask the couple what they wanted to discuss first.

POWER IMBALANCE

Power, like conflict, is neither good nor bad. How power is used defines whether it is constructive or destructive. Some very wealthy people may use their wealth to build hospitals, whereas others may use their wealth to buy weapons for terrorists. Each group has power through their wealth. However, one use is constructive whereas the other is destructive. It is the same between divorcing people and others in a conflict.

All disputes present some level of power imbalance between the people in conflict. In mediation, that power imbalance is defined by the parties and their perceptions. A divorcing mother often sees the father as powerful because he controls the income. The father, on the other hand, sees the mother as powerful because she has cared for the children and knows how to meet their needs. Each perceives the other as having had more power in certain aspects of their married lives. This scenario is very common in divorces. The mediator's role is to help people use their power for mutual enhancement rather than trying to balance power or determine who has more power.

Power arises out of relationship. Power may be one person acting in such a way as to gain unfair advantage over the other. Power is frequently played out verbally in discussion, psychologically in attitude, or actively in behavior. Sometimes it is very apparent. At other times, it is subtle. Sometimes it is intentional, sometimes people do not realize their own power. Silence, for example, may be experienced as a use of power that just frustrates the other, though it may not be intentional. A verbal request voiced with great emotion may be perceived as a use of power to either emphasize a point or to intimidate.

The problem with power balancing is that it assumes the mediator can accurately evaluate who has how much power when, in fact, power is often defined by perception. When one speaks with a loud voice, for example, the other may feel intimidated, but the speaker may simply be hard of hearing and speaks loudly to be sure the other person hears what is said. When one speaks intensely and with deep conviction, the other may perceive it as a powerful demand.

Dealing with power is especially difficult when parties have had a long relationship and know each other intimately. In these cases, the clients carry into mediation the power strategies that made each other feel uncomfortable in the relationship. One's facial expression may devastate the other, and the mediator might be oblivious to what happened that made that person so upset. Each person has subtle ways of pushing the other's buttons that are not readily apparent to the mediator.

One of the early criticisms of divorce mediation was that women should not mediate because there is an inherent power imbalance between the wife and her husband, the wife having little or no power. We were addressing a meeting of the Chicago Bar Association's family law section in the early 1980s when someone challenged divorce mediation on this basis. We had both been mediating divorces successfully for several years. Steve gave the following response, "Well, if you want to keep women weak and powerless forever, never let them speak for themselves." One could hear a pin drop in the room, until lawyers one-by-one began to understand that mediation was a forum that educated wives and husbands about all aspects of their divorce to a far greater extent than adversarial posturing, thereby preparing them to make well-informed decisions. Research about divorce mediation supports this with findings that women are more satisfied with the mediation process because of what they learn in mediation (Ellis and Stuckless, 1996).

Another criticism of divorce mediation has been that a person should not participate in mediation when there is not a level playing field. We have found that there is seldom a level playing field in divorce mediation. Because there are so many topics that need to be discussed and decided, it is not surprising that a person may have more or less information or feeling about any number of them. When the power imbalance has to do with one person having all of the information about a particular topic, that person's agreement to fully disclose all information necessary to the decision making seems to resolve the issue. If one person has only some information, but the other has a full understanding of it, this affords an opportunity to share their information and their understanding. However, they may need a neutral third-party expert to educate and explain the details, implications, and options for decision making. Divorce mediation is about offering the opportunity for each person to be fully informed about the issues to be decided in divorce, before making those decisions.

At any given point in a mediation, one spouse may have more power than the other. Each person demonstrates power at different times and in different ways. The question is how each person uses that power. It is the mediator's responsibility to learn how to recognize and deal with expressions of power. Power carries no threat, even when one has always controlled all financial resources, because in mediation there is an agreement to share the resources and provide documents to verify them. However, if one person misuses power, it may be an indication of reluctance to share information and income, thereby halting the mediation process.

Misuse of power is often based on a need or a fear. When one person misuses power and threatens the other, the mediator first needs to attend to each person's emotional safety. Next, the mediator addresses the person who misused power to learn what he or she intended to accomplish. This is achieved by asking the person, "What do you need?" Often, the person who misuses power by intimidating, swearing, name calling, anger, or however that person plays out the misuse, is fearful of losing something or fearful of the other person. When asked, "What do you need . . . ?" the person's fear or pain is recognized by the mediator, and the mere acknowledgment is usually comforting and provides an opening for that person to talk about an underlying need. The person may welcome this opening and begin to discuss the motivation for misusing power, or the person may want to continue to cover the fear and not respond to the question. Sometimes, the mediator will work harder to engage that person in a more constructive dialogue that begins to get to the underlying needs that drive the use of power. For example:

Rachael and George seemed to get along quite well in the first mediation session. During the next session, they were doing their budgets anticipating a discussion of child support. They had two boys, ages 5 and 7. Every time Rachael listed her expenses, George faulted her by insisting she was inflating them. Rachael, not wanting to make waves, changed her number just to please him even though she did not agree with him. George's behavior was very intimidating and unexpected because in the first session he and Rachael cooperated quite well and were kind and respectful of each other. The mediator intervened and asked if they could take a five-minute break. After the break, the mediator began the session by making an observation about George's manner of questioning and criticizing Rachael every time she gave her budget number. The mediator said, "George, I am puzzled about your questioning each of Rachael's figures. You seem very upset about what we are doing today. It is important to do the budgets to know what you will each need to support yourselves in the future. I am not sure we can accomplish that until we understand why you are so critical of Rachael's ideas about how much she needs in each category." George looked down, put his head in his hands, and wept. Choking he said, "I know that I am stalling the process, but I just didn't want to move forward. I knew that the next subject was to discuss custody, and that I am going to lose custody and never see the boys again because Rachael is getting married, and the boys will have a new father." Rachael, dumbfounded, said, "I would never take the boys away from you! You are the only father they have. You can't be replaced in their lives; they love you and need you."

The above use of power was recognized by the mediator as intimidating to Rachael and a possible road block to further work on the budgets. Therefore, the mediator intervened by calling a break and opening the discussion with an observation. George actually used intimidating behavior out of a fear that Rachael's future plans would supplant his role as father to the boys. In analyzing this misuse of power, it is apparent that each perceived the other as having power that interfered with their decision making in mediation. A mediator must have antennae always alert to how power is being used in the mediation process. It is another aspect of the mediator's role.

CONCLUSION

The role of the mediator is to facilitate conversation, discussion, and communication. Although the role may sound simple, it is in fact very complex. A mediator is called upon to facilitate an outcome agreeable to all involved. President Jimmy Carter once told us, "I believe that if you can mediate a divorce, you can mediate any conflict in the world." We believe that he is quite correct. The levels of complexity of the role of the mediator discussed in this chapter illustrate this very point. In Chapter 5 you will see how the mediator's role is applied to conflict in the workplace and to other applications. Once a mediator has learned to mediate divorces, we believe that the role and the skills transfer well to other types of disputes.

CHAPTER 4

The ABCs of Divorce Mediation

INTRODUCTION

B Y NOW, you are certainly familiar with the process of mediation, but you may not be as familiar with divorce mediation. You may have thought that it involved some sort of effort to save a marriage. In fact, it does not have much to do with reconciliation, but it does have a lot to do with easing the pain of families going through divorce and with helping the millions of children now moving between two homes under a court custody order. Adversarial divorce procedures operate on the assumption that divorce ends the relationship between people. In fact, divorce only ends the legal fact of *marriage*. The spouses are viewed to be in such high conflict that the only way to resolve the conflict is to treat the other spouse as an enemy or adversary and not a person who can be expected to cooperate after the divorce. These notions are misguided, and the result is that the adversarial process creates more conflict and alienation especially for parents who, because of their children, must continue a parenting relationship with each other after the divorce.

Divorce mediation is about ending the old warfare of divorce and creating new beginnings for people. Divorce mediation is also about impacting the big business of divorce in the United States, because providing help to the 2.4 million people who divorce each year has created a very large industry. To the delight of some and to the dismay of others, divorce mediation is dramatically changing that industry by giving the public better, less costly choices about the way they divorce. It has also opened the business of divorce to other professionals outside the legal profession and, as a result, divorce is no longer a monopoly controlled exclusively by lawyers and the judicial system.

This new way to divorce has evolved because divorce has become pervasive and touches essentially everyone, and the old way was destroying families and overwhelming the court system. In the past, the process of divorce was more devastating than the pain couples experienced leading up to the decision to divorce. This pain touches the lives of more people than the couples going through divorce. It is estimated that 50 percent of the children born in the year 1999 will become the subject of a custody determination during their lifetime. For many of these children, existing custody laws mean that they will either have bitter, angry parents or they will end up with just one parent. For those wanting to ease the pain children experience, this book will provide some answers. It explains how some mediators have been able to virtually eliminate custody battles by using client-centered mediation, an entirely new process that results in new ways of thinking and acting. This process avoids the traditional custody-battle approach by asking parents to create new roles for themselves.

Bill, a grandfather and the patriarch of a strong Irish family of six children and 15 grandchildren describes it this way: "Marilyn mediated two of my children's divorces. I can't believe how well it turned out. At my grandson, James', award banquet last month, every one was sitting around the table talking as if they were all friends. His mom and her husband, his dad and his wife were present, and they were all getting along without a fight. I still can't believe it. And, of course, you should see how well James is doing as a result of all their hard work. It's just marvelous. Marilyn is something else."

What Bill doesn't realize is that it is more than just Marilyn. Rather, it is the process of client-centered mediation that helped James' parents preserve a strong parenting relationship. A growing number of the 1.2 million divorces that occur each year are being mediated. Questions of custody, support, and property division are being settled by husbands and wives meeting in the same room with a neutral mediator who helps them decide the terms of their settlement and establish a workable parenting relationship for the future, when they have children. The mediator helps them put aside their anger and negative emotions so they can save or eliminate attorneys fees, create better planning for the children, and end up dividing their property fairly. This is not exciting material for a movie producer thinking of another *Kramer vs. Kramer* or *War of the Roses*, but it is exciting for the professional who serves divorcing families. More significant, it is incredibly important for the 2.4 million people each year who get divorced.

WHAT IS DIVORCE MEDIATION?

> **It is not just an alternative to litigation, but a completely different method of reaching decisions about children, support, and property division.**

As previously stated in this book, divorce mediation is an alternate way for people to obtain a divorce settlement. It is based upon new thinking about divorce and conflict resolution. Instead of relying on the traditional adversarial court process, by first commencing a lawsuit and then settling on the courthouse steps a year or two later just before trial (and after spending thousands of dollars preparing for trial), mediation relies on the ability of divorcing couples to discuss and work out their own agreements with the help, encouragement, and guidance (but not advice) of a professional mediator. The process offers divorcing couples new and very different choices that are better and less destructive than adversarial choices. These choices have been invented by the practicing divorce mediators who have learned in the trenches what works and what does not work with high conflict couples in the midst of painful divorce. Mediation offers these couples the opportunity to learn how to cooperate with each other, rather than encouraging them to compete as adversaries when negotiating and living with a divorce settlement. It offers them the opportunity to use attorneys, therapists, and accountants, not as hired guns, but as experts who assist the couple to achieve fair and workable results. To the surprise of many, mediation actually becomes a vehicle to teach cooperation and to create healing.

Divorce mediation is different than traditional divorce procedures, even when traditional steps taken by attorneys lead to a settlement of the case without a trial. In fact, what occurs in divorce mediation is 180 degrees from the adversarial process at virtually every point. The philosophy of mediation is that all sides should achieve a victorious outcome, in contrast to the adversarial divorce philosophy of winner prevails due to the loser having a weaker case. Even with collaborative attorneys, the traditional approach still follows the win-lose assumptions of the court system that one parent gets the children and the house and the other parent makes child support payments. Even when attorneys stop short of using the total firepower of the adversarial process, people operating within the framework of adversarial thinking still make divorce decisions by competing to determine whose case is stronger. Their thinking goes something like this on almost every issue: "Can I or my client prevail on this particular point, and what will the law give me or make me do?" On the other hand, the mediator encourages thinking like, "You can only get a good result when you help your spouse get a good result."

In the adversarial divorce process, each person usually hires an attorney and that attorney is required by the canons of ethics to advance the case strictly on behalf of their client. Given that mind-set, the attorney will represent the client by presenting the facts and law in the light most favorable to the client. This is not called stretching the truth; in legal parlance it is zealous advocacy. The attorney who represents the other spouse will, of course, do the same. It is no surprise they have different predictions about what their clients are entitled to. The differences in their predictions may not be huge, but the differences are usually enough to stoke the competitive adversarial fires for some time to come.

Because the lawyer also may not know what to expect of the other side in the early stages of representation, one of the first instructions a lawyer gives to a client is to not speak with the other spouse. This suggestion is designed to prevent sharing information that could be useful to the other side in a trial. In some jurisdictions, each attorney tries to outdo the other attorney to initiate the divorce action by being the first to serve a summons and petition for divorce. Aggressive attorneys will also schedule a temporary hearing even before determining whether there is an opportunity to negotiate a settlement of the temporary living-arrangement issues. There is really no reason for starting the civil action at this stage other than to get the earliest date on the trial calendar or to freeze assets if there is a fear that someone is going to leave the country with the children or the bank accounts. Such a fear is unlikely to manifest itself because to leave the country would also result in leaving behind the children, real estate, and retirement assets.

Of course, if one spouse is unwilling to sit down with the other at the mediation table, it may be necessary to commence the legal action as outlined above. However, in our years of accepting referrals from various jurisdictions after the couple has spent considerable time engaging in adversarial battle, the most common refrain from the couple is, "Why didn't we know about mediation sooner?" In far too many cases, the attorney's first step is to initiate the legal action by serving the summons and petition instead of informing clients of mediation. Instant billable hours are also a result of immediate filing. Serving the summons and petition is somewhat like putting the key in the ignition and starting the engine. People often don't realize that if you are driving a battlewagon, there is still a lot of distance yet to be covered. If the summons and petition is not answered by the other side within 20 or 30 days, depending upon the jurisdiction, the other side defaults, giving up all rights to object. This rarely happens except in cases where a spouse abandons the other by leaving the state. After all this is completed, there is usually an open file with the court and an assigned case number. In mediation, filing the documents in court usually occurs after the drafting of the mutually agreed settlement. This costs considerably less because there is no need to file a formal answer and counter petition, as the action is settled by the filing of the settlement agreement, which is the result of mediation.

Another problem with the adversarial approach is that it encourage spouses not to trust each other. The major assumptions of the adversarial divorce process are that the other side will not tell the truth about the marital estate, will hide assets, and will inflate liabilities. Each person may be encouraged to listen to their dark side, to believe that the other party is an unfit parent who will try to get out of their legal obligation to pay support. This cultivation of one's fears usually sets off the other person. Fueled by their fear, each tries to outmaneuver the other. Because neither side trusts the other, the attorneys need to send interrogatories to the other side. Interrogatories are a set of questions that ask for any and all information each side believes it needs in order to proceed. Sending interrogatories tends to be a game of keep away, because each attorney is permitted to advise their client to answer the questions with as little information as possible. After each side has completed this exercise, and neither has gained any helpful information from the other side, the attorneys request depositions. Depositions are another way of trying to obtain information, except that these require the other person to answer questions under oath with a court reporter recording everything that is said. Once again, each person is advised by their attorney to give as little information as the rules allow. Because one side has deposed the other, then the other does the same.

The most egregious of all battles is the custody battle, for what could be more important than one's children? If the parents are fighting over who will get the children, attorneys will ask each client to find friends, relatives, and others to help discredit the other parent. To accomplish this, the friends, relatives, and others are asked to sign affidavits, which are negative statements about the other parent's ability to parent the children. These affidavits are designed to prove that the other is an unfit parent, and they are the most hurtful maneuvers that occur in the entire realm of adversarial divorce (Ellis & Stuckless, 1996, p. 59) These affidavits are used to prove a parent has acted against the best interests of his or her children in the past, as a basis for awarding custody of the children to the more fit parent. The affidavits contaminate the well water for many years to come, making it difficult for parents to cooperate as they must after the divorce.

We could go on and on about adversarial divorce, but enough has been said to make it clear that the adversarial divorce process is inherently destructive. In fact, many people are beginning to realize that if we set out to invent a very costly and damaging system for families affected by divorce, we could not have done better than to invent the present system of adversarial divorce. Is it any wonder, then, that divorce mediation has emerged? Not only has it become the alternative to adversarial divorce, we believe that it is a better way to divorce than even collaborative lawyer-negotiated divorce.

WHY DIVORCE MEDIATION IS A GROWING FIELD

It is not a contradiction to talk about strengthening and improving relationships even in the midst of divorce. Most couples do not want to leave the marriage relationship devastated and alienated whether they have children together or they are childless. In mediation and in divorce-education classes, we have used a visual illustration of this concept to help spouses understand that their marriage does not have to end in disaster; it can end in dignity. When couples understand and accept the concept of how a relationship changes, they understand what they can do to close their marriage with dignity. They try to change their relationship from intimacy to businesslike respect.

RELATIONSHIP CIRCLE

The relationship circle is used to illustrate how a marriage relationship evolves into a separation or divorce. It begins with a period of friendship or dating. This period, illustrated in the first quarter, is the getting-to-know-you time when each person is evaluating their attraction to the other and assessing whether this relationship is serious enough to result in a marriage. The second quarter illustrates the period of positive intimacies characteristic of early marriages. During this period the relationship is dominated by positive intimacies: appreciating each other; sharing inner secrets; togetherness; trust; common interests; knowing what each other is thinking, going to say, or do—it is generally positive. Disagreements are resolved or forgotten. The relationship gradually changes between the second and third quarter when more and more conflict occurs and bad feelings enter the relationship. The relationship is dominated by negative intimacies when more and more conflicts are unresolved, and resentments and anger become commonplace. The negative intimacies dominate the relationship, with such behaviors as blame, cheap shots, name calling, and disrespect.

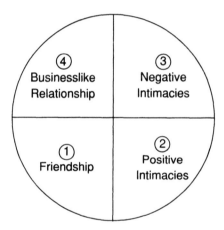

Because a divorce does not end a relationship, the next quarter illustrates a new relationship, a businesslike relationship. A businesslike relationship is dominated by rules and understandings that have been agreed upon by the former spouses about their future relationship. The businesslike relationship has only to do with how they will relate to each other after the divorce.

Spouses without children may have a continuing relationship because of the financial dependency of one upon the other, called spousal maintenance. As part of their divorce negotiations, they establish the details of how much will be paid, for how long, and any special circumstances that would end or continue maintenance. Because only about 17 percent of divorces have spousal maintenance payments, the couple without children may have other reasons to have a relationship, like having common friends and relationships with each other's family members.

Spouses with children of any age will need to establish a businesslike relationship to continue their parenting relationship, which a divorce does not sever. For example, they may have agreements about parenting minor children, and how they will conduct themselves in each other's presence at the children's special events in the future.

MEDIATING PARENTING AGREEMENTS

Concerns about parenting are at the center of the growing recognition that divorce, as it has been conducted in the court system, harms children. Divorce mediation demonstrates a preferred approach that is less harmful to children, and therefore, is more than a passing fad. Almost two million children each year experience their parents' divorce. In addition, with the explosion of unwed births, a growing number of children whose parents are not married experience the conflict between their parents who try to raise them in separate homes. Divorce mediation and mediation with unmarried parents provide hope for these children, because mediation helps strengthen and improve parental relationships for parents who live in two separate places. Providing a means to address the issues of separate parenting is of paramount importance in a country where such arrangements are now the norm. Some professionals point to the increase in youth violence as due, in part, to the vast number of children caught in their parents' divorce conflict. These are children who typically are raised in only one home because the traditional adversarial system of divorce has stated to the other parent:

You are a noncustodial visiting parent and, at best, you are only needed on every other weekend and a few weekday evenings each month. We want you, however, to support your children with your money. You won't be able to have a say in how the money is spent. Just send it to the parent who has been proven to be better than you. In addition, now that we think about it, you really can't be trusted to send it on your own, so we will take it from your paycheck through a wage-withholding process. If you object, we will publicly expose you as a dead-beat parent!"

No wonder so many children of divorce have problems.

Most parents have an innate understanding of the need to strengthen and preserve the parental relationship after divorce, and most parents clearly understand that the adversarial system of litigation does not meet these needs. How many times has the therapist, clergy, or divorce mediator heard the statement, "We had it all worked out until we went to our attorneys"? When divorce is seen as the beginning of a new stage of life rather than an end, divorce mediation is truly a common-sense concept easily understood and embraced by a majority of people.

WHAT'S THE DIFFERENCE?

Client-centered divorce mediation is not the practice of law, because it assumes there are many standards of fairness to choose from, not just state law. Although mediation may produce therapeutic results, it is not the practice of therapy. Although client-centered divorce mediation builds upon the theory and practice of both law and the behavioral sciences, it has developed its own unique conceptual framework that differs from either in that its purpose is narrowly defined as assisting the husband and wife in reaching a settlement of all of their divorce issues that is fair to each by *their* standards of what is fair. In the process of engaging in client-centered mediation, it becomes therapeutic for the couple to create order out of the chaos that may exist for them, yet the mediator is not practicing therapy. Similarly, the mediator may help the couple create fair results after discussing how state law might work as a standard of fairness, but the mediator is not practicing law. The mediator does not assist either or both of them in resolving personal problems or behaviors, dysfunctional relationships, or other emotional afflictions such as addiction. Likewise, the mediation does not predict legal outcomes in court. A by-product of the mediation is that they may be able to understand and apply how the child support guidelines may apply to their circumstances, even though they may choose to deviate from the child support guidelines law. Another by-product of mediation is that they may begin to resolve some of the dysfunctional behavior in order to become better parents after the divorce.

Several skills unique to the role of a client-centered mediator follow:

- An ability to develop an empathic, respectful working relationship with both husband and wife;
- An ability to demonstrate keen listening skills that hear clients messages through the static of the high conflict of the enmeshed negatively intimate relationship;

- An ability to listen for commonalities and agreement in their discussion;
- An ability to listen and clarify to understand what the client is communicating;
- An ability to refrain from judgment, and rather to try to understand motivations and needs;
- An ability to model respectful, interested curiosity;
- An ability to reframe a client's message by taking out the negativity, blame, and fault so that it is more manageable and better understood;
- An ability to learn the content of divorce issues and how to focus on issues when emotions are dominating the discussion;
- An ability to learn the power of asking questions that open discussions and encourage clear logical thinking;
- An ability to be responsible, ethical, and honest;
- An ability to be neutral even when raising a difficult issue that clients may not be comfortable discussing;
- An ability to be well prepared and organized to help clients make sense of the chaos in their lives;
- An ability to use a calm, even demeanor as a technique to settle clients who are very anxious or angry;
- An ability to have a healthy sense of humor and know when to use it;
- An ability to demonstrate clear, concise writing skills that best communicate clients' agreements;
- An ability to be creative without pushing an agenda on clients;
- An ability to allow clients to struggle to find their solutions even when the solution may be obvious;
- An ability to appreciate the value in clients making their own decisions;
- An ability to understand that clients may not be candidates for the parent-of-the-year award and still be good parents;
- An ability to separate the problem from the people;
- An ability to find something to respect in each person no matter how difficult they are to appreciate;
- An ability to recognize that what may work for them may never work for you, and that's fine;
- An ability to be aware that the law does not necessarily fit with how clients need to operate in the future after the divorce;
- An ability to understand and accept the laws as guidelines and per-

haps as a last option, rather than trying to fit the clients' lives and situations to the laws; and

- A desire to seek to know the literature and research about divorce
  and divorce mediation.

HISTORY

Divorce mediation burst upon the scene in the mid-1970s. The current
mediation movement can be traced to the efforts of a small group of people in the early 1970s who set out to prove that divorce mediation
worked for couples in the midst of the high conflict. In 1969, an Atlanta
attorney named Jim Coogler went through a bitter divorce that left his
family torn apart. Both he and his wife were left close to bankruptcy because of their attorneys' fees. His experience convinced him there must
be a better way. As a visionary who encouraged other early believers, including these two authors, he is considered the founder of the divorce-
mediation movement. He often talked about how he was convinced that
the adversarial system of litigation was actually more dysfunctional than
his own marriage.

Jim strongly believed that a divorcing couple need not view each other
as enemies. He felt it was important that couples cooperate in order to
build a good separate parenting plan, because they would most likely be
connected in the future around their minor or adult children. They also
needed to cooperate to have a sound unhooking of their financial futures
and a fair division of the property. From his attempts to help others avoid
the destructive impact of what he experienced, the divorce mediation
movement began and subsequently spawned other mediation applications in the area of business, school, and community disputes.

Jim and a Presbyterian minister, Will Neville, decided to try mediation
to see if it was possible for a couple to stay out of the court system and
reach agreement face to face with the help of a neutral. At the time, their
idea was quite controversial because it had never been done before and
because the legal system, seeing itself as the sole manager of the business
of divorce, was threatened by this new idea. No one had tried to extend
mediation beyond the narrow realm of labor-management conflicts before their efforts in the summer of 1974.

Coogler and Neville, in an attempt to be nonadversarial, did not use a
courtroom procedure nor a process like labor mediation. There were no

opening statements by the parties and there was no caucusing separately in an attempt to coerce the two people to compromise. Coogler strenuously objected to the notion of caucusing because it felt too much like his own divorce, in which he and his wife were required to sit outside the family court while their two attorneys met privately with the judge and settled important matters about their children and their future.

Coogler and Neville also attempted to be nondirective. They discovered that the less they told the couple what they ought to do, the more likely the couple would be to come up with their own fair solutions. They also provided a framework of rules for the couple to follow that excluded fault from the discussions and focused on general concepts of fairness unrelated to blame and wrongdoing. The focus was future oriented, and surprisingly, it worked exceedingly well. This framework has been refined in subsequent years by the use of asking different questions, but the basic philosophy of the process started by Coogler and Neville remains nondirective, future focused, and nonadversarial.

The current mediation movement can also be traced to an important book written by Professor Morton Deutsch in 1973. Professor Deutsch's book had a great impact on several of the early divorce mediators because it gave legitimacy to the idea that the legal adversarial system itself was the major cause of the harm and intense conflict experienced in divorce, not the conflict between the couple. He suggested something quite bold: Conflict itself is not bad, the problem arises from the way we *manage* and *resolve* conflict. In other words, the approach to conflict resolution is what is most important. He believed that managing conflict using a competitive process was destructive, whereas managing conflict using a cooperative process was beneficial and productive. He observed that

> the crux of differences between cooperation and competition lies in the nature of the way the goals of the participants in each of the situations are linked. In a cooperative situation the goals are so linked that everybody "sinks or swims" together, while in a competitive situation, if one swims, the other must sink. (Deutsch, 1973, p. 20)

Deutsch went on to say:

> In a cooperative situation when a participant behaves in such a way as to increase his chances of goal attainment, he increases the chances that the others, with whom he is promotively linked, will also attain their goals. In contrast, in

a competitive situation when a person behaves in such a way as to increase his own chances of goal attainment, he decreases the chances of the others. (p. 22)

For the couple divorcing, it really does get down to basic goals. Will they hire a mediator to help create a cooperative environment, where they choose to share joint goals that help achieve the benefits of shared parenting, separate financial futures that work, and fair division of property or will they each hire an attorney who has sworn an oath to uphold the canons of ethics in an effort to gain all for one client at the expense of the other? Deutsch's observations about shared or separate goal attainment seem grounded in common sense, but these views actually form the basic difference between a cooperative mediation process and all other competitive systems of conflict resolution.

After Deutsch's book, the idea that divorcing couples were not inherently flawed nor always prone to engage in destructive conflict gained strength. Instead, it became more evident that the legal process they were using was destructive because it was based upon an adversarial (competitive) model. Deutsch took the position that conflict by itself is an ordinary and necessary aspect of our existence. Without conflict, society could not function because everyone would be the same with no differences among them. The problem then is not the existence of conflict. It is the improper management of conflict using competition, which is inherently destructive. When we manage conflict using cooperative principles, Deutsch argued, there is the opportunity for positive growth. From this assertion, the early divorce mediators went a step further and argued that the adversarial court system is itself destructive. If a couple could be persuaded to enter a mediation system in which cooperative principles and processes were used, the possibility of settling the conflict increased. In addition, the couple benefited from participating in a cooperative process. Later writers, most notably Bush and Folger (1994), focused on the benefits of the mediation process by arguing that mediation is better than an adversarial competitive process of conflict resolution, and also has the promise to transform relationships and, thereby, change society.

Today everyone is talking about Alternative Dispute Resolution (ADR), mediation, and cooperation. We are finally starting to act as our brother's keeper. Perhaps we will see the day where the type of terrible, destructive conflict that has affected families and communities for thousands of years will become a thing of the past. We will get there by using mediation to transform the way we relate to each other, and applying the healing powers of a cooperative mediation process to use conflict as our helper rather than our destroyer.

Detractors, however, advise extreme caution. They say that although mediation is a nice addition to our existing legal settlement techniques, it has major drawbacks. They advise caution whenever mediation is used and say that mediation should never be used if there has been abuse in the relationship. After all, some people will persist in using dirty tricks against you and, well, to be honest, if you are not very, very careful about mediation, you can end up worse off than before because of your naive thinking that cooperation will work. (Remember that Lucy always pulls the football away just as Charlie Brown attempts to kick it!) Other detractors take a different approach and argue that mediation is the practice of law and that a mediator can get into trouble in complex matters that have traditionally been the province of lawyers. They claim that only lawyers should be allowed to be mediators.

What does all this mean for the therapist, attorney, or other professional who is interested in mediation? Moreover, what does this mean for the consumers who spend an estimated $34 billion a year on an antiquated and inefficient adversarial system that does not really resolve conflict? It means, in a word, change. Just as the Internet is rapidly and dramatically changing the way we share information and do business, mediation is rapidly and dramatically changing the way we resolve conflict. And just as there is a lot of confusion and disagreement about how the Internet is changing our society, there is also a great deal of confusion, controversy, and disagreement about how mediation is changing our legal system. This book helps to clear up that confusion.

THE REASON DIVORCE MEDIATION WAS NEEDED IN THE FIRST PLACE

The idea that a mediator can help a couple find cooperation in the midst of their divorce seems a bit preposterous if one considers only the narrow legal goals of the settlement. Because they are divorcing, the couple may say,

---

"There is nothing about us that says we should sink or swim together. We are getting divorced, and since we will not be living together, why should we cooperate? We have not been able to cooperate in the past and because of that, we are now getting divorced. Why on earth should we need to cooperate now?" If there are children, family courts traditionally have said, "If they can't live together as husband and wife, they certainly can't raise their children together. We had best put one of them in charge of the children and call the other a visitor." If the divorcing couple lived in Louisiana or South Carolina and one of them was seeking alimony, the courts would say, "We will deny the request if it can be shown by the other side that the spouse seeking support engaged in adulterous behavior during the marriage relationship."

In some states, shared marital property was not awarded to the spouse whose actions caused the marital breakup. In many states, the court has said that it will divide property in such a way that the spouse who earned more money during the marriage has the right to receive more of the property upon divorce. If one adheres to traditional legal definitions of fairness, mediation and cooperation seem preposterous when applied to conflicts over who will own the children, who committed adultery, who worked the hardest, or who earned the most money during the years the couple was married.

These legal approaches to ending marriage actually create more conflict than anyone could imagine. Research shows that the level of the parents' conflict has a positive correlation with children's inability to emotionally adjust following divorce (Kelly & Wallerstein, 1980). Then on top of all of this, until the early 1970s most states allowed the spouse who didn't want the divorce the opportunity to show that the grounds for divorce were not met in order to stop the divorce. On the other hand, if there were grounds for divorce, the spouse often said: "Give me the kids, the property, and anything else I can get and you can suffer." By asking these types of right/wrong questions and establishing goals that are impossible to share, the legal system actually created the sink or swim battle mentality that encouraged a greater level of intense and destructive conflict.

From an historical perspective, Coogler and Neville's approach makes excellent sense. At the time, the early divorce mediators were not sure about all their methods and interventions, but they knew they were doing something right. People began to tell others about the mediation process and, perhaps more strikingly, hundreds of professionals began calling the offices of the Family Mediation Association to ask for training.

Our most memorable call came from an Ohio attorney who related how he had practiced exclusively as a divorce attorney for 30 years but was now burned out. After faithfully attending AA meetings for the past six years, he had recently concluded he could not continue working as a divorce attorney. When we asked him why, he gave two reasons: (1) Almost all of his clients were dissatisfied with the outcomes. Even if he achieved more for them than they realized, they invariably felt they had lost as a result of the conflict. (2) He recently realized he could not reconcile the continued practice of law with his 12-step recovery program, which required rigorous honesty, little blame, and focusing on the future rather than the past.

CLIENT-CENTERED DIVORCE MEDIATION

The awareness of the need for divorce mediation arises from both current research (Ellis & Stuckless, 1996) and common sense that shows the adversarial divorce process is destructive and harmful to ongoing family relationships. New thinking is needed to prevent harm to children and families when they decide they cannot continue to live together. Client-centered mediation embodies that new thinking in a way that is helpful to couples facing the inevitable conflict of divorce.

To understand client-centered mediation, it is helpful to understand what happens to a person who is in the midst of divorce.

Susan intends to divorce her husband of 23 years, but she is scared. When people have fear, they generally feel incompetent and act as if they have no power. Her husband is also probably fearful, but perhaps in a different way. Because the marriage is ending, they will both begin to recall horror stories about divorce, and as a result, harbor thoughts that the other could turn on them. They may each visit attorneys and be told that they could lose their house, their children, and a lot of money fighting a battle if things get ugly. Old thinking says that they really have differing interests, and if each does not have an advocate to protect these interests, they will be taken advantage of by the other. However, Susan is not so much angry at her husband as she is sad that she cannot do anything to prevent the divorce from happening. She worries that the children will be harmed by the divorce process and also worries that she will not have enough money once they start living apart. She is willing to con-

sider a new way of thinking in order to try to get through the divorce
with the least amount of conflict. After all, she is getting divorced to
make things better, not worse.

Susan is one of a growing number of people who recognize that they
do not want to enter the legal system and engage in battle with their
spouse, yet they know that they are unable to complete the divorce
process without someone's help. Susan has never been through a divorce
before and decides to see a mediator because she has heard that it is a
better, healthier, and more economical way to obtain a divorce.

THE COMMUNITY OF PROFESSIONALS

Whoever said that divorce is a family matter? A divorce is the ending of a
marriage, which affects a husband and wife and their children. It also affects the extended families of the husband and wife. It affects the children's teachers, classmates, their friends, their parents' friends, teams
they play on, clubs they participate in, extracurricular activities they are
in, their work supervisors and colleagues, their religious organizations,
and related classes and groups, their health, emotional and physical, and
their quality of life. Divorce becomes their never-ending story.

In every divorce, the husband and the wife are responsible for the effect of their divorce on everyone who has been or is in their world. Most
husbands and wives do not understand this, however. In fact, not until
the growth of divorce mediation have husbands and wives begun to understand their responsibility for the effects of their divorces on others.
Most husbands and wives do not understand that they, and they alone,
have the power to make the effect of their divorce on everyone in their
world either positive or negative.

Husbands and wives, who choose to be responsible for the effects of
their divorce on everyone in their world, can make that choice based
upon the method they use to make all of the decisions in their divorce.
They are getting divorced to make things better, not worse for themselves, their children, and everyone else in their world. Because divorce
does not occur in a vacuum, it is very important for divorcing couples to
recognize that they may need a lot of professional help to get divorced
so that everyone in their world is more positively than negatively affected by their divorce.

As you have read so far, client-centered divorce mediation respects and encourages the best efforts of the divorcing couple to end their marriage with dignity and fairness. It is based on Morton Deutsch's conflict-resolution theory, family-systems theory, Carl Rogers' theory of person-centered therapy, the early teachings of Jim Coogler, and the work and experience of many mediators, therapists, and other professionals who have worked with divorcing families. The role of the mediator described in Chapter 3 is complex, not simple. Some skills and techniques of mediators may be taught, others need to be learned through experience. Yet the field of divorce mediation grows and thrives having a major, positive impact on the divorcing public more than any other divorce-related service. Divorce mediation could not grow or thrive without all of the other professionals having input into the mediation process and assisting divorcing family members outside the mediation room.

In the mediation process various professionals are needed to provide information to the divorcing couple as they prepare to make major life decisions. Some of the professionals who are more routinely involved in divorce mediation are therapists, accountants, financial planners, and lawyers. Others who are very helpful though required less often are child psychologists, career consultants, business appraisers, real estate appraisers, mortgage bankers, actuaries, employment counselors, doctors, and others. In mediation, couples ask professionals such as these to be neutral experts advising them in their best, unbiased professional judgment regarding a particular subject in the divorce.

NEUTRAL EXPERTS

When discussing the role of the mediator and the mediation process, it is necessary to also discuss the role of the neutral expert in mediation. Some very creative uses of neutral experts have been pioneered by mediation.

In adversarial divorce, when expert information or advice is needed, each attorney hires an expert to issue an opinion, and if necessary, to testify in a light most favorable to their side in court. With each expert reinforcing the side of the attorney who hired him, there is still a contest between the opposing opinions of the experts.

In mediation, when an expert opinion is needed, the mediator gives the couple three names. The clients then interview the experts and agree on one they will mutually employ to give an opinion as a neutral expert. The professional neutral expert will usually send the couple an engagement letter that explains their role as a neutral in the mediation process. The neutral expert asks the couple to agree not to call the expert as a witness should the matter result in court action. The expert also asks the couple to pay the expert's fee either by each paying one half or having the fees paid out of joint monies.

Different experts may be necessary depending on the subject area being discussed. It is not unusual for an expert opinion to be necessary regarding the value of a defined benefit pension plan, for example, or to appraise the marital and premarital portions of a retirement plan. Most people need to have their home appraised to determine the fair market value. In mediation they are asking their expert to give an honest, neutral value, neither high nor low. Sometimes an expert will give a range of value and then the clients negotiate a fair value that they can both agree to.

THERAPISTS

The Child Psychologist

One of the most devastating uses of therapists in adversarial divorce is their use as custody evaluators. A therapist is asked to investigate the parents and interview the children and others who may have information helpful to the therapist making a decision about which parent will have custody of the children and which parent will become the noncustodial visiting parent.

In mediation, couples who are conflicted about parenting may choose to employ a neutral therapist to meet with them and their children for the purpose of assisting them to create a plan that will meet the needs of the children and each of the parents for the parenting of the children after the divorce. This type of neutral expertise is especially helpful for parents who are having custody disputes after divorce.

Many of the conflicts parents have regarding their children stem from their fears about the impact of the divorce on the children. They may have doubts about parenting schedules, worrying that the children will not fare well when they go back and forth between their two homes. Parents may be reassured by consulting with a neutral therapist or early childhood development expert about the effects of parenting schedules on their children and other issues related to how they can best parent their children when they live in separate homes. These experts assist them in decision making and help them avoid competing with each other to win or own the children.

The therapist may be helpful by meeting with the parents, and then having the parents bring information from the therapist about the needs of the children into their discussions in mediation. In other situations, therapists may come into the mediation sessions to share with the parents their ideas about what will best meet the needs of the children and the parents.

Working with Roberta and Ted, the parents of Liz, 16, and Ryan, 13, the mediator asked them what they needed to decide. Roberta explained that for the last two years she had the children living with her during the week and every other weekend. They lived with their dad, Ted, every other weekend and during the summer weekdays. Both Ted and Roberta are remarried. Ted complained that Roberta and her husband were planning to move to Ohio for one year for Roberta to complete her master's degree. Ted wanted Ryan to stay and live with him. Ryan was very close to his step dad and enjoyed many of the same interests. Ryan was less comfortable with his step mom whom he described as very strict with him and Liz. Their dad was also a professor and very disciplined, but not very close to Ryan. Ted and Roberta each said that Ryan had indicated to each of them he wanted to stay with the parent he was talking with at the time. The mediator observed that Ryan was probably telling each parent what he believed they wanted to hear, and the mediator suggested that they consult a neutral child psychologist. They agreed, after discussing it with Ryan, and made an appointment for Ryan to talk to a psychologist. The psychologist agreed to meet with Ryan, talk to each of the parents, and inform the mediator about what Ryan needed prior to the next mediation session. On the day of the session the psychologist called the mediator and said he and Ryan had each spoken separately with Ryan's parents. The mediator inquired, "What do you think Ted and Roberta should do?" The psychologist said, "They need to listen to Ryan and make their decision." Opening the mediation session, the mediator asked if the parents had talked with the psychologist and Ryan. They said they had, and dad very sadly said, "I know Ryan loves me, and I now know that he really wants to go with his mom for this year. He didn't want to tell me that because he didn't want to hurt me. I think he should go, and we should plan blocks of time when he can come home so he and I can get to know each other better, and I can begin to understand and appreciate him for the good person that he is. It does hurt me, but I am the adult and can learn from this and not hold it against him."

The intervention of the psychologist was crucial to the parents resolving this conflict. The psychologist didn't have to take sides or even advocate for Ryan, except to help the parents to understand the situation from Ryan's perspective. The psychologist as the neutral expert helped Ted and Roberta make the decision, and in mediation they went on to make specific plans and decisions about the parenting arrangements for the next year.

Marriage-Closure Therapist

When parents are highly conflicted, the mediator may comment to them that they may have great difficulty parenting their children after the divorce if they continue to be in conflict and do not learn how to co-operate with each other about the children. The mediator may suggest to them that they see a neutral therapist to assist them in achieving more clarity about each letting go of the marital issues and the bad feelings they each hold toward the other. A marriage-closure therapist can help the couple look at their marriage relationship to begin to understand the patterns that led to divorce. This marriage-closure therapist is neutral in the sense that he or she does not offer an opinion about divorce, but takes the couple through their history, toward a better understanding about why their marriage broke down. The therapist then explores with them ways they can resolve their bad feelings and resentments toward each other. We have found this type of therapy invaluable to divorcing couples and their children. When couples participate in marriage-closure therapy, they are better able to participate in mediation. They usually do this simultaneously with mediating their divorce or postdecree issues.

ACCOUNTANTS AND FINANCIAL PLANNERS

It should be noted here that many accountants are also financial planners, but financial planners are not necessarily accountants. We suggest that accountants be Certified Public Accountants, and that financial planners be Certified Financial Planners.

Some of the most complicated divorces are more easily settled in mediation when an accountant or financial planner is hired by the couple as their neutral expert. The financial expert functioning in this role enjoys the ease of being called upon to do their best work to assist both the husband and the wife in the development of a division of the marital estate. The mediator first works with the couple to decide their standards of fairness regarding these issues. Then the financial expert gathers from them all the data necessary to work in mediation, discussing all the information and creating options based upon their standards of fairness, tax planning, and financial security for each in the future. It is not unusual in these types of cases to have the financial expert present throughout the mediation process. The mediator facilitates the discussion, asks questions, assures that the husband and the wife are each clear about the information being discussed, then drafts their agreements. Toward the conclusion of the mediation process, their attorneys join them in mediation and assist in the final decision making. We have found that couples with very large estates are especially appreciative of this way of using accountants or financial planners as neutral experts in their divorce.

There are many other situations in which a neutral accountant is also extremely helpful. If there is a closely held family business, a neutral accountant may evaluate the business at a cost that is less expensive than if he or she were hired by an attorney to represent one of their interests against the other in a litigated divorce. For the mediation process, the accountant does not have to build into the appraisal his or her defense of the appraisal assumptions, values, etc. as if anticipating a court trial. The accountant as a neutral has the couple each sign an engagement letter describing the role of the neutral. It states their understanding that the work generated by the accountant is for mediation purposes only and will not be allowable in court.

Roger and Nancy sought mediation to settle their divorce. Roger had moved out of the family home into a new home he built in their area of town. Their two children, Kelly, age 17, and Max, age 14, lived with Nancy and had open access to Roger and his home. Roger was the owner of his business, which was valued at $6.5 million. He had an annual income of approximately $300,000 plus other perks. Nancy was a very talented artist, recognized by the public for her watercolor paintings. When they came to the mediation consultation, Roger said he did not want any attorneys involved in their divorce. He wanted to keep the business, buy out Nancy's interest, and pay generous support for Nancy and the children. Nancy was less specific about what she wanted, but trusted Roger to do the right thing. The mediator responded to Roger's plan, "You certainly may make decisions in mediation without attorney's advice or counsel if you each wish to do so. However, you may find it helpful to have a neutral accountant work with you in the mediation process to value the marital estate. The neutral accountant would explain what all the items are and give you ideas about the ways that the marital estate can be divided. The neutral accountant can advise the two of you on how you can assure Nancy of a fair buy out of the business and help you create spousal maintenance and child support arrangements that consider the tax ramifications for both of you. With the advice of a neutral accountant you can make sure the distribution of property is secure for each of you and that it meets each of your needs now and in the future." They both agreed that they would be comfortable with a neutral accountant helping them in mediation.

The mediation process went well for them with the neutral accountant providing very creative options for them to consider as they made decisions. The mediator facilitated the discussions, clarified their understanding of the details and the information, and recorded their decisions in a very detailed memorandum of their agreements. When they were finished they asked for referrals to an attorney for each of them who would respect all their hard work and not make any major changes in their agreements. They interviewed and chose attorneys referred by the mediator. The attorneys joined the last mediation session where the memorandum was thoroughly reviewed with the couple, the accountant, and the mediator. The attorneys commented that this was the most creative divorce they had ever seen and complimented the couple on their work.

This is an example of how the accountant as a neutral expert can assist divorcing couples with their decision making about financial matters in the marital estate. There are also many other issues that a neutral expert can assist divorcing couples with that are not so complex, such as:

- Determining a reasonable stream of income for the person employed by the family business;

- Valuing stock options;
- Projecting each of their retirement incomes based on various options of dividing the marital estate;
- Determining the value of premarital and marital retirement accounts;
- Analyzing financial records and accounts to assure the couple that all their assets are accounted for;
- Advising parents of ways to set aside money for college funds for their children;
- Assisting couples with options to restructure debt; and
- Advising couples of the options and consequences of using home equity or retirement assets to pay off debt.

REAL ESTATE APPRAISERS

Many married couples today own their home. Some even have recreational property such as a cabin or a vacation condo. In the divorce they will need to establish a market value of their real estate for making decisions about its future ownership. A real estate appraiser can be a neutral expert when employed by the couple to appraise their property and establish the present market value. The appraiser usually generates a report that is used in mediation to verify the value. If the couple does not agree with the value, they may hire a second appraiser as a neutral expert to do the same. They can then use both reports to negotiate a value between them.

MORTGAGE BANKERS

Often a divorcing couple decides that they will each own a home after the divorce, or one will agree that the other may own their home only if there is an arrangement for both to own homes after the divorce. This issue is played out differently for everyone, yet it usually results in one person needing to purchase a new home. In mediation the husband and wife try to figure out their options for one to buy out the other's interest in the homestead and the other to buy a new home. They do this either by refinancing the present home to provide a down payment or by agreeing on another asset to be used as a down payment. Once they have established what the down payment is to be, the person buying a new home may consult with a mortgage banker to determine whether the person qualifies for a mortgage on his or her own, and if so, what amount of mortgage. If the person does not qualify alone, the husband and wife may consult together with the mortgage banker about the other person helping the one qualify and what their options are. Although this process may seem cumbersome, the mortgage banker often has ideas about how to make it work. The mortgage banker as a neutral expert can be helpful to both in generating options that will meet their needs.

CAREER CONSULTANTS

When one person has not worked outside the home or is under employed, the couple may see that there is not enough income to support two households after a divorce. In fact, this is usually the case when both are employed! As they discuss the budgets of their monthly living expenses and compare them with their monthly net incomes, they will find they have only four choices:

1. They need to decrease their expenses.
2. They need to increase their incomes.
3. They need to borrow from their assets to pay off some budget items, such as auto loans, etc.
4. They need to do tax planning such as assigning the exemptions for the children to the higher income spouse to obtain maximum tax advantage.

Most couples find that they have to increase their income. This may call for the person who is unemployed or under employed to have a career evaluation. The mediator will suggest that they hire a career consultant as a neutral expert to meet with this person, administer some career assessment tests to determine the person's interests, skills, and acumen in certain areas. The consultant interprets tests and compares the information with career paths that are compatible with the person's skills, interests, and abilities. The consultant then prepares a report that shows what types of employment the person is able to enter at what income levels, or what further training is necessary, the time it would take to be trained, the costs of training, and what positions would be available at what incomes once trained. This information offers the couple some options about how the nonworking spouse can become gainfully employed or employed at their skill level. When the consultant is a neutral, no judgments are made about what the person should do, but, instead, options and possibilities are offered for the couple to consider.

BUSINESS APPRAISERS

Whenever there is an ownership interest in a business by one or both spouses, that interest needs to have a value placed upon it unless the couple agrees that they will each own one half of the interest after the divorce. When they need to place a value upon the business, they need a neutral expert who can determine the value. Sometimes couples will choose to have a business appraiser, a person who specializes in appraising businesses, be the neutral expert. Business appraisers may be lawyers, accountants, or brokers who buy or sell businesses. Sometimes the business will have a stock value because it is a public corporation, and in such cases, the ownership interest is the value of the stock owned by the couple. In a private business there also may be stock, and the value of that may be determined by the book value placed on the stock by the accountant of the business. If the company is a service business, such as a professional practice, the value is often more difficult to determine. A neutral expert, after analyzing the books and accounts of the business, can be very helpful by showing different ways of approaching value and discussing the issue of what is called blue sky (the intangible value of the business). They can then be clear about all the details and options in the business valuation, and, they can make an informed decision based upon the neutral appraiser's report. Sometimes the neutral appraiser comes to the mediation session to assist them in deciding on a value by answering any questions that arise.

ACTUARIES

An actuarial expert calculates the present value of money to be received in the future. When there is a defined benefit plan owned by a husband or wife, it needs to be appraised for its present value for purposes of discussing and dividing the marital estate. If the husband is a public employee, for example, and he has a defined benefit plan that will pay him $1,500 per month beginning at age 65 and for the rest of his life, the question is, "What is that worth today when he is age 45?" An actuary can calculate this by using proper life expectancy tables and a reasonable percentage to calculate the growth of money. Depending on the plan, there may be other factors to apply such as a cost of living adjustment. The actuary then calculates the gross value and discounts it to today's value. When a couple employs an actuary as a neutral expert, the actuary will give a value that is as accurate as possible. Contrast this to an adversarial divorce that would employ two opposing experts each of whom would use a formula most favorable to the side each represents.

DOCTORS AND OTHER MEDICAL SPECIALISTS

Sometimes in a divorce one spouse is incapacitated or unable to work due to a physical or mental condition. In such cases, a medical neutral expert may be necessary to evaluate the person and the condition to determine employability and whether there are special conditions that would limit the person's ability to be gainfully employed. This removes the issues of blame and fault from the discussions and allows the couple to plan appropriately.

CHEMICAL-DEPENDENCY COUNSELORS

There are often allegations of chemical abuse when discussing parenting issues in a divorce. These surface when parents talk about each having the children overnight and on weekends. One spouse may question whether the other will be drinking or using other mood-altering chemicals. When this issue is raised, the person being charged with abuse of alcohol or chemicals is usually angered and denies that there is any problem. The mediator may ask if they need to get an answer to the question of the person's use of alcohol or chemicals, and can offer the opportunity for the accused spouse to see a chemical-dependency counselor who can evaluate whether one is chemically dependent. This will end the couple's conflict about this issue. The neutral chemical-dependency counselor must be independent of a health management organization (HMO) and a treatment center, therefore having no bias based upon an HMO discouraging treatment or a treatment center having openings for new patients. When clients have used the neutral chemical-dependency counselor they have also agreed in advance to follow the recommendation of the counselor. This means that if the person is not chemically dependent, the other person will no longer complain about it, and if the person is chemically dependent, he or she will abstain from use of chemicals and follow the treatment plan prescribed.

HOW TO BECOME A NEUTRAL EXPERT

Neutral experts are crucial to divorce and other types of mediation processes. To be a neutral expert, it is necessary to examine your biases about being neutral, much as a mediator does. It may be helpful to enroll in a mediation training course to learn how to be neutral and how to work with people who are in the midst of conflict. If possible, mentor with a mediator to become comfortable with others' conflict and pain. Talk with mediators about how they see your expertise being helpful to clients and what the mediator would expect of you acting as a neutral.

If you are a neutral expert, your first challenge is to figure out how you will approach clients when they first call. As a neutral expert, it is important that you do not form a relationship with one person. Each person will want to give you their perspective of the issue you are being asked to assist with. It is important to establish your neutrality when you are first contacted, just as the mediator must.

The next challenge is to create your letter of understanding as a neutral expert. You will need to send each client this letter describing your neutrality, your work, and your fees. This letter is usually your agreement with them to become their neutral expert. There is always a clause in this letter addressing the confidentiality of your relationship with the clients, and a clear statement that your work is part of a mediation process. Conducting your work as part of a mediation process assures confidentiality of your work, limiting its use to the mediation process, and protecting you from being called as a witness in a court proceeding should the case not be settled in mediation. The letter of understanding also explains that your fees are less because they do not include testifying in court to defend your work.

The final challenge is marketing yourself as a neutral expert. Networking is a good way to apprise mediators and lawyers about your interest in becoming a neutral expert. Talk to colleagues in your profession about it. Find out if any of them are working as neutral experts and if they would be willing to share some tips with you.

Being a neutral expert is satisfying work to add to the other professional work that you do. Expanding your practice to include being a neutral expert will give you more variety and a new challenge. You may find, as mediators have, that working as a neutral is not only satisfying, it is less stressful and greatly appreciated by your clients.

Until mediation, divorce was handled by two lawyers and various experts competitively supporting each side of the issues. Because mediation has become a mainstream method of settling divorces, couples who are divorcing find themselves surrounded by numerous professionals constructively supporting them in determining what is best for each of them and their children. It takes a community of professionals to help couples create the best divorce settlements possible. Mediators are at the center of the divorce with the clients. Other neutral professionals surround the couple with their compassion and expertise. With everyone working together, the couple can make the best choices and have lasting agreements that assure them a successful divorce that will serve them well in their separate futures.

The neutral experts listed in this chapter are the most commonly used in divorces. As neutrals they give their best professional estimate of what is being asked of them. Aside from these experts, clients are often also influenced by others about the issues in their divorce. Others may include all of their well-meaning friends and relatives who will freely offer advice. Often such advice is unsolicited. Sometimes it is requested. We call this the audience effect. Each person has an audience to their divorce. This audience is there to listen, console, understand, and, unfortunately, to give opinions. Their opinions are naturally biased and can cause more difficulty than help. Their listening and emotional support is welcome and necessary to the divorcing person and family. However, the use of neutral experts is usually the best way to generate reliable information for the couple to make decisions in mediation.

It truly does take a whole community of professionals to assist a couple to divorce. When couples use professional experts as neutrals they receive information that is as reliable as possible. Each divorce requires different experts; some do not require any. However, for the most successful divorce, it is most wise at least to counsel with a therapist, and consult with an experienced family law attorney. Hopefully there will be a day when all of the other people touched by a family's divorce will be able to assist and support each person as a neutral, without taking a side and finding fault with another family member. In this way the community will have healthier, happier postdivorce families.

CONCLUSION

From its earliest beginnings in 1974 to the present, divorce mediation has arguably impacted more lives than any other type of mediation. Divorce mediators' influence can be seen in the adoption of new state Parenting Plan laws as well as in the way courts and lawyers now must first emphasize early settlement efforts instead of relying on tactics that take the case to trial, with settlement occurring on the courthouse steps. Without those early efforts of Coogler and Neville in 1974, one wonders how long it would have taken to realize that it is not only possible for people to cooperate around the ending of a marriage relationship, it is also necessary for the sake of the children. As a result of mediation, the business of divorce is no longer exclusively the province of lawyers.

CHAPTER 5

Mediating Workplace and Other Nondivorce Disputes

INTRODUCTION

It used to be different. We used to talk to each other before all the lawyers warned us not to talk once an incident was being investigated, because anything we said could be used against us at the hearing.

—Robert Van Eldon, Senior Supervisor

When compared to divorce mediation, employment mediation is quickly becoming an even greater area of opportunity for mediators. Like divorce mediation, employment mediation also focuses on close relationships that have gone sour and are in conflict. Mediation's rapid expansion in the area of employment disputes mirrors the explosion of interest in divorce mediation. Like Susan, the young woman mentioned in Chapter 2 who wanted to avoid the stress and cost of destructive conflict in her own divorce, businesses and organizations are seeking similar benefits. In their book *Controlling the Cost of Conflict*, Slaikeu and Hasson (1998) observe that the benefits to businesses of establishing and using a collaborative conflict management system are immediately measurable:

... reduced legal expenses (50 to 80 percent); reduced turnover; strengthened long-term business relationships; reduced stress; and most important, assurance that the organization's mission will be accomplished as employees, managers, partners, and customers work together to achieve common goals (p. xii).

Because it is mutually advantageous for both the employee and the business or organization, collaborative client-centered mediation is fast becoming the preferred method of resolving workplace conflicts. In fact, it is quickly becoming clear to businesses and to families that the legal system is not really much help at all. In many cases, it only causes more harm. Like the divorcing family that is devastated by destructive divorce litigation, workplace conflict also has a devastating impact on the company and the careers of those affected by the conflict when costly litigation is used instead of collaborative methods.

THE PROBLEM

State and federal workplace laws have created tremendous exposure to significant employer liability if workplace discrimination occurs or if other types of workplace conflict result in harm to an employee. Title VII is a federal law that prohibits discrimination based on race, color, religion, sex, or national origin. This law and recent Supreme Court decisions require employers to take affirmative steps to prevent such wrongdoing in the workplace as well as to immediately respond to complaints about such conduct, or the employer can be held liable for damages. In addition, most states have enacted human rights acts that overlap or add to the requirements of Title VII. A complex layering effect has been created for the average employer trying to keep up with all the laws designed to make the workplace a model environment. The new Americans with Disabilities Act (ADA) requires reasonable accommodations for employees with disabilities. Union contracts may require good-cause standards for discipline or termination and common-law tort laws may create other causes of action within the workplace. Virtually any lawyer can usually find and allege a legal claim on behalf of an employee who wants redress for workplace conduct deemed offensive.

As the lucrative field of personal injury litigation gets overcrowded by new lawyers, a growing number of lawyers are specializing in employment litigation. If you think about it, there are an infinite number of workplace conflicts that require investigation, litigation, and settlement negotiations.

Most would argue that harassment, discrimination, and hostile work environments should be a thing of the past. The problem with workplace conflict is not so much that this behavior continues to occur, but that we have an archaic way of responding to it. A priest observed that with divorce, the Church likes to shoot its wounded. Likewise, the problem of workplace conflict is more our response to it than the original conduct that caused it. The standard legal approach is to investigate, find blame, and then fix the amount of damages on whoever has the deepest pockets. (A cardinal rule of the adversarial system is never sue anyone unless they have deep pockets.) This has resulted in tremendous cost to both the employer and the employee. Workers are often unwilling to start the drastic action of litigation, but they have no other options than to bring a claim if their complaints go unanswered by management. Frequently, because the approach has been to determine who is right and wrong, the process quickly becomes adversarial and results are not satisfactory to either party. Filing a workplace lawsuit is the wrong tool. The new way to resolve these disputes uses collaborative conflict resolution systems that focus on the shared goals of the people who inhabit the workplace (both management and workers) and use mediation principles as the preferred method of dispute resolution. For example, the Shell Oil RESOLVE Program incorporates mediation into its steps for early resolution of conflict (Slaikeu & Hasson, 1998). The following, taken from the Shell RESOLVE Employee Brochure, is one of the best examples of how new thinking is affecting businesses at the highest levels:

> Disagreement, misunderstanding, and conflict are natural parts of any relationship. Whether in society, in our homes, or in the workplace, we each bring to the table our own ideas and experiences. Conflict will occur. That's okay when it leads to constructive dialogue and ultimate resolution. It's not okay when it's left unresolved.
>
> Unresolved conflict in the workplace, as in any setting, hurts everyone who is involved and often touches those on the sidelines as well. Left unchecked, conflict rarely goes away on its own. It can disrupt our relationships, prevent us from effectively performing our jobs, and lead to costly, time-consuming litigation.
>
> With this in mind, the Company began over a year ago to examine how we address workplace disputes at Shell and whether those methods could be improved. Discussions with employees confirmed that, as an organization, we tend to avoid conflict. What's more, our existing methods for identifying conflict and facilitating resolution are not always effective. We also learned through benchmarking with other leading employers, as well as

consultations with experts, that there are now sound alternatives to the court system for resolving workplace disputes.

The result is Shell RESOLVE, a three-part program that provides a new approach to conflict resolution at work in an approach that is flexible, quick and fair. Our program was effective May 1, 1997.

Using Shell RESOLVE, we can transform our culture from conflict-averse to conflict-aware and create an environment that allows us to approach disagreements as opportunities to learn, gather information and ideas, and find solutions. Further, dealing with conflict in an open, constructive way can strengthen understanding and commitment to the larger purpose of the organization and free us to focus on our goal of becoming the premier company in the U.S. (Slaikeu & Hasson, 1998, p. 125).

Many other large companies have adopted conflict resolution systems that encourage collaborative efforts. General Electric, Brown and Root, as well as Bally's Resorts have all adopted some form of collaborative dispute resolution program early on in their processes.

The largest employer in the United States, the US Postal Service, with over 900,000 employees, has aggressively decided to eliminate the phrase *going postal* from our nation's vocabulary by adopting a mediation model as a first step in resolving all Title VII discrimination lawsuits and other types of workplace conflict. Their brochure explaining the program is very clear. It states that "the Postal Service strongly supports the use of mediation to resolve disputes" (US Postal Service, 1998, p. 1).

Most companies using collaborative dispute resolution systems have adopted a simple model of mediation that relies on face-to-face mediation sessions and, in the case of the US Postal Service, that permits only one mediation session be held. If the case cannot be resolved in one session, no further mediation sessions will be scheduled. Another important characteristic of the US Postal Service mediation model is that it focuses primarily on the relationship between the parties and is not intended to mediate legal issues, nor is the mediator permitted to be directive or coercive about results.

Although many people just learning about mediation assume the mediator must be able to make judgments about the case in order to influence the outcomes, nothing could be farther from the truth. In fact, once a mediator begins to be judgmental, the mediator has started down the slippery slope toward losing neutrality.

CASE STUDY

Let's take a look inside a typical workplace mediation to clear up some misconceptions and see how a client-centered, rather than a law-centered, approach can solve a typical, intractable employment dispute.

BACKGROUND

Jack was a 22-year employee. He was a union steward in his younger days and the company he worked for recently adopted a dispute resolution program conditionally approved by the union. Jack was written up many times and had been docked for a total of over six months of pay as a result of a series of incident reports against him. When I was asked to mediate the case by human resources, the person scheduling it jokingly said, "wear a flak jacket." I wasn't really sure what he meant by that remark, but I asked, "Should I really be worried about people's safety?" He said Jack was a pretty mean dude and he had filed a series of EEO claims alleging discrimination in various forms. He apparently had sustained a back problem and he claimed he was not being properly accommodated for his injury. In addition, he alleged age discrimination and he alleged sexual harassment by a female supervisor. If there had been any more boxes to check on the EEO complaint form, he probably would have filed under more headings. He was quite angry and as I learned at the mediation, mostly what he did was silently glare at anyone who worked along side of him on the line. He was somewhat of a legend and was becoming a real annoyance to management. In fact, management felt it really had to do something, and mediation was the first step. It became quite clear Jack felt mediation was the first step in the process of getting rid of him permanently, and the two supervisors in the room also viewed mediation as the first hoop to jump through before terminating his employment. It had become impossible to assign any of the younger employees and particularly the women employees to work beside him because he would glare at the new employee. If she happened to be female, she would complain to the unit supervisor, saying she was afraid of working near Jack. This prompted a new round of investigations and incident reports.

Although some mediators like to read all the investigative files and attempt to learn as much as they can about the dispute before beginning the mediation process, most client-centered mediators prefer to let the facts unfold in the mediation room. This is because too much review of the past can turn the mediator into more of an investigator or a judge. In Jack's case, there happened to be about 250 pages of investigative incident reports prepared by various supervisors. In addition, the union representative who attended the mediation also compiled his own investigative reports. Jack was also in the habit of recording in small notebooks the exact time and date of any conduct by a supervisor that he felt was illegal according to the union contract, the ADA, or under his interpretation of the State Human Rights Act or Title VI of the EEO rules. Had the mediator insisted on reading all the information that everyone had compiled, it would have taken days to sift through everything before sitting down with the parties.

Among professionals, disagreement exists over the question of how much advance information about a conflict is needed by the mediator. Our own view is that less information, rather than more, is the proper amount required by the mediator before the sessions start. For a person who uses a directive, law-centered approach to mediation, obtaining as much information and history as is possible about the conflict will be essential because the mediator's views about the outcome will be very important as the case progresses and the mediator directs the settlement outcome. To properly obtain this information usually involves many hours of reading investigative reports and conducting separate interviews with the parties involved in the conflict. Taking our lessons from what has been learned in the field of divorce mediation, we discovered that a mediator need not have a great deal of background information about the facts of a particular case in order to be successful. This is because the client-centered mediator is more inclined to focus on creating the proper environment for the parties, as opposed to judging and ruling on the settlement outcome of the case.

Usually, a client-centered mediator will meet with all the parties together at the same time and begin by making some introductory comments:

ORIENTATION

MEDIATOR: Good afternoon. My name is Steve Erickson and I have been asked by human resources to mediate in your dispute resolution program that was recently adopted by the company, the workers, and the union in an effort to create early resolution of employment conflicts. I don't believe I have ever met any of you before, and that is how I always like it because I want to have this be my first contact with all of you to preserve my neutrality. In fact, in order to preserve my role as a neutral, the only information I know about this case is who will be attending the session and that it involves some claims of discrimination under the Equal Employment Opportunity Act brought by Jack Arneson, an employee. Could I ask which one of you is Jack?

EMPLOYEE: I am. And I want to know why he is here, because I don't have my attorney present. I thought there weren't going to be any attorneys present.

MEDIATOR: Who do you mean by he? Wait a minute, I have a good idea, why don't all of you introduce yourselves.

At this point, everyone in the room introduced themselves. Two from management were present, Jack's immediate supervisor, Eileen Swanson, and the head of the division, Robert Van Eldon, introduced themselves. Fred Harris introduced himself as the union representative for Jack, and Jack then introduced himself. Finally, Dick Solheim introduced himself as corporate counsel acknowledging that he wasn't really sure if he should be there, but because he noted the union steward was present as a representative on behalf of Jack, he thought it appropriate to see if the two supervisors needed representation at this hearing.

I immediately corrected his use of the word hearing by pointing out that mediation sessions really are not considered hearings because that is a term generally used to describe a courtroom adversarial process or a fact-gathering process. This mediation session, if I was going to have anything to say about it, would not become an investigation or a hearing. I told him it was my general policy to have either everyone or no one represented by counsel at a mediation session. Anything in between tended to cause problems because there was an imbalance and the unrepresented person might feel at a disadvantage. The union steward interrupted by pointing out that the reason the union was willing to go along with this experimental mediation program instead of insisting on the standard grievance procedure was only on the condition that an employee be entitled to have a union representative present at the mediation session if requested by the employee. I asked him if he was an attorney and he said no.

DECIDING WHO SHOULD ATTEND

MEDIATOR: I need to ask Eileen and Robert a question. As long as no one is going to keep any record of this proceeding, and as long as nobody gives up any rights, do you need to have someone from corporate counsel's office present?

ROBERT: I was involved in the original discussions that established this program and I think the program is a sound idea. There really isn't any reason we need an attorney present unless corporate says it is necessary.

MEDIATOR: Good, I will then ask Dick Solheim to excuse himself. But before you go, Dick, I want to provide you with a copy of the Agreement to Mediate form I will be using, which requires strict confidentiality of the mediation process. Your office should have received copies of this because I sent them over several weeks ago.

The above interchange is a perfect example of the tension that often exists between corporate counsel staff (or outside counsel that advises the company) and management or human resources staff. Corporate attorneys tend to be skeptical of any process that does not immediately follow the three steps of (1) investigate the complaint, (2) interview as many witnesses as possible, and (3) create a defense for any possible lawsuit. However, the increasing use of mediation and other informal steps to resolve conflict is an important recognition by businesses of the value of early intervention in the life of a dispute. Such understanding relates to the notion that it is better to promote healing and understanding before people feel their only recourse is to file a formal complaint or start a lawsuit. Many companies, instead of hiring outside law firms to investigate complaints, are adopting early mediation as an immediate response to workplace conflict. If the mediation does not resolve the problem, everyone is still left with the same litigation alternatives as they have always had. Mediation should not be seen as replacing any existing remedies or as taking away legal rights. Nevertheless, there will always be tension between advocates of an investigatory adversarial response to conflict and those who advocate early intervention through the use of collaborative procedures such as mediation. In many Fortune 500 companies as well as smaller organizations, the forces of cooperation and collaboration appear to be winning out.

DISCUSSING CONFIDENTIALITY

MEDIATOR: I am pleased that we were able to quickly resolve that issue of corporate counsel being present. Because this is a new program, it occasionally happens that people do not quite yet understand their roles. Had he not volunteered to leave, I would have had to consider asking him to leave because I want to make sure all of you understand that this is not a hearing where anything you say could later get turned around and used against you in court. Rather this is a mediation session, where nothing that occurs here can be used against you in court. I am passing out to all of you the written rules of mediation that I will ask all to sign if you wish to go forward with this mediation. You will see in the section on "Confidentiality of the Mediation Sessions" that the only exceptions to the guarantee of confidentiality would be if any one of you threatened harm to yourself or another. That might make it necessary for the confidentiality to be broken in order to protect someone from harm.

SUPERVISOR EILEEN SWANSON: If everything is supposed to be so confidential, why is it then that the union representative is taking detailed notes of everything that each one of us says?

MEDIATOR: I'm sorry, I didn't notice that. The concern you raise, Eileen, has also come up before many times. Could I ask you, Fred, if you would, to put the pencil down and not take any detailed notes of this meeting?

FRED: As the union representative and as Jack's representative, I need to be able to remember what was said by everyone so I can properly defend Jack against the illegal behavior of the company. At every turn, this company has violated his rights and abused the protections the union contract and the federal workplace laws are supposed to guarantee to him. We fought long and hard to win the right to not lose our jobs except for good cause, and we are not about to let management try to water that down, as they are always trying to do at every turn.

MEDIATOR: Certainly taking detailed notes would be important if you were able to use anything that was said in this room at a later hearing if one were needed. But one of the absolute cardinal rules of mediation is that nobody should be harmed by any effort made at settlement and healing. Therefore, because you may not use any statements or

documents created in mediation for the purpose of advancing your litigation case, there really is no need to keep such complete notes. If
you are willing, what I would rather ask you to do right now is to put
down your pencil and listen to what I have to say and see if this
process makes any sense to you.

In any mediation setting, but particularly where possible lawsuits or vi-
olations of federal or state workplace laws are at issue, it is essential that
the mediation process not be a place for the legal system to retrospectively
peer into and see if there is any ammunition that can be used to further litigation. The mediator in the above exchange is trying very hard to help
the participants in the mediation room understand that mediation is quite
different from any other discussions in which they may have previously
participated. It is not a process designed to get the goods on Jack and
show that he should be fired. It is not a competition to see whose case is
potentially stronger or weaker. It is not a place to determine who was
right or wrong, who violated which laws, or whose conduct caused the
conflict or the harm to occur. It is truly the safe harbor where the parties
may, for the time they are in the mediation room, create an environment
for open, honest communication to occur, hopefully leading to cooperation, healing, and ultimately change in the dynamics of the conflict. Because mediation is off the record and not subject to being used in
litigation, it allows people to loosen up and say what is necessary to create
healing and settle the case. Without a court reporter or tape recorder taking down everything that is said, people become more willing to say, "I
am sorry" or "I understand how you feel about what I did and I am sorry
I caused you the harm I did." "What can I do to help make it right?" Think
about how a lawyer would use these apology statements to hammer the
other side in adversarial litigation. If mediation allowed the use of these
statements outside of mediation, nobody would ever consider engaging
in mediation, because they would be afraid to say anything at all for fear
of it being twisted around and used against them in some future hearing.

SETTING THE STAGE FOR COOPERATION

MEDIATOR: I want to continue to explain what it is that I am trying to do
in this room. As a mediator, I will not sit here and evaluate the evi-

dence for or against any of you. Rather, I will try to create a safe environment where the four of you can really attempt to resolve this problem yourselves. If you want me to help you, I am going to ask all of you to negotiate in a new and different way. I want all of you to recognize that you can only get good results for yourselves if you also help the others obtain fair and just results for themselves. I am also interested in managing this room so that most of what you are doing is listening to each other rather than talking at each other. Sometimes, when things go well in this room, healing and repairing of torn and damaged relationships can occur. If that does happen, it is then likely that you will also find a solution to the conflict that brings us together this afternoon. I should point out that my goal is not necessarily to get everyone to feel good about each other, but it is my goal to help all of you figure out what you need to do to resolve the conflict that seems to have brought all of you to the point where you can hardly sit in the same room without fearing that something bad will happen.

In the foregoing monologue, the mediator is attempting to create an environment where the people in the room truly begin to grasp that mediation is not going to be more of the same old game of who is wrong or right played out by management and workers. On some new level of thinking, the mediator is trying to change the game from head butting, posturing, and alleging violation of rights to a new game of listening, discussing, and collaborating. The statements made by the mediator were probably not expected by most people in the room. Because they were not expected, they may have some impact. However, at this early stage, most of the participants are still pretty skeptical of any process that encourages such an unconventional attitude. The introductory comments and the choice of words by the mediator are clearly designed to set the tone for something different to happen.

Etheridge and Dooley (1994) describes this function as creating a mood or tone. Of the mediator's role, they observe:

A mediator's first role is to establish a mood and tone that leads the parties toward collaboration. In effect, the mediator directs the disputants away from the war and toward the peace conference, encouraging them to stop posturing and to start thinking about resolution. Setting the tone of collaboration is an essential characteristic of the process (pp. 5–6).

Creating the mood and tone of collaboration often starts in the minds of the participants. The mediator offers the opportunity for them to create a different mind set. One way to help the parties create a new mind set is to tap into their desire to solve the problem themselves. By asking them if they wish to begin mediation, the mediator reinforces the notion that they will be choosing this out of their own free will and they are not there simply because a judge or a court rule may have required them to attempt mediation.

SIGNING THE AGREEMENT TO MEDIATE

MEDIATOR: Before we begin, I think it would be a good idea if we could all sign the Agreement to Mediate. Jack, you are the employee who is affected by this mediation. Has what I have said in describing the process made sense to you? Is this something you wish to do?

JACK: I might be willing to sign the agreement to begin mediation, but I'm not signing anything else. Everything I have done lately has been turned around and used against me. I really can't stand working here anymore and I think they are just out to get me fired. I hate this place and these people are bunch of f------

MEDIATOR *[Interrupting]*:   Well, I just want to say again, that nobody may use anything said here today either offensively or defensively in any later court proceedings. Is that understood and agreed to by everyone? As you can see here by the two-page agreement to begin mediation, it specifically prevents anything that is said or written in this room from being used in court. And as I said at the beginning, this mediation session will be very different from any of your other attempts at settlement. If you voluntarily choose to go forward, I will try to help you, but nobody is forcing any of you to be here. What we are doing today has to make sense to all of you.

After signing the agreement to mediate, the mediator usually asks the people in conflict to describe their situation. This is much like telling their story, but not in a blaming or fault-finding way. A client-centered mediator will try to avoid a situation where the people at the table think they are making opening statements as if in court. Rather, the mediator encourages them to tell their story. In employment mediations, it almost always works out best to start with the employee.

UNFOLDING THEIR STORIES

MEDIATOR: Jack, could you start by telling about your situation?

FRED: Ah, I'm going to step in here and say that I have advised Jack to not talk and I will do the speaking for him. I am the union representative here on behalf of Jack and I have investigated all the complaints against him and you should know . . .

MEDIATOR: Excuse me Fred, but I have to interrupt here. The reason Jack needs to talk is because this is about Jack, not you. The reason his immediate supervisor, Eileen, needed to talk instead of the corporate counsel talking for her is that I am trying to get all of you to not just talk to each other but to also *listen* to each other and, hopefully, to quit investigating each other, to begin to change your future behavior instead of trying to determine whose conduct was the most offensive in the past. You know, I was asked if I wanted to read all of those incident reports. If I had said yes, then I would have had to come to you, Eileen, and read your 175 pages or so, and, of course, to be balanced, it would have been necessary for me to review all of your union reports to get Jack's side of things. Then I suppose I would have had to talk to Jack, because I see he has kept his own large notebook of things that have happened to him. Fred, could I ask you to at least give Jack a chance to speak for himself? Certainly, you can also take time to speak for yourself. In this way, perhaps, everyone can then begin to start listening to what each other might say. Jack, are you willing to give your side of what is going on?

One of the more important aspects of a client-centered mediation process is that the history of the dispute is less important than what the parties are going to do about their dispute in the future. This is because with many conflicts, the conflict itself begins to take on a life of its own long after the start of the original problem. In many employment disputes, because of the law's requirement that all complaints be quickly investigated, more effort is put into the investigation to determine the original cause of the dispute than into resolving the dispute or improving the parties' relationship. Indeed, this distinction is one of the most important characteristics of a client-centered process. Unlike what happens in a law-centered mediation approach, more time and effort will be spent in the mediation room discussing and determining what must be done to improve the relationships and resolve the conflict; very little time will be spent by the client-centered mediator addressing the exact factual details of the dispute. Although it must be kept in mind that some past factual information is sometimes crucial to the dispute, much of the material contained in Jack's incident reports were merely each side's version of who was right and who was wrong. Because it is always so difficult to determine who was right and who was wrong, a client-centered mediator simply believes that right and wrong are not really that important. There are in fact two important questions: What are the parties going to do to resolve the dispute; and, How can the mediator get them to talk about their needs instead of talking exclusively about causes?

MANAGING THE DISCUSSIONS

MEDIATOR: Jack, are you willing to start by giving your thoughts about what has happened?

JACK: These people that run this place are really a bunch of jerks. I have been here 18 years and all I get for it is a pile of incident reports. I once was a union steward and I know their games. In fact, I used to be in charge of training new workers. It's clear to me that all they want to do is get rid of me. This is just a waste of time, and if it weren't for the fact that this mediation session was on the clock, I would tell them to shove it and leave right now. I just want my day in court and then I will tell them how bad it has been.

MEDIATOR: Jack, would you please tell me how bad it has been?

JACK: First of all, they don't care about my back injury. When I came back from rehab, I asked to be assigned to the stapler, and they turned me down, saying there were no openings. Then, when I asked if there were any openings on the supervisor's list, they told me that I was not a candidate for supervisor. They said if I wanted light duty, I would have to work the third shift. Do you know what that would do to my family? Since my wife died, I have been the sole provider for my boys, and I am not about to put them into day care just so I can work the third shift.

EILEEN SWANSON: Well Jack, as your immediate supervisor, I have to tell you that you've got an attitude problem. You're a good worker, but your anger gets in the way all the time.

JACK: Hey, don't I get to finish my story? Why do you let her interrupt me?

MEDIATOR: Jack, please continue.

At times, much of what a mediator does is somewhat like a traffic cop, supervising the flow of the discussions. James Laue, a long-time mediator who, before his death in 1994, was the director of the George Mason University Conflict Center, would often say, "Just getting them to the table is 80 percent of the battle." So, in our case with Jack, he continued to talk about how he was upset with the way management treated him. When pressed about what specifically irritated him, it seemed to boil down to the fact that after coming back to work from a back injury, he had been assigned to another work group and was being supervised by a woman he did not like, whom he felt was constantly riding him and always going by the book. He felt that her petty complaints about his work were unfair and his way of responding was to sulk and glare. Because he was 6-foot, 3-inches tall, had a lot of tattoos, and was also a Vietnam vet, the word got around to the new line employees that Jack had posttraumatic stress disorder syndrome and was a time bomb waiting to go off. This rumor got somewhat out of hand and took on a life of its own. Jack did not help himself by letting his anger get out of control any time he was frustrated, which was now becoming most of the time. Eileen Swanson spoke next with her story after Jack finished. She took her time, laboriously going over every incident report that she had written concerning Jack. This was apparently her first assignment after being promoted to supervisor, and she wanted to make sure she had all the t's crossed and the i's dotted. She was careful to point out that the latest incident report involved Jack being told to leave work and go home early after he got out of control. She described how one of the newer women on the floor came to her and complained about Jack staring at her. Eileen went over to Jack and told him that someone had complained about him again. When he asked who, Eileen refused to tell him, and Jack started to yell about his constitutional right to confront his accusers and how he was being mistreated. When Eileen told him to go home, he refused to leave. She then wrote him up for insubordination and asked company security to escort him to the parking lot. After security forcibly led him away, Jack filed a race discrimination claim charging that he was called "white trash" and a "tattooed honky" by the two black security guards. He also filed a complaint under the Americans with Disabilities Act alleging that his back was reinjured by the force used to escort him to the parking lot. At this point, Fred, the union representative, spoke up.

UNCOVERING NEEDS AND INTERESTS

FRED: I have been patiently waiting to speak and I was wondering when I would get my opportunity.

MEDIATOR: What do you want to speak about?

FRED: I want to rebut management's version of the incident reports Ms. Eileen Swanson has been reading.

MEDIATOR: Fred, there will be time for that later. Could we first hear from Robert Van Eldon, the director of the division?

ROBERT: I have reviewed all of these reports, and I have only one thing to say. Jack needs to learn how to get along.

JACK *[Pointing to his immediate supervisor, Eileen]*:   I think she needs to learn how to get along.

EILEEN: I have documented 12 instances where co-workers have come to me and stated that they are afraid of Jack. And I have also documented other instances of. . .

JACK *[Pulling out his notebooks]*:   Well, I count 14 instances in the last six weeks where you have violated my rights.

MEDIATOR: Can I ask you a question, Eileen? How does all of this affect you?

EILEEN: What do you mean by affect? I thought this was a mediation session, not a therapy session.

MEDIATOR: Well Eileen, I am not a therapist, I am a mediator, but I am dead serious about the importance of this question. I recall you saying earlier that this is your first assignment as a supervisor. I suspect that you want to be successful as a supervisor. I also suspect that most new supervisors would like to avoid a situation where this type of conflict occurs on their watch, particularly their first watch. And here you are, running into this buzz saw and everything you try just doesn't seem to work. What has it been like for you?

EILEEN: Well, I can tell you this. I don't sleep very well anymore. I know that Jack's conduct is good cause for his termination, but, of course, that is not up to me.

MEDIATOR: What do you mean, Eileen, you don't sleep well anymore?

EILEEN: Just that. I have tried everything with Jack. I have sat down and gone over the incident reports. I have given him copies of every incident report as required by the contract and by what legal tells us to do, and I have done everything to protect his rights. Nothing seems to work with him.

MEDIATOR: Jack, did you know that this was really bothering Eileen, too?

JACK: What do you mean?

MEDIATOR: Eileen is just as troubled about this mess as you are. It affects her by disrupting her sleep and it affects you by getting you frustrated and angry. Did you know that this was affecting her in that way?

JACK: Well, no, I guess not. But I'll tell you how else this is affecting me. It has cost me almost three months in lost wages and pay reductions as punishment. They're almost forcing me to leave.

MEDIATOR: Jack, what do you want?

In the above exchange, the client-centered mediator is trying to help the people in the dispute understand the difficulties of the other. Again, as in any conflict, there is a strong tendency by the parties to turn the discussions to the past in order to justify their behavior. Because of the influence of legal system, everyone is prepared to discuss and defend their own version of the investigations about the past. If left unchecked, the discussions could easily turn into a legal debate over whose past behavior was worse and who was justified in doing what. In reality, all of them strongly believed they were justified in acting the way they acted. During some of the exchanges in this case, which are not reproduced here, Fred, the union representative, made a pretty good case about how the company had treated Jack poorly just after his injury and how it failed to honor the provisions of the union contract that required accommodations for an injured employee who was having trouble returning to work. In a private caucus session with both sides, management hinted that they really believed Jack was using his injury and seniority status to avoid going on third shift where there was the greatest need for an employee with his skills.

However, above all of the noise, an important event occurred in the above exchange. Jack heard Eileen say that she was having trouble sleeping, and Eileen heard Jack's concern about his pay that had been docked.

At some point, the mediator can return to those two interests in an attempt to get them to talk further. Recognizing the other's pain is an important step in the effort to humanize the process. By asking Jack what he wants now, the mediator sets the stage for moving into interest-based bargaining.

CONSIDERING OPTIONS

MEDIATOR: Jack, perhaps you didn't hear me, I said, "What do you want?"

JACK: Well, I've asked for $250,000 in damages.

MEDIATOR: I know Jack, but what do you really need?

JACK: I need them to get off my back. I also need them to restore my suspended pay because I need the money to pay bills.

MEDIATOR: Could I ask everyone in the room the same question? How do you ever get anything done around here when all you do is spend all your time investigating each other and then writing up all these incident reports? You must need a pretty large typing pool. Or do you type them all yourselves?

ROBERT VAN ELDON: It used to be different. We used to talk to each other before all the lawyers warned us not to talk once an incident was being investigated, because anything we said could be used against us at the hearing.

MEDIATOR: How did that work? Tell me more about what it was like then.

ROBERT VAN ELDON: Well, I started here back when Jack's father still worked for this company. If somebody got out of line, the supervisor would go over and say, "Hey you guys, knock it off." And if that didn't work, we could always find the union rep and then together, we would go to the guy and say, "Hey, knock it off." We could always figure something out. Now it's nothing but typing out investigative reports in triplicate.

MEDIATOR: Do you think you could ever do it like that again?

ROBERT VAN ELDON: Well, first we would have to have the cooperation of the union.

As seen in this final segment of the dialogue, two important things have happened to change the dynamics of the conflict. First, the mediator asked the powerful question, "What do you need?" The first response by Jack was to parrot his legal claim, but then the mediator follows that response with the question, "What do you really need?" This opened up the discussions in a way that could not have been predicted and in a way that often happens in the mediation room when the environment for creative thinking is established by the mediator. The response by Jack was that he needed something very simple: He needed to resolve the conflict and he needed his back pay restored. The second important event occurred when the mediator used humor to influence the course of the discussions. The mediator's comment about how difficult it must be to get things done when everyone is investigating everyone else sets the stage for an important discussion about how things really could be different now. As the supervisor began to explain how it used to be, Fred jumped in on behalf of the union and said it would be possible to work with management on the floor to resolve problems as they came up. However, he disagreed with management's position that it always have the final say because of corporate counsel's advice against sharing power with the union. As Van Eldon continued to talk about the way it used to be, it soon became clear that it did not involve endlessly spinning a web to either create a defense to a potential lawsuit or a paper trail to justify termination of an employee. It became clear listening to Van Eldon that there really was a time when people tried to solve problems by listening to each other instead of investigating each other.

CHOOSING OPTIONS

MEDIATOR: So tell me how it would work. Suppose you have a new employee come up to you, Elaine, and she says, "Jack is glaring at me again." What would you do?

ROBERT VAN ELDON: Well, hopefully, there will be no chance that will happen again because Jack will have completed his ten weeks of anger management counseling with human resources, and he is working here under our rules or he is no longer working here. Which will it be Jack?

JACK: I can go to any seminar HR wants me to go to, but I have to be transferred to a different unit with a new supervisor and I want all my back pay restored.

Once the discussion gets to this point, it is quite likely the parties will find something that will work for them. However, the mediator still has to keep working and, in this case, it was necessary to prod the union representative for some brainstorming on how union could be helpful if a problem occurred on the floor. The real mediation that this case is based upon resulted in a final 45-minute discussion between the union rep and the two management people concerning the actual mechanics of having the union steward immediately becoming involved to assist Eileen anytime a conflict might surface around Jack. Jack also had to understand that he was on thin ice. In exchange for accepting a type of probationary status under the union grievance procedures and by his agreeing to complete anger-management counseling, he was assured that he would get his back pay restored. At this point, tough old Jack, the very person that human resources feared might go ballistic at the mediation session, broke down and cried saying he just wanted a chance to do his job. The people at this company still mention Jack and his case when explaining how it came about that management and union decided to conduct mini-mediations on the floor anytime a serious dispute arose.

CLIENT-CENTERED COMMUNITY MEDIATION

Client-centered mediation applies to many situations as illustrated by earlier examples in this chapter. It is also applies to large-group conflicts in communities and organizations. The following is a community mediation conducted by co-author, Steve Erickson, involving a large congregation in a small town:

Pastor Iverson had been given my name by the bishop. When Pastor Iverson called, he was frustrated. He reported how the entire town was being torn apart by conflict over whether or not to keep the Christian school open another year. Like many churches in small-town America, the school had always been an integral part of the Church. During the early 1980s, it was experiencing declining enrollments and had to be supported by the congregation, which was providing over $60,000 per year just to help keep the school open.

The Church finance committee decided it could no longer provide the level of financial assistance the school needed and notified the education committee that the school would not receive the same amount of financial aid as in the past. Responding, perhaps too quickly, the Church education committee summarily dismissed the principal and the remaining six part-time teachers and closed down the school, citing lack of commitment by the Church. This brought out the save-our-school committee, and the church broke into two factions: those who favored keeping the school open at all costs and those who had tired of having church dollars continually spent to shore up a school with declining enrollments and little prospect of recovering.

Almost forty people squeezed into the large meeting room in the school for the first mediation session. I welcomed them and silently hoped no more would show up. They labeled themselves the Mount Hope mediation group, and I complimented them on their interest and enthusiasm. I asked them to give me authority to determine who would speak and when. Just then I was interrupted by one of the members who announced she had a prepared statement that she wished to read. I asked her if she could please hold off reading any written statements for a moment. I tried to assure her that if she would just wait, we would probably be able to cover everything she has in mind to speak about anyway.

When mediating large groups, the process can quickly deteriorate if everyone is permitted to speak when they want to. Indeed, it is almost impossible to make any progress unless the discussions remain structured. It seems to work best for me to follow the five steps below and allow each person to speak individually on each one of the five steps. In selecting people to speak, I will always alternate between factions and I start by asking the first person to try to list the most important issue that brings us together so that if that were resolved, we would be on the way toward resolving the entire conflict.

These five steps are:

1. Define the problem. (Issues)
2. Give everyone a chance to state their interests and needs in order to provide a basis for settlement. (Needs) When a person's needs are met, the case will more likely settle.
3. Creatively discuss and list options that would solve our problems and begin to meet our needs. (Options)

4. Select and implement a combination of options by making specific agreements. (Agreements)
5. Design methods to carry out the agreements. (Implementation)

Step One: At the end of their first evening's mediation session, these were the problems that the group listed as their issues:

Issues

Finances
Conflict has affected church relationships
Inability to make a decision
Communication—poor types
Educate the congregation about the true financial picture. Is the school really a drain on church finances?
Lack of support by church leaders
Need to not divert our attention and energy from other important problems
Getting agreement on facts about finances
Lack of open and honest communication
There is a problem with running a larger organization on less staff and money
Must run the school and church more like a business
Our rules keep getting changed and we don't stick with our commitments
Our feelings, our emotions, and our positions contaminate our ability to listen
Seeking more financial support for church programs
Need to examine other (than money) aspects of the school question
Prioritize our expenditures of money with open, honest communication
Too much energy is diverted from spiritual development
Emotional pain of the past has stopped communication
Need to be more creative about communication with the entire parish
Parent support lacking
Avoid positional bargaining
Confusion of roles
Learn to be more effective at board meetings

When listing the issues, some members in the group insisted on stating them in negative and blaming ways. When the Mount Hope save-our-school committee complained about being stabbed in the back by certain members of the Church finance committee, I clarified what was meant and reframed the statement with their agreement as, "Lack of support by church leaders." This method of bringing out the issues is certainly better than allowing the leader of each faction to make an opening statement. Opening statements are generally avoided in a client-centered approach, because they can be a premature statement of one side's positions. Using the method just described, the story unfolds so everyone can begin to see various aspects of the problem.

Step Two: Step two of the process asks the participants in mediation to list their needs. "If you could get one important need met, what would that need be? In other words, if you think of the things that are needed to solve the problems facing this congregation, what is the one most important need that you believe must be met?" The following is the listing of needs from the second evening's mediation session:

Needs

Need more money for religious education

Need the six professional staff members to support the school (more than nominal support)

Need to be more Christlike

Need complete financial information about all programs

Need people in the parish to recognize that funds are limited and hard choices must be made

Need all of us to unite together and find support and money for all programs

Need staff to focus on spiritual development, and then the budget and administration issues will be easy to resolve

Need to become clear about some church decision-making process

Need a joint commitment from staff and congregation to keep the school open, and then money will solve itself

Need to eliminate factions

Need to put school issue to rest

Need unity of purpose in order to set an example for youth

Need to trust that we are all trying our best

Need time to listen and to love

Need to not be judged

Need to know exact finances and other ramifications of a closure of the school

Need to examine numbers in order to solve the problem

Need to build a school we can all be proud of

Need to honor our past commitment to keep the school open

An examination of the group's needs reveals the division within the church. In client-centered mediation, great care is taken to keep the process a safe environment for all sides. The mediator might need to reframe and tone down some of the statements that come from the group. All the needs are purposely written in such a way that does not blame or attack. As might be seen from the letter at the end of this chapter, it is clear that many of the needs just listed were eventually met as a result of the mediation process. Of course, they didn't assign a committee to figure out how each need could be met. Rather, people were beginning to listen to each other and there was beginning to be an attitude shift. This attitude shift came about as a result of realizing that they had shared goals and they would either sink or swim together. Although no amount of prodding and cajoling would have made them cooperative at the beginning of mediation, the interaction of client-centered mediation brought about a transformation.

Step Three: Before ending the second mediation session, we started to list options. Options, of course, are the things people think will meet their needs and solve their problems. Usually, it is helpful to search for options that will allow both sides' needs to be met.

Options (Things to Do to Solve the Problem)

Figure out concrete ways to build cooperative support and generate contributions to the entire church effort.

Might have to make some hard budget choices—involve the parishioners.

Determine the actual amount of money that is needed to keep the school open for the following year.

Explore new ways to generate money, such as latch key or other new uses of the school building (must be self supporting).

The next session was rancorous. Near the end of the session, I remembered an idea from Ghandi's autobiography where he talked about his early days as an attorney in South Africa. He stressed the importance of understanding the facts of each case, and then it hit me. We really didn't know much about the finances of the school and the church. I decided to ask a question about the facts. I said to the entire group: "Does anyone really know how much money would be saved for the church by closing the school right now?" We had been focusing on what it cost to keep the school open and, by default, everyone thought they would save what they would not have to then spend. Someone in the front row said, "Why do you ask that?" I responded by pointing out that even if the school were to close now, they were still going to use the school building for scouts activities and other scheduled uses. There is one cost of keeping it open. In addition, the staff that had been laid off would surely collect unemployment benefits and perhaps they needed to know how much money would be saved by closing the school. Then somebody asked if there were contracts to be met concerning health insurance benefits. Soon, it became clear that they needed to know more details about the operation. I asked if the finance committee would need to meet with the education committee before another mediation session.

At the beginning of the third and final mediation session, the chair of the finance committee stood up and asked if he could give his report. The two committees had met for over four hours on the previous Sunday afternoon and, to their surprise, they concluded that at most, if the school were closed immediately, there would only be a $14,000 to $18,000 savings. The additional costs were due to obligations related to contracts with the teachers, unemployment compensation costs, insurance costs already paid, and for utilities and maintenance on the school building. As a result of this information, the discussions turned to the possibility of keeping the school open on a trial basis for at least one more year. The decision to keep the school open was finally reached when everyone agreed to certain criteria that had to be met in order to continue to operate the school. The criteria are set forth below in the letter that was mailed out to the entire parish.

The letter is reproduced in its entirety with permission from Pastor Iverson. It is an example of how the process of mediation, when conducted in accordance with the principles of client-centered mediation, will transform people from adversaries to partners:

To: Members of Mount Hope Church
From: Members of Mount Hope Mediation Group
Date: August 9, 1983

The purpose of this letter is to communicate with you the results of our mediation meetings. Upon recommendation of the Church Council, mediation was sought to help us reach a decision regarding the future of our Christian school, while maintaining unity within our Church.

Members of the Mount Hope mediation group met with Steve Erickson, a professional mediator. Steve Erickson did not make decisions for us, but rather helped and motivated us to reach some results that all of us in the room could agree on. The process also enabled us to develop positive skills in dealing with conflicts and their resolutions. In addition to our three meetings with the mediator, the finance council, the pastoral council and the education task force met on several occasions to clarify specific issues that were raised at the mediation meetings.

Each member of the mediation group had the opportunity to state their perceptions of the parish's problems, needs and solutions. By the end of our third meeting with Steve Erickson, it became clear that if our school were to remain open, certain criteria would need to be established; namely, what would the Church subsidy to our school be? What would our school income need to be? How low could the enrollment be in order for our school to be viable?

The following criteria have been developed and accepted by our Church Council: The finance council has approved our total budget for the present fiscal year.

The finance council has approved a $30,300 church subsidy as well as the budgeted building expenses of $23,815 on a yearly basis for the support of our school. These numbers may be adjusted yearly, depending on our ability as a parish to do so based on our parish having a balanced budget in the preceding year.

Our school will need to assume responsibility for raising the sum $64,221. Failure to do so will mean closure of our school.

The finance council reserves the right to evaluate the subsidies on a yearly basis in the event that there is a significant deficit.

The Mount Hope Christian school will need to keep an enrollment of at least 40 students in the kindergarten through sixth grades. Any number below 40 will mean closure of our school. The projected enrollment for the coming school year is 52.

As a mediation group, we accept these criteria that have been presented by our finance council, Church Council and mediation task force.

In addition, our mediation group has adopted the following agreements:

1. We agree to think and speak of Mount Hope as a single entity. We are *not* the church and the school. Rather, we are a Christian community with a school.
2. We agree it is better to attack problems that arise in our Church rather than attacking people.
3. We agree that we need to work together by improving communication with the various committees, councils, as well as members of Mount Hope.

We feel that the results of our mediation meetings were very helpful and although it is only a beginning, the communication and agreements made were done so in a very loving and caring manner.

Even though there has been past conflict within our group of believers, we believe that out of our experience of trying to resolve the conflict cooperatively, we have experienced growth and healing and believe there were no winners or losers. We believe that if we work together as an entire parish family we will continue to grow in unity and in our love for God and each other.

We ask that you join us in our efforts to put any past conflicts behind us. In doing so we *will* be a stronger faith community.

If you should have any questions or comments regarding the above information, please feel free to *call anyone of us.*

Sincerely,

The names of the 30 members of the mediation group are omitted.

The final proof of the power of a client-centered mediation approach is found in the letter of September 9, 1983 from Pastor Iverson:

Mount Hope Church
1621 West Oak Street
Pleasantville, Minnesota 54333

Stephen Erickson

Dear Stephen,

I have enclosed with this letter, a copy of the letter that we have sent out to each member of Mount Hope Church with regard to the school. I believe this letter adequately summarizes and spells out the criteria that the entire mediation group has agreed upon for the continuation of Mount Hope Christian school.

I met with the members of the finance council, Church Council, and mediation task force to work out the specifics. We then had our general mediation meeting to adopt and ratify the criteria. The rest of the meeting was spent working on specific action plans to address the 18 options that were put together at our last meeting with you.

I was very pleased with the attitude and openness of the people at each of these meetings. After each of the meetings the people left smiling and very positive in spirit. I can't thank you enough for the great work that you did with our group. Many of them commented on how the mediation process helped them to see that everyone wants the best for our church community. Although it is only the beginning, I believe we now have a solid foundation to work with as we continue to work toward greater trust, communication, and unity.

In Gratitude,

/s/

Pastor J. Iverson

CONCLUSION

Some people predict that mediation has the opportunity to replace current litigation practice, significantly reducing the reliance on adversarial legal wrangling to make the workplace fair. In an informal discussion in 1998 with former Minnesota Supreme Court Chief Justice A. M. Sandy Keith, he observed that civil court filings have declined almost 20 percent since the adoption of mandatory use of mediation or other ADR in all civil cases in Minnesota. He went on to say, "You mediators really don't realize what a dramatic impact you have had on our legal system. It is no longer business as usual for lawyers."

Already, some employers are requiring new employees to agree, as a condition of employment, that the new employee first mediate and then arbitrate all employment disputes. For over 20 years, the New York Stock Exchange has required its dealers to insist that in all brokerage agreements, the client forego traditional court lawsuits and use arbitration.

The trend, however, seems to be moving away from using arbitration as the first step and more toward mediation instead. Employers are finding that arbitration is just as costly and adversarial as is the court system. Indeed, a review of the literature of organizational development and human resource management reveals a strong effort in the direction of collaboration and early conflict resolution before disputes spawn costly and destructive litigation. The US Postal Service, which is the largest employer in the United States, has found that a form of client-centered nondirective mediation has settled almost 70 percent of Equal Employment Opportunity (EEO) filings (Bingham, 1997). Detailed satisfaction questionnaires report that 95 percent of managers and 93 percent of line workers rated the mediation process favorably, even in those instances where the mediation process resulted in no agreement.

CHAPTER 6

Mediation Training

B EFORE EVALUATING the endless number of training courses offered in mediation, it might first be helpful to understand what it takes to be a mediator. What are the special attributes that make a good mediator? Are there any personality traits that might make one better or less-well equipped to become a mediator? Are these traits innate or can they be acquired? These are difficult questions partly because, only in the past 20 years, have we experienced a proliferation of people holding themselves out as professional mediators and charging fees for this unique service. It has also been only in the past 20 years that we have begun to teach others the skills of mediation. In order to teach others, we must first have a conceptual framework to teach from, and, unfortunately, there is not yet complete agreement on exactly what a mediator should be doing in the mediation room. Therefore, there is not complete agreement about who will succeed as a mediator and who will not. With all these difficulties in mind, we think we have some good answers to these very complex questions of what type of person makes a good mediator and what type of training is best. If you believe you already have these necessary attributes to become a good mediator, or you are willing to acquire these attributes, we invite you to begin the journey.

We cannot point to any research on this subject, but we believe one of the reasons some people fail in their efforts to become professional mediators is that they do not understand what it means to be neutral. They forget (or are unwilling to learn) that it is not their job to judge the behavior of others in the mediation room and that it is not their job to advise what outcome is best for the people in front of them. Judging is for state and federal court judges, not for mediators. Committed, professional mediators who take their job seriously know the importance of remaining neutral in the midst of high conflict. They know that their job is not to make decisions for the people in front of them nor to predict what the legal outcomes will be if impasse occurs. In mediation, mediators understand that their job is to help people find a way to make decisions they have been unable to make on their own. However, as you will see, the job of a mediator is to do much more than just help people make decisions and settle their divorces. In reality, the job of a mediator is to change the course of peoples' lives.

Since conducting the first national divorce mediation training of about 60 mediators in 1980, those of us who continued to train have tried to figure out what makes a mediator successful. Every year, it seems more and more people are attracted to the field because mediation makes so much common sense. Yet, this common-sense aspect of mediation is deceptive. Many who attend a divorce mediation training believe it will be easy to be a mediator and that anyone can do it. In fact, learning to be a mediator is challenging. If you are willing to discard old ideas in order to acquire the important attributes of a good mediator, the rewards of the profession will far outweigh the hardship experienced as a result of choosing to become a teacher of peace.

CHARACTERISTICS OF A MEDIATOR

There are important personality traits, attributes, and characteristics that are conducive to becoming a client-centered mediator. They can be broadly summarized as follows:

Be nonjudgmental in the face of discrepancies;
Be willing to listen holistically;
Be willing to manage conflict and be comfortable in the presence of others' conflict;
Be able to clarify communication and communicate clearly;
Be intuitive and willing to go with your hunches;
Be a creative thinker and encourage clients to think creatively;

Be nondirective, expecting clients to decide what is best for them;

Be passionate about what you are doing;

Believe it is better to embrace your adversary than to destroy him.

If you have these abilities and are willing to cultivate them, then the next part of this chapter will make even more sense. It examines the motivations for entering the field and explores how to select a training program that will meet your needs and interests. Although most people who invest time and money in mediation training intend to enter the field as a professional, many take the training for their own personal growth. In our experience, nobody has ever been disadvantaged by spending a week intensively learning peacemaking skills from a professional mediator. As you begin, you will want to select a training program that best suits your particular interests and abilities.

BEING NONJUDGMENTAL

Perhaps the single most important characteristic of a client-centered mediator is the ability to build rapport with people in conflict while being both nonjudgmental and compassionate. This is not an innate skill or personality trait. It requires a great deal of effort to develop the skill. Judge Jack Etheridge has said that in his capacity as southern regional director of JAMS (Judicial Arbitration and Mediation Service), he observed that only a minority of judges makes the transition from judging to mediating. He said that in his opinion a judge's greatest downfall is the propensity to judge, a trait that is hard to break, and an attribute that does not fit in mediation practice. Maintaining a nonjudgmental attitude is even more essential because a mediator hears the most egregious stories of spousal behavior while each spouse simultaneously clamors for sympathy.

The following scenario illustrates a mediator's work with a high-conflict couple and why the mediator must be nonjudgmental:

Jim and Betty are a typical couple who attend an initial consultation about mediation. They are both anxious about their divorce and extremely angry with each other. As the mediator begins to explain the major areas of decision making and starts to discuss the children, Betty interrupts to say that Jim is an excellent parent when he is not using alcohol. However, she thinks he should not be allowed to have the kids overnight because of his history of drinking and blackouts. Jim instantly becomes upset at this statement and vehemently denies having a drinking problem. He concludes by saying this confirms his fear that Betty was going to create a ruse about his drinking to use it against him in order to take the kids and anything else she could get her hands on.

This is the point where the mediator steps in.

MEDIATOR: Jim, what kind of relationship do you want the children to have with each of you?

JIM: I think they should live with each of us half of the time.

BETTY: You've got to be crazy! You can't even take care of yourself. How do you expect to take care of four kids? Besides, the kids are not little anymore, and they know what's going on with you. They've seen you drunk. And what about last week when you were stopped while driving with the kids in the car, and the officer warned you about drinking and driving! You should have been arrested! You only got off because the officer is the brother of one of your drinking buddies.

MEDIATOR: Well, making decisions about the children will be an important part of the divorce. How are the children handling all of this?

JIM: They're great kids. They are doing fine, but it's my wife who is not doing very well. She is willing to call me an alcoholic just to keep the children from me.

BETTY: They are very disturbed by everything. They are worried about Jim and afraid to talk to him about it out of fear he will just get mad. *[Turning to the mediator]* You understand how devastating it is for kids to have to walk on egg shells around their dad. His drinking and his temper scare the kids. You must know how bad that is for kids.

JIM: That's not true. They think you are breaking up our family, and they want to live with me. *[Turning to the mediator]* You should ask them, then you will believe me. We can have the children come into mediation and talk to you, can't we?

MEDIATOR: Often kids have difficulty with divorce. Most do not want their parents to divorce. Depending on where they are developmentally, they may each have different reactions to the divorce. However, the greatest difficulty for your kids is probably the conflict between the two of you. Research findings support that what affects children the most in a divorce is the level of conflict between the two of you, and how long that conflict continues. So, perhaps the most important question for the two of you is, How will you each let go of what you hold against each other? Because once you begin to do that, the children will benefit. They will not have to feel that something is wrong with them if the two of you begin to build respect for each other once again. This is part of the mediation process. In this room you have the opportunity to address all the issues of the divorce while I facilitate that discussion, without blame and fault. In that light you may address not only the children's needs, but also the issues of support and the division of your assets and liabilities.

The foregoing vignette is typical of what a family mediator will encounter with a couple caught in the middle of high conflict. The mediator must learn to respond to their plight without being drawn to either side. Being nonjudgmental requires strength and concentration. It also helps to have the experience of hearing and seeing both sides of the coin as they are played out in the room. Notice that one of the techniques used by the mediator in the foregoing vignette is to redirect the discussion so that it focuses on the children and what *they* need. Whenever the mediator is making an observation about the universal needs of children, it is easier to remain nonjudgmental. As you read the foregoing vignette, you might have asked yourself why the mediator didn't discuss how unhealthy it is for children to stay overnight with an alcoholic father. You might have also asked yourself how the mediator will ever get the wife to quit using the drinking ruse to control the husband's access to the children. By considering these two questions, you learn how difficult is it to remain nonjudgmental.

BEING A HOLISTIC LISTENER

Although each person has a different story, each has the same motive: to have the mediator listen to that person's story, agree with his or her concerns, and then take sides. This is not what a client-centered mediator does. Even in the midst of incredible hurt, anger, betrayal, mistrust, and suspicion by those entering mediation, the mediator respects each person and looks for the light within each of them that may need recharging through a caring glance, a willingness to listen, and a fully open posture that invites them to participate. The mediator remains interested, non-judgmental, and empathetic. The mediator's goal is to help the couple create their own agreements, not to tell them what they should do, or what the law says they should do.

A client-centered mediator listens intently to the couple's stories without considering who is right or who is a better or worse parent. Instead of trying to figure out who is more at fault, the mediator asks them what they want to happen in mediation. Sometimes the couple returns to their accusations and acrimonious monologues about the other. Again, the mediator does not take sides or give advice but might share the following observation: "*If your children experience what you have just described to me, they must be torn apart inside. Your children know they are made up of half of each of you, so when one of you puts the other down, it often makes them feel that half of who they are is bad.*" With this observation, mediators compassionately describe their own pain as they listen to their conflict. Such an observation is a very powerful tool in helping the couple face the conflict and how that conflict can negatively impact their children. Because the mediator's words are communicated compassionately and with great respect for each person, the couple usually hears what the mediator says. A client-centered mediator listens carefully for opportunities to reach out to each person's heart by making comments about the dire consequences of their conflict without judging. Heartfelt listening creates the groundwork for building rapport and trust with the clients. Without rapport, mediation is very difficult, if not impossible.

BEING WILLING TO UNDERSTAND AND MANAGE CONFLICT

A client-centered mediator does not avoid conflict. Rather, the mediator understands that conflict provides an opportunity for change, growth, learning, and understanding. If managed constructively, conflict presents opportunities for positive outcomes. For example,

---

MEDIATOR: Betty, if you believe that Jim has a chemical addiction, what do you think needs to happen to resolve this issue? And Jim, how can you get Betty to quit raising it?

BETTY: I need Jim to go to treatment before I will let the kids stay overnight with him.

JIM: I don't have a problem. She and her family think the whole world is addicted. Just get off my back.

MEDIATOR: I certainly don't know whether or not Jim has a drinking problem. However, there is a way for both of you to resolve this issue. Would the two of you agree to go to a chemical dependency evaluation for Jim? Upon completion, would each of you abide by the recommendations of the evaluator's report? That way, Betty, if Jim doesn't have a drinking problem, you can no longer accuse him of that. And Jim, if the report finds that you do, you agree to go to treatment. That will not only be healthy for you, but will greatly enhance your relationship with the children. Whatever the results, it may get the two of you off the subject in the future, so you can begin to concentrate on what is best for your children as you divorce and plan your separate lives. Is this something you would each consider?

Every problem has a solution, and mediators believe that conflict presents an opportunity for change and growth. For every fear or concern that is expressed, there are usually several avenues the mediator can encourage people to consider. Unfortunately, most people in conflict think they are simply stuck in their positions. The above exchange is a good example of the mediator understanding how to manage the conflict so the parties may move beyond this issue and begin to tackle other ones. For every sticking point, the mediator may suggest ways that they can move beyond that point. It is up to the couple to decide whether they wish to journey down the avenue suggested by the mediator. They may decide to take a different route, or they may simply stay mired in the mud as they were when they entered mediation. Whatever course they take, it is *their* choice, not the mediator's. The mediator is merely the guide providing the map and pointing out many places they may go on that map. The mediator will encourage the couple to craft their own solutions. Thus, the mediator honors the outcome chosen by the couple, even if their choice entails doing nothing differently. Remaining in conflict is also a choice the couple is free to make. The mediator will always respect the choices made by the couple.

BEING ABLE TO CLARIFY COMMUNICATION

Yogi Berra once said, "It's not too far, it just seems like it is" (Berra, 1998, p. 100). Like Yogi, most couples think they are making sense, but when you observe them closely, you find that they are not even speaking about the same thing. The ability to clarify communication is another attribute of a client-centered mediator that requires a great deal of concentration and effort. By the time a couple enters mediation, communication between them has usually deteriorated. They have become deaf to each other's words and concerns, and sometimes act as though they are from different planets. When the mediator models good listening skills, the husband and wife often begin to listen more closely to each other. When the mediator clarifies what one of them is saying, the message is also clarified for the other person. This process of concentrating on the words and phrases and having people repeat what they have said in slightly different ways creates opportunities for each to hear what the other is saying without emotional contamination. Like the wine that is continually moved from one cask to the other in an effort to clarify it to brilliance, the mediator will make many attempts at clarification to remove some of the impurities that obscure their ability to hear clearly.

Tom and Jean came to mediation after their divorce to work out parenting conflicts. They had a five-year-old boy, Jonathan, who lived with each parent about half time, with mom having a little more than half and dad a little less. Jonathan was having difficulties moving between their homes, and was acting out in school. Both parents were very concerned about this.

JEAN: I don't think this parenting schedule is working for him. I think he needs to live with me and see his dad every other weekend for three nights and have dinner with him on Wednesday evenings.

TOM [very angry and hurt]:   I knew you'd pull this! Jonathan and I get along great. I am involved in his T-ball, gymnastics, and swimming. We are always doing things together. I read to him before bed every night and help him with his prayers and make sure he always remembers you in those prayers. You have always been so perfect, and you just can't accept that I have a significant role in his life.

JEAN: He is not doing very well in school, he has no friends, and the day-care center is concerned that he is wetting his pants! There is something wrong, and I think he doesn't have the security of having one home, which is what he needs.

Tom: Since when is he wetting his pants? I didn't know anything about that!

Jean: Well, you would if you stayed around at day care instead of just rushing in, picking him up, and rushing out all of the time.

Tom: I still think they should have made a point to tell me. I know that when he gets excited sometimes, he holds himself and I have to make sure he gets to the bathroom right away, but he hasn't had any real accidents when he is with me. How about you?

Jean: Well, the other day he did, and I can't figure out why. He threw a temper tantrum during his shower. He got upset when I told him he didn't have to use rinse on his hair!!! He said you told him he should always use rinse, and he got absolutely unruly.

Tom: Well, he was right, he always uses rinse. He began when he saw me use it, and thought it was something that men and boys use, so he was excited to use it.

Mediator: Wait a minute. I don't understand. He got upset because he couldn't use rinse at your house, Jean?

Jean: Yes, and later that day he wet his pants!

Tom: Well, maybe he should just live with me more of the time. He does fine with me.

Mediator: Is this the first you two have ever talked about this? When do you talk together about Jonathan?

Both: We don't, except here.

Mediator: How can you parent Jonathan if you don't talk to each other?

Tom: We never talk to each other. When we used to talk, we always ended up fighting, so we decided we would not talk to each other anymore. So we use faxes and e-mail.

Mediator: So Jonathan never experiences the two of you getting along?

Jean: No, he never sees us together, and we don't talk about the other in his presence.

Tom: We thought it would be best for him this way.

Mediator: Has it worked for him?

[They both looked at each other and tears welled up in their eyes.]

Tom: What should we do?

Mediator: Perhaps the two of you need to talk about that. I can't tell you what to do. You have to make your own decision about how to make things better for Jonathan. Is he in counseling?

Jean: Actually, that is one thing I wanted to discuss with Tom today. I would like Jonathan to see a child psychologist.

TOM: I have always opposed this. After all, we are both highly educated people. We should be able to help him. But hearing everything to- day I don't know if he needs the counseling, or if maybe we do.

JEAN: Maybe we all do.

MEDIATOR: Do you remember from the parenting classes that the conflict between parents is what harms children in divorce? Well, even though you tried to keep your conflict from Jonathan, is it possible that he perhaps felt the tension, and got the message, by your not talking about the other to him, that he didn't have permis- sion to have the other parent with him even in his thoughts and heart while at the other's house? So maybe your idea about the two of you going to counseling together is worth considering. What do you think, Tom?

TOM: I do remember that from the classes, but it never occurred to me that Jonathan could sense our disdain for each other. He is so young to carry all of this. I think we need to see a counselor as soon as possible. My God, what have we done?

The mediator listened carefully to their conversation, and first tried to clarify by asking a question about what was hard to understand. When that did not help Tom and Jean, the mediator again listened and asked if they ever talked to each other. This was done to find an opening for changing the discussion from blame and fault to how they communicate with each other. The mediator kept asking questions to clarify their rela- tionship and to learn how they communicate with each other as parents. Next, sensing a deeper concern for Jonathan, the mediator changed the questioning to focus on Jonathan's experience of his parents' relationship by asking, "Has it worked for him?" This question helped Tom and Jean look at the whole situation differently, and for the first time in this con- versation they began to reach each other and talk constructively about Jonathan's needs and their own roles as parents. The role of the mediator was to help them become more clear. Then, on their own, they were able to begin to figure out what they needed to do.

BEING INTUITIVE

Intuition is another attribute of a client-centered mediator. Although in- tuition is seldom discussed in the professional literature, experienced mediators routinely rely upon their intuition. They read their own feelings as the mediation process unfolds, and when they feel something or feel something happening, they go with their intuition. Client-centered mediators follow hunches and ask questions to see what lies underneath the topic being discussed. More often than not, what lies underneath is crucial if an issue is to be fully understood. Mediators do not use intuition as a therapeutic intervention, but rather use it to remove the blocks to creative thinking that are preventing the couple from resolving their differences. Occasionally, intuition serves to unlock the puzzle that is presented.

Susan had an MBA and directed a well-known agency. Charles was a university professor. Both were articulate, self assured and knowledgeable of the marital estate and finances. The initial consultation went well with both contributing to the conversation and asking questions. During the first session, they talked about their children, and they agreed on an exchange schedule for each week as well as for holidays, vacations, and how they would communicate with each other. The next session focused on their budgets. They were in the process of working on both of their separate budgets of their monthly living expenses and trying to allocate what each was spending on the children. Susan had great difficulty doing the budgets, and whenever she gave her line item cost, Charles criticized her. She would respond by changing her budget expense to what he thought was more appropriate for her. This was very unusual behavior for both of them, considering how they operated in the first session.

MEDIATOR: You both seem to be having difficulty with this budgeting. Susan, you seem to be well prepared with your budget, but, Charles, you seem to be questioning her expenses, and listing your own as what Susan feels are extremely low figures. Is there something else we need to talk about before continuing the budgets?

SUSAN *[very irritated]:*   I'm so glad you brought this up! What is going on here?

CHARLES   *[quite disturbed and quiet]*: I'm sorry. I just learned that the university is cutting back in our department, and I'm on the list for job termination. I don't know what I am going to do! It will be hard for me to find another teaching position in my specialty here, and I may have to move somewhere else to work.

SUSAN [stunned]:   Oh, I'm so sorry. Should we just delay everything, or what should we do?

MEDIATOR: Now I think I understand why you were questioning Susan's budget. But how does this impact your decision to divorce?

SUSAN: I believe we are still getting divorced, but now we need to rethink all our assumptions about how it will work out. Charles, why don't we both scale down our budgets for now? We could even think about selling the house so we could each purchase a less expensive house with a lower mortgage payment. Then I think we can still make it. Even if you have to move, you'll still need a home for the kids when they live with you. We just have to figure out a different parenting arrangement.

CHARLES: I never thought of that. We just have to look at things differently. I really thought I'd lose the kids through all of this. And I still can't fathom losing my job! I've been there for 17 years!

MEDIATOR: Sometimes when there are changes you have no power over, they actually can be an opportunity to improve one's situation. I'm impressed with how you each are willing to make everything work in spite of this news.

If it is true that one of the main roles of the mediator is to change the interaction between the parties, then intuition gives the mediator permission to ask why something is amiss. Experienced mediators trust intuition to be that small guide in the back of the mind when they are uncertain about where to go next in their discussions. Intuition is a valid skill that comes with experience. It is enhanced when used with the other skills of listening, clarifying, understanding, and not judging.

BEING NONDIRECTIVE

Mediators do not *direct* the discussions toward a premeditated outcome, nor do they *direct* the clients based upon the mediator's desires or beliefs about clients or process. Being nondirective means that the mediator does not drive the process and clients according to the mediator's needs and desired outcome. The mediation process is fluid, and the mediator takes direction from the clients about the issues, their needs, and their desires. When the clients are conflicted about the direction, the mediator clarifies what the conflict is about and opens a discussion about what to do. At times, the clients will defer to the mediator to make the decision, in which case the mediator is following their desires.

Being nondirective does not imply that the mediator sits quietly and waits for clients to talk. Clients engage the services of a mediator because they want someone to facilitate their discussions, to be actively involved in the process. Otherwise, clients would resolve their issues on their own.

Mediators can be nondirective and still be confrontive and firm, particularly when conflict becomes potentially harmful, with name calling, insults, or demeaning, hostile, or threatening behavior. A mediator may intervene and insist that the behavior stop and use this opportunity to help them figure out why this happened.

LOIS: You jerk! Who do you think you are? You think you can get away with dissing every woman in the office. Well, the buck stops here. You are the sleaziest excuse for a man ever! Where do you get off? You should be locked up in a cage and paraded in front of all the women you have harassed so they can laugh at you and treat you the way they have been treated!

MEDIATOR: Lois, please stop. You are obviously very upset. Did something just happen?

LOIS: He just rubbed his foot against my leg under the table, and I will not sit here and have him continue to abuse me!!! This is what the lawsuit is all about, you'd think he'd learn.

MEDIATOR: Sean, what's going on!?!

SEAN: I just bumped her leg when I moved. I didn't mean to. You've got to believe me.

MEDIATOR: It's not me you have to convince. How are you going to convince Lois?

SEAN *[to Lois]*: Lois, I'm sorry. I didn't mean to bump your leg. I'm sorry you think I'm such a despicable person, because I'm really not. Since the first day you began work, I was attracted to you. I obviously did not show it in the right way. I'm generally an introvert, and thought that I would never get your attention unless I got out of my shell. So I sent you flowers and bought you gifts anonymously. Okay, maybe the gifts were too personal, but I really didn't intend anything by them. I heard from one of the other workers that you were very upset about the gifts, and about having a secret admirer, rather than being flattered as I expected you would be. Then when I told you as discreetly as possible that I was your secret admirer, you became enraged. I don't know how to make you believe me.

MEDIATOR: Lois, do you believe him?

LOIS: I've heard all this before. You see, he just doesn't understand how awful it felt to have someone secretly send very personal gifts to me. I felt dirty, and like every guy in my life could not be trusted! It is so hard to believe him when the feelings won't go away! I am so frustrated and angry at him for robbing me of my privacy. It has been so hard to trust anybody since this happened. I'm sorry I flew off the handle at you, because in a way I am treating you the way I felt you treated me, with total disrespect. I'm sorry, that is not how I usually act. Thanks for stopping me.

BEING ABLE TO THINK CREATIVELY

Conflict may give rise to creative thinking, but it can also create paralysis. Morton Deutsch (1973) discusses creative thinking as having several phases:

> (1) an initial period that leads to the experiencing and recognition of a problem that is sufficiently arousing to motivate efforts to solve it; (2) a period of concentrated effort to solve the problem through routine, readily available, or habitual actions; (3) an experience of frustration, tension, and discomfort that follows the failure of customary processes to solve the problem and leads to a temporary withdrawal of the problem; (4) the perception of the problem from a different perspective and reformulation in a way that permits new orientations to a solution to emerge; (5) the appearance of a tentative solution in a moment of insight, often accompanied by a sense of exhilaration; (6) the elaboration of the solution and the testing of it against reality; and finally, (7) the communication of the solution to relevant audiences. (p. 360)

Curiosity is closely related to intuition. Creative thinking requires new and varied patterns of thought that can be flexibly combined into novel patterns. This can be achieved through curiosity. When client-centered mediators pursue their curiosity and ask clarifying questions, they often hear: *"I was always curious about that but thought it best not to mention it for fear it would cause anger or be discounted by the other."* Although this may open a Pandora's box, more often it opens the discussion about an underlying fear, need, or interest that is key to understanding the conflict. A willingness to go to the heart of the conflict may initiate a response that the other person in the conflict hears for the first time. Client-centered mediators pursue their curiosity with interest and great respect, not judgment, in order to obtain more information about underlying needs. That curiosity also presents opportunities to the couple to say more about something that offers a deeper understanding about a conflict that eventually leads to "the perception of the problem from a different perspective" (Deutsch, 1973, p. 360).

BELIEVING PASSIONATELY IN THE VALUE OF MEDIATION

Another characteristic of a client-centered mediator is a passionate belief that resolving conflict constructively is the best way for couples to have a successful divorce. That passion for doing the right thing sets client-centered mediators apart from others and drives them to do their best to help couples divorce. Jim Coogler, (1978), when asked why one should consider becoming a divorce mediator, always replied: "Because it is right." Mediators must have that same passion about divorce mediation, and act out of that passion, because it is the right thing to do.

BELIEVING IN THE CAPACITY OF PEOPLE TO MEDIATE

So much of mediation is dependent on the beliefs and attitudes the mediator brings to the table. To mediate between adversaries, the mediator must believe they can sit in the same room, address what has happened, and then proceed to make things better. Clients would not seek mediation if it were not to make things better. The mediator would not mediate if the mediator did not believe that people can overcome their differences and heal. Assisting people to embrace their adversaries is what mediation is about, for when they do, in a nonadversarial setting, they begin to understand each other, let go of what they hold against each other, and create the opportunity for positive change and resolution of their issues.

WHAT MOTIVATES SOMEONE TO BECOME A MEDIATOR?

People have frequently asked us for information about becoming a mediator. We usually respond by asking, *"What is your primary motivation in considering this profession?"* Each person has responded differently. Some motivations are helpful, others are signals to stop and think further. Not everyone is suited to become a mediator.

First we ask where you are in your own life's journey. We suggest that you take an introspective look at why you are drawn to this field. Many people are interested in divorce mediation because of their own divorce experience. This may be helpful, but it can often be detrimental. We have found it difficult to have a recently divorced person in mediation training. If you are close to your own divorce, you may view the training from that perspective and ask questions for the purpose of figuring out what went wrong in your own divorce, rather than learning how to mediate other people's divorces. Or you may compare your divorce settlement with what you are learning in mediation training and become upset with what happened to you. You may also challenge what is being taught and become argumentative. Such a situation can be harmful to you, and it often detracts from the training for the other participants. Therefore, in general, we advise anyone going through a divorce to wait until they have been divorced for at least two years before you take divorce mediation training. We advise an even longer delay if a person has a great deal of unresolved anger about their divorce.

A second motivation we have observed is the need to do good for others. Although altruism is usually heartfelt, we question who would be gaining from the mediation experience. Would it be the altruistic person or their clients? This is a more complex motivation to address. We have had people in divorce-mediation training who want to help others and believe that the way to help couples in the midst of divorce is by giving advice. However, client-centered mediation is not about imposing the mediator's ideas and solutions, but about assisting clients to find *their own* solutions. We find that some aspiring mediators have difficulty understanding this seemingly simple concept.

Many have entered this field because of their strong beliefs that couples should have the opportunity to resolve their divorce issues with a mediator instead of in the legal adversarial process. This was actually Jim Coogler's main motivation. If you see yourself as a nonjudgmental facilitator helping to create a cooperative environment for couples who are divorcing, then this motivation to do good is more in line with what a client-centered mediator does.

Another motivation for some is the constructive potential mediation has for divorcing couples. They have read extensively about divorce mediation or have known people who successfully mediated their divorces. They may be therapists or attorneys who are troubled by their own professional method of dealing with divorce. As they come to believe that mediation is a better process, they feel a genuine excitement about the positive impact mediation can have on peoples' lives and a desire to learn how to do it. This excitement encompasses a respect for people's desire for self-determination in divorce and for appreciating a new approach to resolving conflicts. Their passion is driven by a common belief that the adversarial divorce litigation process only leads to greater distress, destructive outcomes, and alienation between parents, which negatively impacts children of all ages. This person usually believes in the innate goodness of people and that good can prevail in the divorce decision-making process, even when people are at their worst. Most of the people we encounter in our mediation training courses are this type. Their past professional experience, their hearts, and their positive perspective drive their passion to learn how to mediate.

We have found that people who are passionate about the social value of divorce mediation frequently come from professions in which they were expected to provide the answers to their clients' problems. For example:

- An attorney advocates for one client's best interests and advises the client in that regard.
- A therapist listens to peoples' personal problems, gives them direction, and advises how they can overcome the problems and feel better about themselves or their situations.
- A teacher is accustomed to helping people learn by explaining information and methods of handling situations.
- A minister helps people bear their burdens and learn to forgive others.

With these and other professionals, clients often follow their advice and then find fault with it when things do not work as they expected. Either way, professionals who work with clients in high conflict eventually burn out. They often welcome an opportunity to provide service in a new way that helps clients make their own decisions. They are motivated to learn new ways to help people without making decisions for them or leading them in a direction the clients may not follow. They have seen how dependent and disempowered their clients were in their practices, and they are anxious to become more successful helping clients through mediation.

A fourth motivation to become a divorce mediator is to earn a good living. This is the I-need-to-make-money motivation. If this is a primary motivation, mediation may be a disappointing career. It is not yet a profession that will support a person with a full-time professional income equal to other professions. It is more a profession for the entrepreneur or a professional service to be added to another profession, such as law or therapy. Only persistent, highly motivated mediators can earn a living through mediation alone, and that happens only after working uncompensated while getting a practice started. We spent many years building our mediation practice.

To our dismay, some people who have had their professional licenses revoked because of an ethical violation have turned to mediation as a new profession. Mediation attracts those people because it is still unregulated. The following is an example of such an instance:

A psychologist who had just completed a 40-hour divorce-mediation course called to ask where he could obtain malpractice insurance. My first response was to tell him to ask his present malpractice carrier to add a rider to that policy to cover mediation, which is usually possible. He said he no longer had a malpractice insurance policy for his psychological practice. He went on to say he had been found guilty of malpractice and his license had been withdrawn. He described this action as grossly unfair. I inquired about the grounds of the violation, and he replied, "It was just a little 'boundary issue'; you know how that goes." Well, actually, I didn't know how that went, but I did wonder why he dismissed it so lightly! Needless to say, we did not encourage him to pursue mediation any further.

Disbarred attorneys have also turned to the mediation profession to make an income.

One person who opened a mediation practice had a lot of money and was able to market herself very well. However, she was disbarred from the practice of law for mismanaging client funds, and now had a reputation for doing the same as a mediator. She also had a reputation of intimidating clients into making decisions she thought best for them. In addition, she advertises herself as a Christian mediator.

Numerous clergy have become trained in mediation as a means of leaving the ministry and entering a profession that is consistent with their commitment to serving others in a meaningful way. Although most have become excellent mediators, some have made mediation a platform for continuing their religious mission. They advertise as ministers who mediate, but they act as ministers, not mediators. They tend to make negative judgments about divorce and encourage couples to reconcile. The difference between many former ministers who have become excellent mediators and these people is that the successful mediators have learned to separate their ministry from the role of mediator. See Chapter 3 for more information on the role of the mediator.

A similar problem occurs with other mediators who view mediation through the lenses of their former profession. For example:

- An attorney may view each mediation case from the perspective of how the law would apply to the facts of the case.
- A therapist may view each mediation case from the perspective of diagnosing each person's psychopathologies.
- An organizational development specialist may want to give every couple in conflict a Myers-Briggs Inventory.
- A feminist may view a mediation case from the point of view that women are less powerful and most often the victim of male dominance.
- A men's resource center counselor may want to give all men more time with their children.
- A retired judge may want to tell couples in mediation what to do.
- A psychologist may view 50-50 joint custody as damaging and may try instead to persuade parents to do 50-50 time sharing of their children.

If you want to become a client-centered mediator, your first task will be to remove the lenses of your former profession and view everything from a new perspective.

Consider your reasons for wanting to enter the field of mediation. It may be helpful to discuss those reasons with a professional colleague who will be honest with you. You might consider calling upon mediators in your community and learning about their mediation practices and their motivations for becoming mediators. When you feel that you are well informed about mediation practice, and if you are still passionate about what a mediator does, that is the time to check into some training courses. It is important to find out what training programs are available, the conceptual framework of each, who the trainers are, and what their reputations are in the field of mediation. This is a lot of work, but it is wise to be well informed before selecting a training program. After all, the mediation training will lay the ground work for your new career. The following section offers more detail about how to approach the task of finding the best training.

CHOOSING A CLIENT-CENTERED MEDIATION TRAINING

To find a quality mediation training course, it is important to examine several criteria: the trainers, the curriculum, the conceptual framework, their theory of conflict resolution, an experiential component, and the course accreditation. These criteria are very important, and will provide the information necessary to make a good choice.

THE TRAINERS

The information about mediation training courses is plentiful, but it may not provide specific information about the trainers, their backgrounds, and their credentials. A close look at the training curriculum should reveal whether it is comprehensive and contains the trainer's conceptual framework of divorce mediation, philosophy about conflict resolution, and the trainer's experience and background. Training programs range from excellent to very poor, but the person seeking the training will not know the difference because one seldom takes more than one course of training. This is why it is so important to research courses before choosing one.

When investigating a mediation training program, first inquire about the trainers. Because mediators are not licensed at this time, the trainers' credentials are very important. Many training brochures contain names of leaders in the field, but this does not necessarily mean that those people will be training. Ask if those people highlighted in the brochure will actually be conducting the course.

Background of Trainers

Some trainers will send out a vitae for prospective trainees to review; others may send a short biography. Because mediation is such a new field, it lacks official regulation. Presently consumers of mediation services and training are the only regulators. Do not hesitate to ask about trainers' former professions and if they have been disciplined or lost their license to practice. This is a very important question because, as we noted earlier, the mediation field has attracted professionals who are prohibited from practicing in their former professions.

It is important to learn about the trainers' backgrounds as practicing mediators and find out when they were trained, and by whom. If they were initially trained as mediators less than two years ago, we would question their experience in training and in mediation. You should also find out if the trainers received training through a course that was approved by the Academy of Family Mediators (AFM), Family Mediation Canada (FMC), the Society of Professionals In Dispute Resolution (SPIDR), the Association of Family and Conciliation Courts (AFCC), or if they are certified by a state supreme court or statewide court administration. If the answer is yes to any of these, then a state, national, or international organization has scrutinized the training they attended and approved it. Because the training a trainer has received determines whether that trainer is qualified to conduct mediation training, it is important that the trainer demonstrate that he or she attended a training program that was approved by an appropriate organization. We recommend that people only take training that has been approved by one of the organizations listed above.

Professional Memberships

Training brochures frequently state the trainers' professional memberships. You may wish to inquire further about their membership status in each organization: Are they professional members? Ask what the criteria is for being a professional member. The criteria usually includes a number of hours of initial training, a number of hours of additional training, yearly continuing education units, a number of cases mediated, amount of experience as practitioners, and a number of hours of supervision to be approved as professional mediators.

The major professional membership organizations, as mentioned earlier, are the AFM, SPIDR, FMC, and, for court-affiliated mediators, the Association of Family and Conciliation Courts (AFCC). All have different levels of membership, so it is important to inquire about the level of membership that trainers hold, to know if they are professional members. If the trainers do not hold membership in any of these organizations, you may question their experience and commitment to the field of mediation.

Mediation Experience

Most people who train others to become mediators have a wealth of practical experience as mediators and have extensively studied the field. When you are considering taking a training course, we suggest that you research what experience the trainers have. After all, an important part of the training program is for you to learn from the trainers' experiences, insights, and knowledge, not just to hear a discussion of the most recent articles and books about mediation.

Training courses approved by the AFM must have at least one trainer who is a Practitioner Member of the academy. A practitioner has at least 100 hours of training, and has mediated at least 10 cases. The Practitioner Member has also been supervised by a consultant of the academy, and has had several memoranda reviewed by the academy. Therefore, a training approved by the AFM provides assurances that the training course has met specific experience-based criteria.

If the course is not approved by the AFM, you may want to inquire about the trainer's mediation practice, including the average number of cases the trainer mediates each year, and how many active cases the mediator is presently mediating. Because mediation is growing as a profession, more trainers who have little or no mediation experience themselves are conducting training programs. They may advertise that they are professional trainers, but they may not necessarily practice mediation. If this is the case, decide if you want to be trained by a professional trainer who is not also a practicing mediator. Two questions to consider are: (1) Do they attend seminars to stay current with the profession? and (2) How do they answer practice-based questions, give case examples, or conduct role plays as a mediator? We concur with the generally accepted principle that trainers who conduct mediation training programs must also be practitioners, at least part time.

THE CURRICULUM

A basic divorce-mediation training course consists of at least the following topics:

- Discussion of conflict resolution/transformation
- A conceptual framework
- The mediation process
- The role of the mediator
- Listening skills
- Mediator skills and strategies
- Comparison of mediation and the adversarial process
- Child custody—legal labels
- Effects of divorce on children
- Parenting plans and schedules
- Separate parenting agreements
- Budgeting
- Child support and spousal maintenance
- Marital assets and liabilities
- Concept of nonmarital property
- Distribution of marital property
- Domestic violence
- The emotional divorce
- Managing high conflict
- Tax implications of divorce settlement
- Strategies to avoid impasse

The curriculum is extensive and intense. When inquiring about training programs ask for the curriculum and training schedule. Compare the information with curriculum topics just listed.

Initial divorce-mediation training programs are usually conducted for a period of at least 40 hours, often in a five-day period of time. There may be some variations on the format, but the number of hours is still the same to cover the curriculum.

CONFLICT-RESOLUTION THEORY

One of the most important aspects of a good divorce-mediation training program is how it addresses conflict. Conflict is natural, neither positive nor negative. The way conflict is managed can be either constructive or destructive. Therefore, when inquiring about a training program, it is important to determine how much emphasis is placed on the theory and resolution of conflict.

Conflict-resolution theory should be discussed from the perspective of constructive or destructive conflict that can be addressed either by a competitive or a cooperative approach. This should lead to an analysis of competitive and cooperative methods of conflict resolution. Conflict resolution is viewed as competitive, issues are defined in terms of win-lose, and clients' perspectives of the conflict are described in negative and destructive terms. This competitive approach to conflict resolution destroys the possibility for open, honest discussion and for conflict to have a constructive outcome. When conflict resolution is viewed as cooperative, the goal is to provide a means to create understanding between clients about their differences so they do not have to employ conflict destructively. Therefore, inquire about whether the trainer is able to explain cooperative management skills or if the trainer believes that the mediator forces a compromise between two competing parties.

Applied to the interpersonal conflicts of divorce, mediation offers a means of addressing clients' differences constructively and creates the opportunity to view conflict as a chance to transform their interactions into productive outcomes. The mediator, as a facilitator, assists clients in the process of examining their differences, making choices about the issues so that the outcome is constructive and helpful to them and their children. The mediator does not assess the strengths and weaknesses of each side and then pressure them to move to the middle.

Mediation training usually begins with a topic dedicated to conflict and how conflict is addressed in the mediation process. This section is often introduced with an introspective analysis of how you perceive conflict in your own life. This is intended to help you understand your natural responses to conflict when it occurs in your personal life and in the world. This is critical to learning to be a professional, client-centered mediator whose work continually encounters people in conflict. When you begin to comprehend how you respond to conflict in your own life, and understand your own comfort level with conflict, you can decide if you want to learn other ways to address it. When we struggle with our responses to conflict in our own lives, we become better able to empathize with our clients' struggles with the conflicts in their lives.

The mediation process is about addressing clients' conflict and assisting them to change how they respond to it. Learning how to mediate begins with learning about conflict in others' lives and offering them the opportunity to respond to conflict more constructively. The mediation process offers them the opportunity to forgive each other for the past damage they have created in their lives. Because conflict is a normal part of human interaction, and not necessarily unhealthy, those of us who mediate need to be comfortable with others' conflicts in order to mediate their differences.

If the mediation process is about addressing others' conflicts, it is not just a system of skills and techniques. It is not a linear process that follows specific steps. Rather, it is a fluid process that is directed by the issues raised, not the mediator's prescribed outline of conflict resolution.

How does a mediator function in the midst of great conflict between the clients? The clients employ the mediator to assist them in arriving at a settlement of their divorce issues, and the mediator has to manage their conflict while helping them get divorced. As mentioned earlier, the mediator listens intently, not for faults or inconsistencies in the clients' stories, but for opportunities for them to better understand each other and transform their conflict into a constructive outcome. The mediator clarifies, asks questions, and offers observations and hunches about what is being communicated. The mediator listens for what might unlock the conflict interactions so clients have the opportunity to change how they perceive the issues and change their thinking, feelings, or perceptions. The mediator learns to view their conflict as an opportunity, not as a block, to achieving their goals.

Mediation-training programs usually begin with the topic of conflict resolution because it is the core of mediation. However, is it resolution or transformation of conflict that occurs in mediation? It is both. Certainly some people resolve some of their differences by reaching agreements after thorough examination of the root of the conflict. Others may not resolve their differences at all, but they may gain a better understanding of them and move beyond them. When they hold things against each other that inhibit the conversation necessary in mediation, they may need to spend some time figuring out what to do to get beyond those deeply held feelings. The mediator will assist in managing their discussions about these topics, and offer ideas in the form of questions or observations about what may move them forward. Sometimes clients conclude that they need to forgive and let go, other times they may agree to try to work on letting go. The discussion, with the assistance of the mediator, is respectful and safe so each can speak the truth as they see it. Even when they do not choose to let go of what they hold against the other, they at least have had a discussion about it and have opened the door to that possibility. Perhaps their relationship has changed by merely having had the discussion, and a transformation of their conflict occurs even if it is not resolved. Clients then are free to own their feelings and carry them as they choose.

Training programs employ various methods to teach about conflict and its role in the mediation process. We offer a comparison of competitive and cooperative methods of addressing conflict based upon Morton Deutsch's work. Tom Crum, an expert in the martial art of akido, has written *The Magic of Conflict* (1987), which describes conflict in picturesque language. He discusses conflict as energy, and he teaches that when we confront conflict by trying to resist it, there is impasse, but when we choose to flow with the energy of the conflict there is the possibility for change. In his book, *Preparing for Peace*, John Paul Lederach (1995) describes training as viewing conflict transformation as a means for people to grow, change, and make decisions that will restore relationships and allow healing to occur. The topic of conflict resolution in training programs then leads directly to the discussion of the trainer's conceptual framework of mediation.

CONCEPTUAL FRAMEWORK OF MEDIATION

The field of divorce mediation has not yet adopted a single conceptual framework. Although there is a good deal of consensus about what divorce mediation is, how it is practiced, and what its goals are, we lack a consistent conceptual framework that can be used to teach others. We recommend the client-centered conceptual framework discussed in Chapter 2, not only because it is our own practice model, but also because it is based upon the principles of Morton Deutsch's description of a cooperative framework. Another model is transformative mediation. It is very close to client-centered mediation. Those who offer training in this model base it on the principles and concepts discussed in *The Promise of Mediation* by Robert Baruch Bush and Joseph Folger (Bush & Folger, 1994). Mediators who practice the transformative model focus on the conflict and offer their assistance to the parties to resolve their conflict, whether or not there is a settlement. This is not unlike the philosophy of client-centered mediation, which says that the mediator does not make decisions, the clients do.

There are many similarities between these two models, and we recommend training in the transformative mediation model as well as the client-centered model. Both concepts focus on the people in conflict and emphasize that they have the capacity to create their own outcomes. The mediator is a facilitator of the clients' conversations and follows the clients' direction about what they need to discuss and accomplish.

Experiential Training

Each training program should include a lot of hands-on learning. Training programs in mediation do not use a didactic method because it is generally accepted in the mediation field that learning to mediate is primarily experiential. As trainers, we have found that each training program we provide is an opportunity for us to learn and it is a good learning experience for aspiring mediators. There are two types of role plays that provide experiential learning: (1) the fish-bowl role play in which a trainer takes the role of the mediator and demonstrates mediating specific issues; and (2) the experiental role play in which the trainees play the parts of mediator and clients to practice mediating. In addition to the role plays, there are experiential exercises to learn certain skills and techniques. Divorce-mediation role plays give you experience in mediating every aspect of the divorce process. The role plays demonstrate how to mediate difficult parenting situations, budgeting and support processes, and asset and liability valuing and distribution.

Participant evaluations of our training programs have consistently reported that learning from role plays and debriefing them is most useful. Debriefing offers a detailed discussion of the specific skills, techniques, interventions, and methods used in mediation. Trainers also learn from the feedback of the trainees in classes, and there is usually a healthy give and take of information and learning.

The experiential learning is monitored by the trainers. Because most people feel vulnerable when role playing or participating in exercises, the trainers set up role plays and exercises with parameters for debriefing and feedback. Role plays in which trainees play the mediators and try out what they are learning are supervised by professional mediators to assure the debriefing is not personally critical or demeaning. Just as mediation is carried out in a safe environment, it is important that trainees understand that the training program is designed to promote emotional safety for them.

Most training programs also discuss the special methods to employ when mediating with a couple who have a history of serious domestic violence. The role plays for these scenarios are the most difficult, and the trainers must be especially careful that those who play the husband and wife in a abusive relationship are sensitively debriefed after the role play so they do not carry the intense emotion they demonstrated. These role plays generate thoughtful discussion and insight into very delicate, difficult situations. The AFM requires all divorce-mediation training programs to educate potential mediators about domestic violence and how to mediate these exceptional cases.

Accreditation

Lastly, we suggest that when you research mediation-training programs, inquire about accreditation. As previously mentioned, there are four major membership organizations for mediators. Of those, only two accredit training: the AFM, and FMC. We suggest contacting these organizations to request their standards for approving training programs and their list of approved trainers and programs. This will provide a starting point for finding a good divorce-mediation training program. When contacting the training programs, we suggest that you take note if the phone is answered by a person who can give some preliminary information. If there is a recording, leaving a message is wise, but if it takes a few days for a reply, you might question whether this is a full-time mediation practice. Sometimes you may be able to talk directly with the trainer. This is an excellent opportunity to ask all kinds of questions, including those mentioned earlier in this chapter. If that is not possible, talking to others who have been trained in a particular program may be helpful.

Divorce-mediation training programs are also certified by many state court administrations to train mediators to receive referrals from the courts. Training programs are usually certified in their own state and may be in other states as well. We suggest you call the state court administrator's office to obtain the criteria used for certifying mediation training and a list of the programs they certify.

Some training programs are accredited by colleges and universities. When you inquire about the training program, ask if it is also offered at a college or university. Some training programs are affiliated with an educational institution, and you may be able to receive academic credits for the program. Receiving academic credits may require a different fee for the training program, and different requirements such as writing a paper or taking an exam at the end of the program and being graded on your work.

If you need continuing education units (CEU), or continuing legal education (CLE) credits, ask the trainers if you can receive those credits through the program. Often you will need to obtain an application for CEU or CLE credit that the trainer submits for your credit. Ask the trainer if they are familiar with the process of securing CEU or CLE credits for the training program.

CONCLUSION

This chapter has discussed becoming a client-centered divorce mediator. The training in client-centered divorce mediation is an excellent basic training. There are also other basic training courses in mediation that are more generic in context. They are especially appropriate if you wish to mediate conflicts other than divorce and other family law-related conflicts. The next chapter introduces you to other applications of the client-centered mediation process.

CHAPTER 7

Building a Mediation Practice

A T THE close of each divorce-mediation training program, people are excited about what they have learned and anxious to put it into practice. Some people have a plan for how they will use mediation in their current profession and some take training as part of an overall plan for business start-up. If you don't yet have a plan, you may be panicked about how to start a practice. Though you have learned the basics, you may wonder what step to take next. Here are some suggestions:

- First, rest and let the training sink in for a few days!
- Assess the areas in which you need more information or training and make plans to further your divorce-mediation education in those areas.
- Become acquainted with divorce professionals including the judges.
- Join local and national mediation organizations.
- Choose a mentor with whom to contract for consultation and supervision.
- Look at mediation practice models to choose the one that best fits you.
- After choosing the model, draft a business plan and a time line to open a practice.
- Meet with a Small Business Administration (SBA) consultant to get more help with your plan and to find out about financial assistance for new small businesses.

- Consult with marketing and public relations professionals or read books about marketing services to gather advice on marketing your mediation services.
- Prepare a marketing plan to help focus and guide your promotional efforts.

This list may look a bit overwhelming. However, as in the mediation process, there are many options within each of the steps listed. Opening a mediation practice is essentially starting a business, so consider these steps seriously and make decisions carefully. After all, the training was the first big step, and the rest will begin to fall in place as you make decisions about the location, market, and business strategies that will best support your practice.

This chapter elaborates on each of the steps and breaks the steps down into smaller headings to cover all the details of starting a divorce-mediation practice. Included are examples of what worked for us when we began our practice, and the many mistakes we learned from. We hope that this will assist you so you won't have to reinvent the wheel. Because there is little opportunity to present all this information in divorce-mediation training, we are pleased to share our experience with you in this chapter.

REST, REST, AND MORE REST

After completing a grueling, 40-hour divorce-mediation training the best next step is to take some time to let it all sink in. Most people are both exhilarated and exhausted after the training, and rest is a great remedy for that. If the training you attended was a concentrated one-week, 40-hour program, it may be helpful to slow down your mind to begin to think about what you learned and experienced.

It may also be helpful to review the training materials and to think through some of the broad concepts. See if they still make as much sense to you as they did during training. Determine what is most interesting and what is most confusing for you at this point. Review the reading list and order a few books that interest you. Reading in order to round out the training will help keep you on track and interested. Most of all, be well advised not to rush into making major career decisions that would eliminate a present source of income.

CONTINUING TO LEARN
ABOUT DIVORCE MEDIATION

Most training programs do not cover everything you need to know to become a divorce mediator. Each person in the training brings valuable education, skills, and experience. Look at your own particular education, skills, and experience to ascertain the strengths that you would bring to divorce mediation, and identify the areas in which you feel you may need more information or training.

For some professionals, people skills are already part of their professional work, but the budgeting and property areas of divorce may be more foreign. Once you assess what more you need, you can begin to research ways to gain expertise in those areas. Once you identify the additional resources you will need to prepare yourself to mediate you can make a plan that will guide you in your process. Because resources include books, journals, videos, informational interviews, internships, and classes, be aware of the way you learn best and make your plan to take advantage of those types of resources.

If you have had little experience in budgeting with clients, then seeking counsel from financial planners, consumer credit counselors, or agricultural extension agents is a must. All of these professionals have information, advice, and data that may be helpful in learning to assist clients to create budgets that become a meaningful cornerstone of their future planning for child support and spousal maintenance.

The mediator is seeking this information to be able to mediate these issues better, not to advise clients about how much should be budgeted for a family of four in your area. Because clients use their incomes so differently for their needs, any assumptions made by the mediator about what they should spend is disrespectful. After all, it is their life to live after divorce, not the mediator's. Thus, when you talk to credit counselors or other financial experts, ask them what information they think you should gather, how they would use it, and how they might be able to assist your clients should you refer future clients to them.

For property issues in divorce, there are as many resources as there are different questions. When valuing the items in the marital estate, there are numerous experts a mediator needs to know as resources for clients:

- Realtors and real estate appraisers will provide values on homes, buildings, farms, and other properties.
- Financial planners and accountants will analyze income and cash flow from a closely held business, stock options, stock portfolios, and bonds. They will help build options about buy outs of assets in the marital estate, such as a closely held business, stock, stock options, and spousal maintenance. These professionals can also assist couples in planning how their income and assets will serve them into retirement, so they can each leave the marriage relationship having information about financial security in their future separate lives.
- Tax accountants and tax lawyers may assist in developing past and future information about the couple's tax situation and advise them of their options.
- Therapists are often helpful to couples that are highly conflicted over the marriage breakdown and may help couples understand and begin to forgive the other for their part in it. This has the effect of lifting the emotional baggage from the mediation room so the couple can address other issues they want to settle.
- A panel of three neutral attorneys may prevent an impasse in mediation when particular issues are presented to them blindly for them to respond with what they think a fair settlement would be and what they believe the court would do.

Approach each of these experts to find out how they might advise your clients should you refer future clients to them. These professional conversations will help you understand what information clients will need for assessment. Some aspiring mediators seek more information about developing their people skills. This is not to say that they do not have people skills. Of course they do. However, they may be trained to be more sensitive to facts and data, finding discrepancies in the other side's case, asking leading questions, giving advice, and in general not getting involved in the client's lives and emotions. Many people in divorce-mediation training begin to understand this difference and wonder whether they will be able to change how they handle clients. Most are eager to make this change, and then wonder how to do so.

There are many ways to improve your interaction skills with clients by changing your way of working with clients in a mediation process. You might ask to meet with a marriage and family therapist to learn how they interact with clients. Support groups for divorce and grief are facilitated by trained leaders and are offered through hospitals, schools, and churches. Consider observing such a group for several sessions. There are also classes in interviewing skills, dealing with hostile people, conflict resolution, and communication skills. All these courses and many more are offered at colleges, universities, and community education programs. There are also many books and articles written on these subjects.

Another area beginning divorce mediators often feel inadequate about is family law. Divorce mediation is always practiced in the shadow of the courthouse, and, therefore, it is important for divorce mediators to understand what the laws are and how they are applied. However, you do not have to be a licensed attorney to gain this knowledge.

Early in our divorce-mediation practice, Bill Haugh, one of the finest family law practitioners in Minnesota, was among the few family lawyers who agreed to represent our mediation clients. One day Bill asked Steve where Marilyn went to law school. Steve, amazed at the assumption, replied that Marilyn was not a lawyer, but rather, had been trained as a social worker. In truth, she had never even taken a family law course! Bill could not believe it! He told Steve he didn't understand how Marilyn could come up with such good settlements. In reality, Marilyn did not devise the settlements but facilitated her clients' ability to create them.

If you are uncomfortable with your lack of knowledge in this area and want to learn more, there are many options available to you. First, you may audit a family law course at a law school. This is limited to the times it is scheduled, and the cost may be prohibitive. As an alternative, you may choose to take an annual family law continuing education course offered by your local CLE organization. This course is usually offered once a year, and in our state it is commonly referred to as the Family Law for Baby Lawyers course, meaning it is a course for inexperienced lawyers. This may be a very good resource for you to learn not only family law, but also the lay of the land of divorce law in your state. There are also many books about the legal divorce for clients. These may be excellent resources because your clients may be reading them. Once you have learned more about this subject area, take a divorce lawyer to lunch to ask any questions you may have about what you have learned.

After training, many have questions about mediating the custody issues. Divorce-mediation training covers the developmental stages of
children, the impact of the divorce on the children, and what parents can
do to help their children adjust to divorce. However, mediators often
want more information about the psychological impact on children and
how to help parents make decisions that will best serve their children in
the future. We suggest that beginning mediators become acquainted with
a child psychologist who understands the impact of divorce on children.
This professional will often answer your questions and be available to
work with families you refer. This is an excellent way to learn more and
gain valuable experience mediating this sensitive area of divorce.

NETWORKING WITH DIVORCE PROFESSIONALS

Hillary Clinton said that it takes a village to raise a child. We say it takes
many professionals to assist a couple to end their marriage. Mediators
are at the center, administrating the entire process. In addition, there are
their lawyers, and many other professionals such as therapists, child psychologists, school teachers, accountants, financial planners, appraisers,
career consultants, day-care providers, domestic-violence counselors,
chemical-dependency counselors, actuaries, and others. Each divorce requires different professional advice and opinions based upon the clients'
particular needs.

At the end of divorce-mediation training we suggest you begin to
build a resource list by taking professionals to lunch. Pick their brains
about their work with divorcing couples and children. As you build these
relationships, you will develop a relationship with professionals to work
with your clients. These professionals will also begin to refer to you as
they experience your work with clients.

As you develop your network of professionals, be sure to include the
judges for the courts that have jurisdiction for your future clients. If there
are questions raised about mediated agreements or ongoing problems,
the judge at least knows of your work and may refer clients back to you
for further mediation. The bench is a good resource for referrals, so it is
important that you have a good working relationship with the court.

The primary focus of networking is to create professional referral relationships that support mediation. Another focus of networking is to
know others in the business community who might provide referrals and

who might also help you locate the business services you need to operate your mediation service. Consider joining a networking group of business professionals who meet monthly for breakfast or lunch to discuss business-related topics. A local weekly business publication will list meetings for networking groups. Groups may also be listed with your local chamber of commerce.

The chamber of commerce offers frequent meetings for members and nonmembers on topics related to local business and marketing. Attending these events will provide you an excellent opportunity to network.

Networking is an excellent way to broaden your list of resources. When you begin to establish your practice, join organizations that will help you meet new professionals who work with divorcing clients. We think it is fair to say that a divorce mediator is as good as the quality of the professionals he or she works with in divorce mediation. Clients depend on your referral network. When you refer your clients to a professional who is competent and helpful, they will have confidence in your work as well.

JOIN MEDIATION AND OTHER ORGANIZATIONS

A mediator will find it helpful to join several community organizations. These include chamber of commerce, a small business network, service clubs such as Kiwanis, Sertoma, Lions, and others. These club members will want to learn more about what you do, and give you an opportunity to make a presentation to them about mediation. You will receive referrals and refer clients to some of the people you meet as well.

Joining the Bar Association offers the opportunity to network with the legal leaders in your community. State and local bar associations have family law sections, which you will want to join if you are eligible, and many have ADR committees, which do not require that you be an attorney to join. It is always good to be proactive by working with these organizations rather than to react to what is being done by them in your absence, because they are more active in proposing legislation that may affect your mediation clients and your practice.

Your state may also have a professional mediation membership organization that is active in the field of mediation. These organizations offer conferences, workshops, and seminars in mediation for their members and the field in general. They also hold networking meetings for the mediation community. Find out if there is such an organization in your state and join it as soon as possible.

There are national and international mediation and ADR organizations that you are encouraged to join. The AFM is an international professional organization of family mediators. Its membership is primarily professional mediators. It publishes a journal, *The Mediation Quarterly*, the only professional mediation journal in the field. The AFM sets standards for and approves training programs in divorce and family mediation. It also has membership standards that require a number of hours of mediation training as well as experience and supervision of mediators. It has confronted the issues of certifying competency of mediators and credentialing since the late 1980s, and still leads the field in this effort. The AFM presents the largest family mediation conference every summer and through its preconference institutes, workshops, and seminars offers state-of-the-art thinking and leadership in the field of family mediation. Networking at the national conference is invaluable. Getting to know many professionals in this field may be especially helpful when you have a question on a case that you heard someone make a presentation about at a conference. Members have learned from each other, which has been a characteristic of the AFM since its inception. Members receive *Mediation News*, a bimonthly newsletter, and the *Mediation Quarterly* as well as special rates at the conference and on the purchase of materials through the academy. The AFM also offers mediator malpractice insurance to its members through Lloyds of London.

Another international professional organization to join is the Society of Professionals in Dispute Resolution (SPIDR). SPIDR members come from a variety of professional backgrounds in the field of conflict resolution including mediators, arbitrators, union representatives, academics, theorists, and others. Its members work throughout the world as mediators and other neutral facilitators. Members of SPIDR receive a quarterly newsletter and membership registration and privileges at the national conference, which is the largest conference of a professional dispute-resolution membership organization in the world. It also cosponsors other conferences in other countries. Professional members of SPIDR also have available malpractice insurance coverage. SPIDR also has several regional organizations of dispute resolution professionals that frequently offer conferences.

We urge mediators to join the AFM and SPIDR, as well as the local organizations. These organizations offer the greatest opportunities for mediators to meet other mediators, acquire continuing education units, and learn the cutting edge issues and ideas in the field.

MENTORING

Mentoring has become one of the key techniques recommended to those starting a new business. Business-development conferences promote the mentoring relationship in seminars designed to help you select a mentor to suit your needs. You may benefit from more than one mentor relationship if you choose one to help you with business start-up issues and one to help you develop your strengths as a mediator.

Steve once attended a seminar presented by an arbitrator who said, "I can't really tell you what I do, but just watch me." He proceeded to role play. In the early years of training mediators, we were always challenged to teach what we did in the mediation room, to analyze and describe our work so that it could be replicated. Role plays have always been helpful, but the observations about the role plays performed by others were most helpful. You will benefit most by watching other mediators work and by having them watch you.

Finding a mentor to work with you may be your most valuable next step. Your mentor can discuss your cases with you, and you may be able to observe your mentor in mediation practice. If you are able to arrange this while you begin your practice, you will learn to mediate without much difficulty. The mentor will be able to give you suggestions, advice, and constructive feedback about your work. We highly recommend that you consider having a mentor to work with as you begin your mediation practice.

The AFM has consultants who are experienced mediators who have taken specialized training to consult with and mentor family and divorce mediators. You can receive a list of the AFM consultants in your geographic area and contract with one to assist you as you begin to mediate.

PRACTICE MODELS

There are many ways to establish a mediation practice. To decide which one will be compatible with your needs and style, you may want to check out several. These are some of the more common models:

- Add mediation to your present profession.
- Offer your services to be marketed with someone else's practice.
- Develop a practice group of mediators to establish a practice to-gether.
- Open a mediation practice as an entrepreneur.

We will describe each of these options in detail for you to consider.

EXPAND YOUR PRACTICE TO INCLUDE MEDIATION

If you already have a private professional practice, you may want to add mediation as a different service that is somewhat compatible with your present profession. Many therapists and lawyers do this. Professional ethics dictate that you cannot wear two professional hats when mediat-ing, so mediators are cautioned against providing more than one service to the same clients. This means that you are not allowed to mediate with clients with whom you have another professional relationship. You may not mediate with your legal, accounting, or therapy clients, or anyone else for whom you have provided or presently provide other professional services. We mention this here because it is a primary consideration when adding mediation to your present professional practice.

If you have thought about this and believe that you can maintain the professional boundaries necessary to expand your practice to include mediation services, here are some things you can do to assure that this will not be a problem for you or your clients:

- Name your mediation services separately from your other profes-sion so there is not confusion on the part of your clients about which service they are seeking and receiving.
- Schedule your mediation clients on different days than your other clients.
- Use a space for mediation sessions that is separate from your other practice.
- Have a separate phone line for each professional practice.
- Have separate informational materials, brochures, and cards for each service you provide.
- Explain in writing and verbally to clients that you will work with them in only one of the services you offer, and if they need the ser-

vices of your other profession, you will refer them to someone else.

- Develop a referral network of professionals who offer the other services you offer to whom you may refer your mediation clients.
- Do not allow yourself to slip into providing your other professional services as a part of your mediation practice.

There are many mediators who have successfully added mediation to their other professional practices, so you will not need to reinvent the wheel. They may welcome your questions about how they have accomplished having two professional practices simultaneously with different clients. We have found that mediators are very willing to share information and ideas, and to help other mediators beginning their mediation practice. A good place to start is with the membership directories you receive when you join the national organizations. Call some mediators and take them to lunch to discuss how they got started and what pitfalls they can help you avoid.

There are several advantages to adding mediation to your present professional practice:

- Offering services that are compatible with your present practice will bring new clients and provide a new routine, variety, and challenge that may be very rewarding for you.
- Making better use of your present office space will save overhead costs, such as rent, utilities, staffing, and equipment needs that may go unused in your present practice.
- Expanding your practice may enable you to call upon some of your same referral resources to refer to your mediation practice.
- Your good reputation in your present professional practice may easily transfer to your mediation practice when offered in the same setting.
- You are your own boss. You make all your own business decisions and do not have to work with others when making important decisions.

You will have to decide for yourself how you will establish your mediation practice, and adding it to your present professional practice may be your best option. As you ponder your decision, it may be wise to consult with not only other mediators but also with your financial advisor. This is a major business decision, so an outside opinion may be very crucial to the success of this endeavor.

OFFER TO WORK WITH ANOTHER PROFESSIONAL PRACTICE

Law firms, human-resources departments, managed-care groups, mental-health clinics, and other professional practices are beginning to add mediation to their services. You may wish to research if there are any such entities in your area that may be interested in contracting with you to mediate in their office or facility. If they are a large practice, they may even be interested in offering a salaried mediator position.

For some beginning mediators, this is an ideal possibility. The practice group is already established. They may see the value in adding a mediation position to their services and be prepared to pay well for the right professional mediator. As a mediator considering this possibility, you may be able to be marketed through their present system, be expected to attend continuing education courses and conferences paid by the practice, have supervision provided by the practice, and even become a leader within the agency by developing this new service.

Sometimes the practices just mentioned may not even know about the advantages for them to offer mediation services. You may find yourself actually selling your program of mediation services to some of these entities as a pilot project or on a trial basis. Put your mediation training to use with the negotiation and mediation skills you learned to create an outcome that is good for them and for you! This may be a great opportunity to be creative in beginning your mediation practice.

ESTABLISH A MEDIATION GROUP PRACTICE

Many mediators are interested in beginning mediation practice as soon as possible after finishing training. One of the quickest ways to establish a practice is to do it with like-minded people with whom you feel comfortable. You may have some preliminary meetings to ascertain the interest of others. If you have a compatible working group, you can accomplish setting up a high-quality, viable practice by pooling your resources and planning your business venture together.

When we began our practice, there were seven of us including two lawyers, a teacher, two social workers, a therapist, and a chaplain. By the end of three years one of the lawyers and the teacher left the practice. Steve, the other lawyer, eventually quit his law practice. The remaining five of us continued the practice with four mediating and with Mylan Brenk, the therapist, consulting and seeing some of our clients in his private practice. He later left the mediation group to develop marriage-closure therapy with many of our clients.

We originally organized our practice as a nonprofit and received a 501-C3 status from the IRS. We applied for grants for start-up expenses, and in the third year we finally received a small grant that enabled us to move the practice to an office building and create more of a business image. We were unable to secure more grants, so we dropped our nonprofit status and incorporated as a sub-chapter S business. In the first four years we only made enough income to purchase office supplies, equipment, pay back our loan, and compensate mediators a very nominal amount for the hours they mediated.

We share this story with you for many reasons. First, if you are starting a practice with a group of colleagues, work together in the decision making. Decide which legal business model works best for you. Consult with an accountant or tax attorney about your options.

It is important to be clear about the sweat equity that each person is contributing and the implications for ownership in the practice. If people in the group each put in the same amount of time and effort, are you equal partners? If they do not, do you assign percentages of interest in the business according to what you agree is each person's nonmonetary contribution? These are a few of the questions you need to discuss when beginning a group practice.

Be very clear about money. If each member of the group is contributing an equal amount of money for the start-up expenses, have a written agreement about how much and how one gets back what one invested. Also decide how mediation income will be distributed when you begin to have clients paying fees. All these considerations about money need to be discussed and decided in the early stages of planning the group practice.

If you decide to pursue a group practice, you may want to use some resources to meet with a business consultant for advice on how to organize and to create a business plan and a formal written agreement. Even when you trust everyone, it is advisable to have some instrument that governs the group members' relationship and responsibilities. A group practice will be only as good as the time and effort everyone invests in creating it. Once this has been accomplished, you may find this a great way to begin your mediation career.

OPENING YOUR OWN MEDIATION PRACTICE

Many who complete mediation training believe as we did that mediation is the greatest thing since sliced bread, and they proceed to set out on their own to open a mediation service. That is exactly what we did in 1977, except that there was no mediation training available at that time except from Jim Coogler and Morton Deutsch. Little did we know how great the struggle would be to create a *viable* mediation practice!

The greatest advice we have for those of you who want to open your own mediation practice is don't quit your day job. Instead, carefully plan how you will start your business. Finance your living expenses with income from your present employment while you work on building your mediation practice. Plan to invest your time and some money in your mediation business.

Take time to work on establishing your practice. Fortunately, there are many resources available to you so you won't need to struggle through the trial-and-error method that we did when we started our practice. Call the SBA in your area and inquire about their services. If there is an MBA program at a local college or university, check to see if there are any students who need a project to do a business plan. This may save you time and money and help you organize your thoughts into a plan that will work for you.

Plan on spending some money to start your own business. It is naive to believe that you will not need to make a financial investment. You can be conservative in your spending, but don't be foolish. Even if you do not invest a lot of money in a business plan, you may need to do so in marketing your business. Again, you can keep these expenses at a minimum if you have time to do a lot of networking and can easily build referral resources.

DEVELOP A BUSINESS PLAN

There are many reasons to write a business plan; two of them will be discussed here. First, the business plan creates a structure and focus to guide you and your partners in business operations. The second is to secure financing from lending sources. Financing is available for small businesses through programs administered by the Small Business Association (SBA). Start-up financing generally requires security but repayment terms are geared to the uncertainties of start-up. Business consultation and oversight are provided by the SBA to help ensure success.

There are many books available to guide you through the development of a business plan. Workshops and seminars are also offered to help new businesses create an initial business plan. Follow the steps outlined to the extent you are able. Do not worry if there are questions that you cannot answer. Leave these sections reserved to develop later.

MEET WITH THE SBA

After drafting your initial business plan, contact the SBA to set up an appointment with a business consultant to discuss financing opportunities. The SBA requires specific information for their application and will want a business plan that supports the application and specifies reasonable goals. The advice they provide is designed to ensure success. The SBA may refer you to a nonprofit or other organization that contracts with SBA to administer the distribution of loan funds. These organizations include neighborhood revitalization programs and programs that serve minorities and women. They also offer excellent business consulting services. Sometimes there is a fee for the initial consultation, but if you obtain financing, additional consulting is provided as part of the loan package.

Financing for start-up can include funds for office equipment, supplies, and marketing. You will be encouraged to take initial steps in start-up that are manageable and that will establish for you a track record of success. If you need financing for start-up, a loan through SBA programs will offer business advice, an external structure, and a financial track record for future financing to grow the business.

PLAN A MARKETING AND PUBLIC RELATIONS STRATEGY

Once you have a business plan, the next step is to acquire a marketing plan that will outline how you will use your limited marketing dollars.

Attend a workshop about marketing (SBA offers some training on this topic) or read about marketing and the process of developing a marketing plan. Once you have a general background so that you can make the decision, decide whether to hire a marketing firm to develop your plan and promote your services or to launch your own campaign based on a marketing plan you develop. If you develop your own plan, the first step will be to define the location and population segment of your targeted market.

We thought the mediation practice would grow quickly as soon as the public knew what we were about. Marilyn quit her day job as a county social worker, and we set up the mediation office in our home. We had a business phone line, borrowed money to develop a logo, letterhead, and a brochure.

For our first marketing initiative we mailed hundreds of brochures to all the lawyers, therapists, and clergy in the metropolitan area announcing the opening of our mediation practice. Then we waited for the phone to ring. The first phone calls we received were from lawyers and therapists asking to be on our referral list for our clients! But we received no referrals from that effort.

We regrouped and decided upon another strategy to attract clients by advertising in the newspaper. A business friend of ours said to put an ad in the business section of the newspaper on Monday when there was little other business news after the weekend. We spent $300 on that ad, again with no response. Our money was dwindling, so we decided to put a small ad in the personals column that read:

DIVORCE?
Less Cost - Less Time - Less Stress
Call Family Mediation Services
612-555-5555

We began to receive phone calls from people disgruntled with their divorce. Some callers just wanted someone to talk to. One day a man called with a lot of questions. He was genuinely interested in mediation, and then he asked, "So how many divorces have you mediated?" Marilyn was somewhat embarrassed by the question, but thought quickly and responded, "Well, if you begin, you will be our first!" The man appreciated the honesty, and he and his wife were our first clients. They settled their divorce in mediation, and we got our practice off the ground.

We suggest that you approach marketing in a much different way. As already outlined, first learn about marketing, then consult with a public-relations professional to learn what you can accomplish by having them create your marketing plan. Often this is the best way to begin, though it may be relatively expensive compared to doing it yourself piecemeal. You may wish to compare the time and costs of each approach and then decide what to do. The do-it-yourself marketing effort will take time and some money, but here are some things you can include in the plan you develop:

Purchase Advertising

Research local newspapers, magazines, newsletters, and any other print media readership to determine if it fits your client profile, namely, those people considering or in the midst of a divorce and those with a parenting and/or family focus. Choose the ones in which you want to advertise and design an ad. When discussing some options about placement and frequency of the ad, speak to the editor about running a story about your new practice simultaneously with running the first ad. This is often an opportunity with some of the smaller, community newspapers. Then when the article about your practice is printed, make copies of it to send to prospective clients and referral sources. It will add to what you already send out and give you more credibility.

Design a mediation ad for the yellow pages. The yellow pages have been a good source of referrals for our practice. You can list your service under Mediation and under the heading of your other/former profession if it is in a related field. The yellow-pages ad is printed once a year and distributed in the yellow-pages phone book to everyone who has phone service. Though there is only one printing, you will be billed monthly for the ad, so be sure to consider the entire annual cost in your marketing budget.

The frequency of print ads is very important. Plan to run the ads over a period of months, and track the calls you receive to learn which ads are most effective at producing responses. Do not do what we did and place an expensive ad once and expect it to produce results. It just doesn't work that way.

When you design your ads and brochures, make sure you write good copy. Here is where you may wish to consult with a public-relations person. The ad needs to grab the reader when perusing the paper. The lead word or phrase needs to catch the reader's eye and interest, so even if you do not wish to invest in a professional public-relations person or firm to do your marketing, it may be wise to consult with such a person about your ads.

There are usually many public-relations professionals and firms available to mediators today who actually understand what mediation is, unlike our experience when we opened our practice. Ask colleagues for some referrals. When you see a brochure or an ad you like, find out who developed it, and contact them. You need to decide if you are going to seek several professionals to do different parts of your marketing plan or if you will ask a firm to work on all aspects of it. A marketing or public-relations firm will be able to offer a spectrum of services from print ads to television appearances. A firm will promote you and your business in as many ways as you wish. However, you need to decide what your budget is for purchasing this type of package, and whether it meets your needs.

Obtain No-Cost Advertising

Marketing books will provide creative ideas about ways to enhance your marketing efforts along with case studies about how companies combine ideas to create a plan that works for them in particular. We cannot give you nearly the number of ideas you will be able to gain from the wealth of marketing books that exist. Consult your library, browse the business section of your favorite bookstore, or check with universities and colleges in your area to find a business advisor who can provide you with these resources.

There are many ways to get free press for your mediation services. Many small periodic newspapers are eager to publish interesting freelance articles. Instead of paying you for your article, they may offer to provide you with a few lines to present yourself and your qualifications to the interested consumer. Associations under the gun to produce a monthly or quarterly newsletter for their members may also welcome a well-written article made relevant for their members. Many organizations now publish their newsletters on a Web site. Contact the Webmaster to propose an article.

Consider writing a press release tying mediation into issues related to current public concerns. Submit the press release to the editor with a cover letter to suggest how this article relates to other issues recently featured in news articles published. If one of your press releases is printed, send copies to smaller papers nearby and offer a follow-up interview.

Join forces with another group that offers workshops, training, or entertainment services, and offer to help pay for their brochure or program printing in return for advertising space.

Public Speaking

Another way to publicize your practice is by offering to speak about it anywhere and anytime. Check out some of the organizations mentioned earlier in this chapter. Professional organizations are also frequently looking for people to speak about new ideas and concepts that may become resources for their members. Because divorce is so pervasive, it touches almost everyone's life at some time. Speaking to almost any organization or group about divorce mediation will likely prove beneficial to your practice. To begin speaking, consider joining Toastmasters, a club that supports growth in professional speaking skills. By attending Toastmasters' meetings, you will gain skill in speaking and while you are doing so you will meet many other professionals with whom you can develop professional referral relationships.

As you practice speaking, concentrate on a specialty related to mediation. Research your topic and become an expert. For example you might choose to be an expert on the initial causes of marital breakdown. Speaking on this topic, you might speak to groups of newly wed couples at churches who hope to make their marriages work. Talking about mediation in that context might not result in new clients, but those who hear you speak may refer friends to you once they understand the benefits of mediation. Later, if their marriages do fail, they also might seek your help. Other topics on which you might focus include stress reduction, causes of addiction, money problems, parenting, child development and discipline, as well as topics on personal and spiritual growth.

One opportunity is to become acquainted with professors who teach conflict-resolution and marriage-and-family courses, and offer to make a presentation to their classes. Also, consider offering a course about your topic at the local community center. They are always looking for different courses that will interest community members. When you make your presentation, introduce yourself as a mediator and provide basic information about mediation services. Tell how your topic relates to divorce and mediation and why it is a concern to you.

Religious congregations have also been very interested in mediation. They tend to downplay divorce because they do not want to encourage people to divorce. However, many do have singles groups or organizations for the divorced and separated members of their congregations.

One of the first presentations we made about divorce mediation was to the Annual Conference of the Catholic Program for the Separated and Divorced sponsored by the local Catholic Archdiocese. We were amazed at the hundreds of people who attended. After all, the Catholic Church does not recognize divorce, but the conference attendees at our presentation were excited to learn about divorce mediation. Afterwards, we felt very privileged to present at this conference. Had we not been invited to present, we may have missed a great opportunity to get the word out about divorce mediation, because we would not have thought of approaching the Catholic Church about divorce mediation.

Many congregations also have adult-education programs when they meet for services. If you do not mind giving up a Sunday morning or a Saturday, you might find a receptive audience in a religious congregation. Religious organizations and congregations do not endorse divorce, but they do include people who divorce. Most have changed greatly their views on divorce. They recognize divorce as a reality and are open to learning more about mediation as an option for their divorcing congregants. At least mediation offers a process much more in keeping with their beliefs than does the adversarial process. That is probably why mediators are so welcomed to present at religious organizations' adult-education classes. Do not overlook these valuable forums to talk about mediation.

Most courts require that divorcing parents attend parent-education classes. Ask your local court administrator how to become qualified to offer the classes. Check the Internet for parent-education programs nationally and collect all the information you need to develop your program.

WEB PAGE

Increasingly, people are using the Internet to find mediators. Do not overlook this as a resource. A growing number of Web sites offer network information, and for a fee you can place information about your mediation practice on the Net.

CONCLUSION

Mediation unfortunately does not sell itself, because it is still relatively unknown. Even with many courts requiring some use of ADR, mediation still competes with several other types of ADR. The other ADR procedures, such as arbitration, have become the favored method of ADR by courts and lawyers who are still most comfortable with adversarial approaches. Even when courts order clients to mediate, judges often refer to those professionals they know and may bypass the list of approved ADR professionals. With courts serving as the gatekeepers of conflict resolution, it is important to market yourself outside the court system to the public. Therefore, it will be necessary for you to go upstream and obtain referrals before people enter the court system.

To build a mediation practice takes great patience, persistence, energy, and a good plan. Most of all it takes the attitude that mediation is an important social value, and you are pursuing it because it is right.

CHAPTER 8

Ethical Standards
and Accountability

J UST WHAT does a mediator do? To an experienced mediator talking to
a seat mate on the airplane, this question has been asked a thousand
times. Although it should be apparent by now that there are many aspects to the role of the mediator, there is less agreement than you would
expect on what is considered proper and improper conduct by a mediator. This chapter discusses the question of mediator conduct from the
perspective of client-centered mediation. Because the mediator is neutral
and serves the interests of all people in the process, the mediator must
maintain neutrality, while helping clients move forward together instead
of apart. This chapter identifies some of the pitfalls of mediator conduct
relating to the Standards of Practice promulgated by the AFM. Those
standards were originally created at a conference in Denver, Colorado in
1984, attended by representatives of many organizations involved in divorce and family mediation. Since then, the standards have changed
slightly, but they are still the standards of practice most widely recognized and respected by family mediators.

The AFM Standards are reprinted in full in Appendix E at the end of
this book. As you read them you will notice that they are written in the
affirmative, stating the obligations and responsibility of a family mediator. Unlike other ethical standards, they do not state specifically what is
unethical. It is assumed that the opposite of the standard is professionally unethical or irresponsible.

To illustrate how the standards relate to mediation practice, we will discuss each section with an explanation about how the standard applies to the role of the mediator. We will add some commentary and examples to put the standards in the context of mediation practice beginning with the preamble.

I. PREAMBLE

Mediation is a family-centered conflict resolution process in which an impartial third party assists the parties to negotiate a consensual and informed settlement. In mediation, whether private or public, decision-making authority rests with the parties. The role of the mediator includes reducing the obstacles to communication, maximizing the exploration of alternatives, and addressing the needs of those it is agreed are involved or affected.

Mediation is based on principles of problem solving that focus on the needs and interests of the participants; fairness; privacy; self-determination; and the best interest of all family members.

These standards are intended to assist and guide public, private, voluntary, and mandatory mediation. It is understood that the manner of implementation and mediator adherence to these standards may he influenced by local law or court rule.

The preamble sets forth what mediation is and the role of the mediator. Almost everything in the preamble is consistent with the self-determination concept of client-centered mediation. We do not refer to *principles of problem solving* when we describe client-centered mediation because client-centered mediation is more than problem solving. Client-centered mediation is based on principles of cooperative conflict resolution, self-determination, and clients' standards of fairness.

II. INITIATING THE PROCESS

A. Definition and Description of Mediation. The mediator shall define mediation and describe the differences and similarities between mediation and other procedures for dispute resolution. In defining the process, the mediator shall delineate it from therapy counseling, custody evaluation, arbitration, and advocacy.

B. Identification of Issues. The mediation shall elicit sufficient information from the participants so that they can mutually define and agree on the issues to be resolved in mediation.

C. Appropriateness of Mediation. The mediator shall help the participants evaluate the benefits, risks, and costs of mediation and the alternatives available to them.

D. Mediator's Duty of Disclosure.

1. *Biases.* The mediator shall disclose to the participants any biases or strong views relating to the issues to be mediated.

2. *Training and experience.* The mediator's education, training, and experience to mediate the issues should be accurately described to the participants.

The standard for Initiating the Process focuses on the role of the mediator at the beginning of the mediation process. The definition and description section prescribes that the mediator discuss with the clients at the beginning of mediation the difference between mediation and other related professions.

A mediator can easily get into ethical trouble when forgetting what professional hat is being worn (II-A), especially if the new mediator has previously worn the hat of therapist or attorney. We suggest that mediators fully explain the difference between their role as a mediator and their other professional practice. Clients want to be very clear that they are not hiring the mediator to act like a lawyer or therapist, so the mediator needs to explain the difference, as well as assure the clients that the other professional roles and practices will not be a part of the mediation process. Sometimes this is challenging, because clients might want the mediator to wear both professional hats simultaneously. That is not ethical mediation practice nor is it ever helpful to the clients. It can be very confusing, and usually ends the mediation without a settlement or resolution of issues.

A characteristic of a client-centered mediation process is that the information exchanged is not biased, inaccurate, or exaggerated, as so often happens when the parties use competitive adversarial tactics to resolve their conflict (II-D1). Deutsch (1973) observed that typically, a competitive process tends to produce communication that is "unreliable and impoverished. The available communication channels and opportunities are not utilized, or they are used in an attempt to mislead or intimidate the other" (p. 353). The rest of this section is self-explanatory and accepted as a practice routine when initiating mediation. Mediators cover these standards as a matter of course in each initial consultation with clients. In Minnesota, these standards are mandated by law to be discussed with clients at the first meeting with the mediator. The procedures are also a standard practice for client-centered mediators.

III. PROCEDURES

The mediator shall reach an understanding with the participants regarding the procedures to be followed in mediation. This includes but is not limited to the practice as to separate meetings between a participant and the mediator, confidentiality, use of legal services, the involvement of additional parties, and conditions under which mediation may be terminated.

A. Mutual Duties and Responsibilities. The mediator and the participants shall agree upon the duties and responsibilities that each is accepting in the mediation process. This may be a written or verbal agreement.

In client-centered mediation the mediator offers an Agreement to Mediate, which outlines basic procedures (III-A) as, the mediation process, expectations of the clients, and the duties of the mediator. These are discussed, modified by agreement of the clients and mediator, and signed by the clients and mediator to formalize their relationship. This agreement addresses the procedures described in this section of the standards. A copy of the institute's Agreement to Mediate is provided in Appendix B for your information.

A mediator who does not use the Agreement to Mediate or any other written statement that defines the mediator's role may get into ethical difficulty. For example, if a mediator is a psychologist and fails to inform the clients in writing or by the Agreement to Mediate of a duty to report child abuse, the mediator is then in deep trouble if child abuse is alleged in mediation. Being ethically bound to do so by the psychology ethical code, the mediator then must violate the promise of confidentiality. This type of complaint has been lodged against a mediator who failed to use a written mediation agreement spelling out the potential exception to confidentiality. We recommend the use in every case of a formal Agreement to Mediate to avoid these types of difficulties. In addition, many states that have a statute on mediator confidentiality indicate that confidentiality does not attach to the discussions until an Agreement to Begin Mediation is signed by the parties.

IV. IMPARTIALITY AND NEUTRALITY

A. Impartiality. The mediator is obligated to maintain impartiality toward all participants. Impartiality means freedom from favoritism or bias, either in word or action. Impartiality implies a commitment to aid all participants, as opposed to a single individual, in reaching a mutually satisfactory agreement. Impartiality means that a mediator will not play an adversarial role. The mediator has a responsibility to maintain impartiality while raising questions for the parties to consider as to the fairness, equity, and feasibility of proposed options for settlement.

B. Neutrality. Neutrality refers to the relationship that the mediator has with the disputing parties. If the mediator feels, or any one of the participants states, that the mediator's background or personal experiences would prejudice the mediator's performance, the mediator should withdraw from mediation unless all agree to proceed.

C. Prior Relationships. A mediator's actual or perceived impartiality may be compromised by social or professional relationships with one of the participants at any point in time. The mediator shall not proceed if previous legal or counseling services have been provided to one of the participants. If such services have been provided to both participants, mediation shall not proceed unless the prior relationship has been discussed, the role of the mediator made distinct from the earlier relationship, and the participants given the opportunity to freely choose to proceed.

D. Relationship to Participants. The mediator should be aware that post-mediation professional or social relationships may compromise the mediator's continued availability as a neutral third party.

E. Conflict of Interest. A mediator should disclose any circumstance to the participants that might cause a conflict of interest.

Although we pointed out in Chapter 1 that the ancient world viewed the mediator as the person to stand between, this role of a neutral is still an often misunderstood concept in our modern society. Acting as a neutral is something that does not come easily or naturally to most people. Because we are living, breathing entities who, from the youngest of ages, have been taught right from wrong, we become quick to judge and quick to point out what others should do. Perhaps the neutral's role is misunderstood because in our society we tend to view things as having opposing sides, and everyone has an advocate to bolster their side. Congress and legislatures are filled with lobbyists for one cause or another, and we are encouraged constantly by the media and even by the mail we receive to join one side of a cause against another. There are farm advocates, welfare advocates, environmental advocates, and certainly every redwood tree in California has perhaps at least one advocate who is willing to climb it to stop a logger's saw. Being a neutral pales in the face of all this competition.

In training, a mediator learns not to become judgmental (IV-A and B) and not to take a side. For some, this is impossible because they will begin to give themselves away by their posture, the inflection in their voice, or by other means, and they will be unable to stay neutral. Staying neutral is important because the continuing act of remaining neutral creates trust and enhances the ability of the clients to be cooperative. The easiest way to understand the concept of neutrality is to distinguish the act of mediating as a neutral as quite different from having to be neutral in one's view of the world.

When "raising questions for the [couple] to consider as to the fairness, equity, and feasibility of the proposed settlement options" (IV-A), a mediator has to be balanced and must evidence concern for all of the people, not any one person. The concept of impartiality and neutrality essentially requires the mediator to understand and have deep compassion and respect for each client's beliefs, regardless of how different those beliefs may be from the mediator's.

Staying neutral and impartial, however, does not mean that the mediator never voices a concern. The following are some examples of appropriate instances of a mediator expressing a concern:

MEDIATOR COMMENTS ABOUT VIOLENCE AND INTIMIDATING BEHAVIOR

One of the most frequent questions asked of us is, "What do you do when people get out of control, angry, noisy, or threatening?" In such circumstances, the mediator takes a stand against violence and expresses that violence is never acceptable behavior, either inside the mediation room or outside of sessions. It is not a violation of mediator neutrality to voice a concern about safety issues. Intimidating and threatening behavior or communication is also discouraged by the mediator. This is achieved in a balanced and neutral manner.

V. COSTS AND FEES

A. Explanation of Fees. The mediator shall explain the fees to be charged for mediation and any related costs and shall agree with the participants on how the fees will be shared and the manner of payment.

B. Reasonable Fees. When setting fees, the mediator shall ensure that they are explicit, fair, reasonable, and commensurate with the service to be performed. Unearned fees should be promptly returned to the clients.

C. Contingent Fees. It is inappropriate for a mediator to charge contingent fees or to base fees on the outcome of mediation.

D. Referrals and Commissions. No commissions, rebates, or similar forms of remuneration shall be given or received for referral of clients for mediation services.

Mediators' fee arrangements are different than other professional fee arrangements. Divorce mediators charge an hourly fee that is similar to fee levels of attorneys in their vicinity. Beginning mediators set their fees close to what beginning attorneys charge, and they raise the fees as they gain more experience to what they believe is a fee commensurate with their skill levels. They do not usually require retainers, but they may charge an administrative fee for case management, word processing, copying, and faxes.

Mediators explain their fees to clients at the initial consultation and discuss how the couple will share the fees. Fees are usually paid at the end of each mediation session for the time used. At no time should a mediator agree to be paid only if there is a settlement. Making the fee contingent upon settlement affects the mediator's neutrality and may cause the mediator to push a settlement that is not client driven or in the clients' best interests. In the same light, paying or gifting a referral source for each referral is improper. This may also bias the mediator to steer the mediation outcome in favor of the person referred.

VI. CONFIDENTIALITY AND EXCHANGE OF INFORMATION

A. Confidentiality. Confidentiality relates to the full and open disclosure necessary for the mediation process. A mediator shall foster confidentiality of the process.

B. Limits of Confidentiality. The mediator shall inform the parties at the initial meeting of limitations on confidentiality, such as statutorily or judicially mandated reporting.

C. Appearing in Court. The mediator shall inform the parties of circumstances under which mediators may be compelled to testify in court.

D. Consequences of Disclosure of Facts Between Parties. The mediator shall discuss with the participants the potential consequences of their disclosure of facts to each other during the mediation process.

E. Release of Information. The mediator shall obtain the consent of the participants prior to releasing information to others. The mediator shall maintain confidentiality and render anonymous all identifying information when materials are used for research or training purposes.

F. Caucus. The mediator shall discuss policy regarding confidentiality for individual caucuses. In the event that a mediator, on consent of the participants, speaks privately with any person not represented in mediation, including children, the mediator shall define how information received will be used.

G. Storage and Disposal of Records. The mediator shall maintain confidentiality in the storage and disposal of records.

H. Full Disclosure. The mediator shall require disclosure of all relevant information in the mediation process, as would reasonably occur in the judicial discovery process.

Confidentiality (VI-A) is a very complex standard. The basic tenet of confidentiality is that the mediation process is private and confidential as agreed to by clients and the mediator in the Agreement to Mediate. This protects the mediation process and allows clients to speak openly and honestly, have personal discussions, and brainstorm options without fear that what is said may be used against them in court. We advise all mediators to use an agreement or contract to mediate to protect the process in addition to what is in the state laws regarding mediator confidentiality. If your state has laws regarding mediation that limit confidentiality (VI-B) or compel you to testify in court under certain circumstances, you need to be aware of the law and include mention of it in your contract with clients.

One of the main benchmarks of a cooperative mediation process is that the discussions are private, confidential, and may never be used in furtherance of the adversarial court process (VI-C). This firewall of confidentiality is meant to separate the adversarial court litigation process of conflict resolution from the cooperative mediation process. A mediator's duty to maintain and foster confidentiality of the mediation process means that it is not appropriate for the mediator to consent to mediation documents or statements to be used in court if the mediation process reaches impasse and the parties move to litigation of the conflict. It is unethical for a mediator to testify in court about what happened in mediation except under some very narrow exceptions when the mediation discussions relate to criminal conduct or abuse of minor children. Some mediators will even contract with the parties to allow the mediator to breach confidentiality if a party threatens harm to self or others.

One disturbing trend that is a constant source of tension between mediators and lawyers is the propensity for the adversarial system to always be on the lookout for something that can be used to advance a client's case in the court system. In a small number of cases that reach impasse in mediation and subsequently move through the court system, some lawyers will try to obtain and introduce evidence about what was said or done in the mediation process in order to advance their client's case in court. Mediators must resist such efforts by citing their rules of mediation adopted and signed by the parties at the beginning of the mediation sessions. Most state courts would reject such efforts by the attorney, relying on the mediation contract as well as state court rules of confidentiality for the mediation process. However, some jurisdictions, perhaps in their zeal for docket efficiency, have adopted a model of custody mediation that requires the mediator to be subpoenaed should the mediation fail. Such a model is criticized by experienced mediators as inappropriate mingling of the two conflict-resolution processes. At the institute, we have had only one instance of a mediator being subpoenaed:

Steve was subpoenaed to testify about a mediation case in which both clients agreed to break the confidentiality clause in the Agreement to Mediate. He replied that the Agreement to Mediate was a contract between him and each client, and just because two parties to the contract wanted to set it aside, because he did not wish to do so, the contract could not be broken. He filed a motion to quash the subpoena attaching the Agreement to Mediate and was asked to be available for a conference call initiated by the judge with the judge and the two attorneys. At the beginning of the call the judge acknowledged to Steve that he received his motion, and then excused Steve from the call. The judge then admonished the attorneys for their action, agreeing with Steve that the contract was valid. Steve was not trying to be difficult, but saw the integrity of the mediation process potentially jeopardized by a court ruling setting aside the Agreement to Mediate. Steve also believed that he had nothing to testify about because a mediator does not take process notes, give opinions, nor does the mediator find it important to keep records of what was said.

Confidentiality also needs to be explained to clients about disclosure of facts (VI-D). Because most facts, like documents that verify income, assets, and liabilities, for example, are discoverable in a legal process, it does not make any sense to limit their use to the mediation process. The mediator must explain to clients that these factual documents are not confidential and that they are expected to be shared with legal counsel to avoid lengthy and costly discovery.

Confidentiality in mediation also covers information sharing with others (VI-E). If clients want the mediator to talk with or provide written or other information to other professionals or people, like friends or relatives, about their mediation, the mediator and the other professionals need to have releases signed by both of the clients in order for that to occur. This extends to discussions with the clients' attorneys. The mediator is prohibited from discussing or sharing other information from mediation with friends and relatives without prior written permission from both clients.

If a mediator decides to caucus with each side (VI-F), the mediator needs to be clear about the protocols before doing so. Specifically, the mediator needs to discuss with clients whether written or spoken information derived from the caucus can be shared with the other person. The clients are free to decide the purpose of the caucus and the limits on how it will affect the mediation process. Because we do not encourage caucus except when mediation has reached near impasse, this issue does not arise in every case. When it does, the mediator needs to establish the protocols with the clients before caucus.

A client-centered model of mediation does not make extensive use of caucusing because separate meetings by the mediator with the parties can create mistrust and suspicion. When one side is sitting alone, there is the tendency to be suspicious about what the mediator is doing with the other side. Nevertheless, occasional caucus sessions can be useful to prevent impasse or to provide the mediator with an opportunity to explore roadblocks being experienced by the parties in mediation. The AFM standard suggests that in the case of a caucus session, "The mediator shall discuss policy regarding confidentiality for individual caucuses" (Standard VI-F). This means that the mediator should clarify in advance of caucusing whether information privately provided to the mediator will be shared with the other mediation participants.

All mediation records, files, flip charts, and memos are confidential (VI-G). The mediator must assure that they remain confidential. The confidentiality extends to office personnel and discussions with the clients' attorneys. Confidentiality also applies to storing client records and files.

We suggest that you have a secure system of storage and of disposal. Consult your malpractice insurance carrier about how long you need to keep client files.

A mediator is responsible for ensuring that all participants in the mediation process have sufficient accurate information, knowledge of necessary facts, and an understanding of options and outcomes in order to make intelligent, informed choices (VI-H). It is the responsibility of the mediator to ensure that the process remains fair, and this requires the mediator to be skilled at managing the information exchange. A crucial role of the mediator is to manage this information exchange and at a minimum, ensure that there be full disclosure of all relevant information.

The mediation process requires full disclosure of all information necessary to informed decision making. This includes information that would be discovered in a court procedure. The mediator needs to inform clients of this requirement and explain why it is important to the mediation process. We ask clients to agree to provide any information that the mediator and either of them need in order to have all the information necessary to make wise decisions. This is discussed in the Agreement to Mediate. If for some reason one does not want to disclose some information that the other believes is necessary to that person's decision making, the mediator and the clients need to decide if mediation can continue, and if so, what to do about the conflict about providing information.

VII. SELF-DETERMINATION

A. Responsibilities of the Participants and the Mediator. The primary responsibility for the resolution of a dispute rests with the participants. The mediator's obligation is to assist the disputants in reaching an informed and voluntary settlement. At no time shall a mediator coerce a participant into agreement or make a substantive decision for any participant.

B. Responsibility to Third Parties. The mediator has a responsibility to promote the participants' consideration of the interests of children and other persons affected by the agreement. The mediator also has a duty to assist parents to examine, apart from their own desires, the separate and individual needs of such people. The participants shall be encouraged to seek outside professional consultation when appropriate or when they are otherwise unable to agree on the needs of any individual affected by the agreement.

Because this book is about client-centered approaches to mediation, it should be expected that self-determination is identified as a crucial element of the ethical standards. Although self-determination plays an important part in most ethical standards promoted by various mediator organizations, there is continuing controversy over how far a mediator should go in trying to obtain a settlement between the parties.

This concept of self-determination is perhaps one of the more difficult standards of practice for the beginning mediator to understand and follow. The dilemma for every mediator is that in an attempt to help the clients, there is a danger the mediator will push too hard in an effort to be helpful. How can a mediator avoid being coercive when, in reality, every single case that comes to the mediator is already at a stage of impasse? (Indeed, why would anyone need to hire a professional mediator if they could resolve the conflict on their own? Therefore, by definition, they begin working with the mediator after arriving at impasse on their own.) How can the mediator move parties toward resolution without coercing them? The answer, from a client-centered mediator perspective, is that the mediator creates for the parties the elements of a cooperative environment by orchestrating the process of mediation and is thus able to help the clients find their own resolution without having to coerce them.

Because the field of mediation is rapidly mushrooming in growth, interest, and usage, there are more and more professionals who call themselves mediators. Many of these new mediators are also practicing lawyers and they may employ a coercive, very directive model of mediation. Their understanding of mediation is more akin to what a judge does at the pretrial conference. These lawyers have probably had many litigation cases in their career where the judge reviewed the file, called everyone into chambers, and butted heads in an attempt to obtain a settlement. This method of mediation is law centered and attempts to evaluate the merits of each side's claim. It is really a form of advisory arbitration by a person who evaluates the case and then tries to convince each side to compromise. This model is not based upon cooperative principles of seeking shared goals. Rather, it is often based merely on the neutral's idea of which side has a stronger or weaker case and what a judge or jury would likely do if the case were tried in court. Such an approach can be costly and it produces results that are seen by the parties as having been forced upon them. These directive models should not appropriate the term mediation because they are about as far as possible as one can get from the concept of self-determination. The following highlights this growing problem.

About the third day of a four-day mediation training for a group of lawyers in a small northern Minnesota town, one of the participants in the training recounted one of his earlier experiences with mediation. He started by saying he was beginning to agree with an observation made on the first day of training (which caused a great deal of controversy) that it is not appropriate for the mediator to investigate and learn in detail the factual background together with determining as much as possible about each side's claims in the case. Rather, the new mediators were being taught to let the facts of the case unfold in the mediation room.

Three years ago, before you heard much about mediation, we had a complex case involving an addition to a school. The addition could have been built on poor soil or it might have been the case that there was a flaw in the design, the construction, or even the concrete, but whatever the cause, the whole addition started to crack and pull away from the main building. It was kind of humorous in that it severed the electrical service and the plumbing started to crack. It created a very costly problem. As expected, the school district sued the contractor, the excavator, the architect, and just about every subcontractor that worked on the project. The contractor impleaded the surveyor, the owner of the concrete plant, and, as is usual with these types of cases, everybody was pointing the finger at everyone else. The judge called all the attorneys into chambers at the conclusion of one of the endless rounds of motions and said, "Do you want to try to mediate this?" It seemed like a good idea at the time, except nobody knew any good mediators. The judge said, "I heard about an attorney in Minneapolis who mediates these cases, but I don't know much about him. Should we give him a call?" As soon as the attorney came on the speaker phone for all of us to hear, he sounded as if he knew what he wanted. He asked every attorney in the room to box up and send to him all the pleadings, interrogatories, depositions, documents, and expert reports they had along with a two-page summary of their theory of the case and a bottom line offer or demand for settlement. He stressed that the offer be the best offer or demand that could be made and he didn't want anybody playing any games with their offers. It should be a good faith effort. We were to wait further instructions from him.

About two months went by and one of the attorneys called the judge's clerk to inquire about what we should do next. The judge replied through his clerk that he was wondering the same thing. About three days later, all of us got the same letter in the mail. The letter thanked us for considering mediation and it continued: "I have reviewed all the pleadings, interrogatories, depositions, expert's reports, and the rest of the documents you have sent me. I have further reviewed with interest each of your separate letters outlining your particular theory of the case. Based specifically on the bottom-line demands or offers that were contained in the letters, I have regretfully concluded that you are all so far apart in your estimate of what would be reasonable damages in this case that it would not be prudent or cost effective for me to travel to (name of city deleted) and attempt to mediate this case. Enclosed herewith is my bill for $2,314—fees for reviewing the files, records, depositions, etc."

The concept of self-determination, which is so necessary to the strength and benefit of the mediation process, is being undermined by a well meaning but naive lawyer turned mediator. In the foregoing case, the mediator assumed that his responsibility was to provide the parties with his opinion about whose claim was stronger or weaker and then proceed to try to force the parties to compromise at a settlement. This lawyerized brand of mediation is more costly because it requires the mediator to spend a great deal of time investigating and gathering background facts, which in turn creates an expectation on the part of the participants that the mediator will then tell them whose case is better or worse and the value of each side's case. This model of mediation is particularly harsh on parents who submit custody disputes to this kind of mediator because the couple experiences a form of shortened custody evaluation without the necessary safeguards of a due process trial. In many ways, such a type of mediation process presents people with the worst of all worlds; expecting some kind of mediation process to occur, they experience instead a coercive settlement type of process where, quite likely, they will never even sit face to face in the same room with the other participants. As we pointed out earlier, many of the ethical problems in mediation relate to the improper mingling of a judicial process and a mediation process.

In a client-centered process of mediation, the mediator refuses to put pressure on the parties to settle by predicting whether they would do worse in court or suggesting that their claim doesn't really merit very strong consideration. Rather, the client-centered mediator encourages the parties to obtain outside information about disputed facts or law by engaging the services of an attorney to advise each of them about outcomes in court. The client-centered mediator will ask the parties to consider obtaining the services of a neutral expert who can advise them about the strengths or weaknesses of their factual claims. When a neutral expert is asked to fulfill this role of advisor, it is less likely that people will experience the extremes of the adversarial predictions that are often nothing more than posturing by an advocate for one side.

One of the other ways a mediator violates the standard on self-determination is by coercing the parties to follow state law. Self-determination is best achieved when the mediator remains noncoercive and nondirective about which standard of fairness must be followed. This approach results in the parties owning their decisions. A noncoercive approach also moves the mediator away from advising the parties about the law and how the law would settle their dispute. Most client-centered mediators encourage the parties to create their own laws of fairness that work for them, rather than insisting they follow some rigid application of state law. Once the parties realize they are permitted to deviate from the law by their own agreements, they are usually able to obtain much more creative and elegant solutions.

VIII. PROFESSIONAL ADVICE

A. Independent Advice and Information. The mediator shall encourage and assist the participants to obtain independent expert information and advice when such information is needed to reach an informed agreement or to protect the rights of a participant.
B. Providing Information. A mediator shall give information only in those areas where qualified by training or experience.
C. Independent Legal Counsel. When the mediation may affect legal rights or obligations, the mediator shall advise the participants to seek independent legal counsel prior to resolving the issues and in conjunction with formalizing an agreement.

A client-centered mediator is committed to a process that produces information that is necessary to the clients' full discussion and resolution of issues (VIII-A). Because the mediator as a neutral cannot give advice, the client-centered process offers the use of neutral experts to produce information and give advice to clients.

It is important to delineate between providing information and giving advice, because the mediator may have information that may be helpful to the mediation process. The mediator is free to provide information that is true and accurate (VIII-B). Clients expect mediators to have information from their former/other profession and from their mediation experience. This is often discussed with clients at the initial consultation.

In client-centered divorce mediation, we *encourage* each client to be represented by an attorney (VIII-C). Most clients do have attorneys by the end of the mediation process. However, some choose not to be represented. This standard is stated too strongly, and it is in conflict with client self-determination when it states *"the mediator shall advise . . . ."* We believe that a mediator has a duty to explain the importance of legal representation, but, *to advise* is to suggest that the mediator knows what is best for the client(s). We find that more and more clients are attorney phobic, and do not want to have any attorneys involved in their divorce. As mediators, we point out the benefits of attorney representation during and after mediation, and we offer clients referrals to attorneys who respect both the mediation process and clients' efforts to mediate.

IX. PARTIES' ABILITY TO NEGOTIATE

The mediator shall ensure that each participant has had an opportunity to understand the implications and ramifications of available options. In the event a participant needs either additional information or assistance in order for the negotiations to proceed in a fair and orderly manner or for an agreement to be reached, the mediator shall refer the individual to appropriate resources.

A. Procedural Factors. The mediator has a duty to ensure balanced negotiations and should not permit manipulative or intimidating negotiation techniques.

B. Psychological Factors. The mediator shall explore whether the participants are capable of participating in informed negotiations. The mediator may postpone mediation and refer the parties to appropriate resources if necessary.

The mediator does not assess the clients' ability to mediate but assumes that they have the capacity to do so if they choose. This is true of most clients, but there are spouses who have had an imbalance in their marriage relationship in which one spouse acted in an intimidating and disrespectful manner toward the other spouse, and the other spouse, feeling intimidated, submitted to the demands of the other. When these dynamics are present in mediation, the mediator has a duty to address them, explaining to the clients the implications for mediation. If this is a case with a history of nonreciprocal spousal abuse, the mediator may insist on protocols to be followed in order for the clients to mediate. The protocols may be necessary to balance the negotiations so that each client can negotiate in his or her best interests. These protocols and agreements by the clients about their behavior in the mediation room are used to assure balanced negotiations (IX-A).

Regarding psychological factors (IX-B), the client-centered mediator *and the clients* discuss the clients' capabilities to mediate and decide under what circumstances mediation will be beneficial to the clients. This differs from the standard, because the discussion of capability is *with the mediator and the clients*. This again addresses client self-determination. The mediator may offer several options for the couple to be better able to mediate, including suggestions such as referral to a marriage-closure therapist, or use of neutral experts. Client-centered mediation deviates from this standard in deference to client self-determination, which leaves the decision about their capability to the clients. The mediator may make suggestions and offer referrals, but if the clients, fully informed of the mediator's concerns about capability, wish to proceed with mediation, and the mediator agrees, we believe that they may proceed. If they accept a referral to a counselor, for example, the mediator and the couple need to decide whether to suspend mediation while they are in counseling.

X. CONCLUDING MEDIATION

A. Full Agreement. The mediator shall discuss with the participants the process for formalization and implementation of the agreement.

B. Partial Agreement. When the participants reach a partial agreement, the mediator shall discuss with them procedures available to resolve the remaining issues.

C. Termination by Participants. The mediator shall inform the participants of their right to withdraw from mediation at any time and for any reason.

D. Termination by the Mediator. If the mediator believes that participants are unable or unwilling to participate meaningfully in the process or that a reasonable agreement is unlikely, the mediator may suspend or terminate mediation and should encourage the parties to seek appropriate professional help.

E. Impasse. If the participants reach a final impasse, the mediator should not prolong unproductive discussions that would result in emotional and monetary costs to the participants.

When mediation ends with an agreement of all the issues, the mediator needs to discuss with clients the legal process and implementation of their agreements (X-A). This includes which of their attorneys will draft the legal documents, how they will pay for drafting, and how various agreements will be completed.

Sometimes clients will agree upon most but not all the issues in mediation (X-B). The mediator does not hold their feet to the fire until all the issues are decided, but discusses with them options to complete the decision making.

Clients are informed at the initial consultation that mediation is voluntary and that they are free to end mediation at any time (X-C). The client-centered mediator offers to assist them in agreeing on how they will complete their divorce, so each knows what to do after mediation ends. The mediator drafts a memorandum of the agreements they have made and encourages them to continue to work toward their shared goals with their attorneys.

There are instances in which the mediator believes the clients are not making progress in mediation and may need to consider suspending mediation while they work on the block in the process. The mediator may challenge the clients to either invest in the mediation process and work on the issues in mediation or end mediation and let the court make their decisions. One of the problems that often accompanies a block of the progress in mediation is that the couple is mediating with one foot in the courthouse and one foot in mediation. That is, they are not fully committed to mediation because their attorneys are continuing the adversarial process while the couple is trying to mediate. This does not work, and clients are asked by the mediator to decide which process they want to use to settle their divorce.

When progress in mediation is halted, it is not unusual to have a spouse B who is in denial and refusing to engage in decision making in mediation. This spouse may use the mediation sessions as a way to continue to see spouse A in hopes of convincing him or her to reconcile.

The mediator may offer some options at this juncture. One method of getting the clients back on track with the mediation process (if it is their desire) is to have a meeting with each of their attorneys present. The attorneys' presence may provide a reality check for spouse B that breaks the denial and helps move the process along.

Impasse in mediation means that the process has stopped. We believe that there are many options available to clients approaching impasse. We have developed many strategies to avoid impasse at the institute. In fact, we do not believe in impasse, except for impasse decided by the clients. Short of declaring impasse, we offer many creative strategies for clients to consider in order to avoid impasse. In 1988 we published the strategies in our book, *Family Mediation Casebook: Theory and Practice* (Erickson & Erickson, 1988, p. 194). We have continued to develop new strategies that have resulted in many of our clients avoiding impasse. If the clients choose impasse, the mediator must respect their decision and assist them in terminating mediation.

XI. TRAINING AND EDUCATION

A. Training. A mediator shall acquire substantive knowledge and procedural skill in the specialized area of practice. This may include but is not limited to family and human development, family law, divorce procedures, family finances, community resources, the mediation process, and professional ethics.
B. Continuing Education. A mediator shall participate in continuing education and be personally responsible for ongoing professional growth. A mediator is encouraged to join with other mediators and members of related professions to promote mutual professional development.

This standard is discussed at length in Chapters 5 and 8 as advice we offer in our training courses. We explain that the 40-hour divorce-mediation training does not sufficiently prepare people to begin to mediate. Newly trained mediators need to round out their training by acquiring more information and knowledge in divorce law, conflict resolution, and interpersonal dynamics in order to be prepared to begin mediating (XI-A).

Once a new mediator begins to practice, continuing education in topics related to divorce and mediation will be necessary to stay current with changes in laws, new research, and mediation practice (XI-B). The AFM requires a number of continuing education units each year to maintain membership status.

XII. ADVERTISING

A mediator shall make only accurate statements about the mediation process, its costs and benefits, and the mediator's qualifications.

This standard is self explanatory. It is important for a mediator to re-spect this truth-in-advertising standard. What this means for the client-centered mediator is that any information about the mediator will be true and accurate on calling cards, brochures, letterhead, in ads, and other media. This is an area in which there have been misunderstandings about how mediators identify themselves. Because mediators cannot wear more than one professional hat at a time, it is important for media-tors to distinguish between being a mediator and being a member of any other profession. On mediator calling cards, for example, the mediator is a mediator, not an attorney-mediator or therapist mediator, because this blurs the line between the professions and muddies the waters about the service being advertised.

XIII. RELATIONSHIP WITH OTHER PROFESSIONALS

A. The Responsibility of the Mediator Toward Other Mediators/Relation-ship with Other Mediators. A mediator should not mediate any dispute that is being mediated by another mediator without first endeavoring to consult with the person or persons conducting the mediation.

B. Co-mediation. In those situations where more than one mediator is par-ticipating in a particular case, each mediator has a responsibility to keep the others informed of developments essential to a cooperative effort.

C. Relationships with Other Professionals. A mediator should respect the complementary relationship between mediation and legal, mental health, and other social services and should promote cooperation with other profes-sionals.

This is the practice-what-you-preach standard. If mediators believe in cooperation, unconditional regard for others, and constructive conflict resolution, then their relationships with mediators and other profession-als should be complimentary. Common sense and courtesy would sug-gest that a mediator would not mediate a dispute being mediated by another mediator. If clients want to change mediators, the former and new mediator should ask client permission to discuss the situation to cre-ate closure with one and an easy transition to the new mediator (XIII-A).

Co-mediation is a method of mediation practice (XIII-B) . Some media-tors insist that it should be the norm, especially in divorce mediation. Other mediators prefer the single-mediator practice and insist that it is the superior method. Client-centered mediation is taught in the context of the single-mediator method although it does not insist that this is the superior method. Co-mediation may be preferred as a method for beginning mediators to offer high-quality services although the mediators are not experienced. When we opened our practice in 1977, we all co-mediated with someone of the opposite gender and profession. This offered clients our best effort of assuring balance, quality, and efficiency. After each mediator became more comfortable mediating, they preferred to mediate alone.

To co-mediate successfully, the mediators must be clear with each other and the clients about their roles in the room. Usually one will be the lead mediator and the other will follow that lead. If either has contact with clients separately or between sessions, that mediator must apprise the other mediator of the contact. The co-mediators need to cooperate with each other in their mediation work both in the mediation room with the clients, and outside the room, preparing for sessions and drafting memos.

As discussed in Chapter 4, mediation does not occur in a vacuum. In most cases there are other divorce professionals involved with the couple. The mediator should encourage all professionals involved with the couple to have client permission to discuss the case, and whenever possible they should work together to assist the clients to achieve their shared goals (XII-C).

XIV. ADVANCEMENT OF MEDIATION

A. Mediation Service. A mediator is encouraged to provide some mediation service in the community for nominal or no fee.

B. Promotion of Mediation. A mediator shall promote the advancement of mediation by encouraging and participating in research, publishing, or other forms of professional and public education.

At the institute we have a policy that no clients will be refused services because they are unable to pay the fees. We will negotiate a fee arrangement whenever necessary to assure clients the opportunity to mediate with a mediator of their choosing at the institute (XIV-A). We include in the Negotiated Fee Arrangement policy that every client will pay some portion of the mediation fees, and will negotiate fees down to a level of $20 per hour. We encourage all who attend our training courses to do the same.

We also encourage mediators to volunteer to speak to high school classes about mediation without fee, and be willing to accommodate other requests for speaking or presenting at a nominal or no fee. We accept this as our responsibility to educate the public about mediation and applications of the mediation process. We also welcome the opportunity to do work that advances the field of mediation and encourage other mediators to do the same (XIV-B).

In summary, the AFM Standards of Practice are clearly written and detailed. They provide a structure to the practice of mediation and enhance the field by setting out the dos and don'ts for family mediators. Although they meet the need for the field to have high ethical standards, there are a few that do not seem consistent with the practice of client-centered mediation. Those inconsistencies, regarding self-determination, for example, do not greatly affect the day-to-day routines of mediators.

OTHER STANDARDS OF PRACTICE

The Joint Code of Standards of Practice for Mediators was developed in 1994 by representatives of the American Bar Association (ABA), SPIDR, and the American Arbitration Association (AAA). It begins with an introductory note explaining it as a general framework for the practice of mediation. The preface describes The Joint Code as having three functions: (1) as a code of conduct for mediators; (2) as a means to promote public confidence in the mediation process of dispute resolution; and (3) as a way to inform potential clients about mediation. The Joint Code defines mediation similar to the definition in the AFM standards, except in more general terms. There are nine sections to the code, which are more specifically addressed in the AFM standards:

I. **Self-determination: A Mediator Shall Recognize that Mediation is Based on the Principle of Self-Determination.**

II. **Impartiality: A Mediator Shall Conduct the Mediation in an Impartial Manner.**

III. **Conflicts of Interest: A Mediator Shall Disclose all Actual and Potential Conflicts of Interest Reasonably Known to the Mediator. After Disclosure, the Mediator Shall Decline to Mediate Unless all Parties Choose to Retain the Mediator. The Need to Protect Against Conflicts of Interest also Governs Conduct that Occurs During and After Mediation.**

IV. Competence: A Mediator Shall Mediate Only When the Mediator Has the Necessary Qualifications to Satisfy the Reasonable Expectations of the Parties.

V. Confidentiality: A Mediator Shall Maintain the Reasonable Expectations of the Parties with Regard to Confidentiality.

VI. Quality of the Process: The Mediator Shall Conduct the Mediation Fairly, Diligently, and in a Manner Consistent with the Principle of Self-Determination by the Parties.

VII. Advertising and Solicitation: A Mediator Shall Be Truthful in Advertising and Solicitation for Mediation.

VIII. Fees: A Mediator Shall Fully Disclose and Explain the Basis of Compensation, Fees and Charges to the Parties.

IX. Obligations to the Mediation Process.

Each standard is followed by an explanation of the standard and then comments that more fully describe the conduct of the mediator.

Family Mediation Canada also has published standards that describe mediator qualifications in great detail as well as standards for trainers and training programs.

MEDIATOR ACCOUNTABILITY

A mediator is professionally accountable to clients and to collateral contacts in the process of mediating. As a private professional, the mediator is also accountable as a member of professional organization(s) to the standards and ethics of those organizations. Most important is the mediator's accountability to self.

CONCLUSION

Credentialing in the field of mediation is limited to the standards that have been developed by the organizations already listed and by other organizations such as state court administrations and the many local conflict-resolution membership and provider organizations, both public and private. The field is still in its infancy, and not yet ready to move into licensure or further credentialing, and it may never be. This issue of whether to limit who may practice mediation has been discussed in the field since the early 1980s when the AFM decided its membership standards and concluded that it was not possible to know what knowledge, skills, abilities, or personality, for that matter, could predict mediator competency. The Test Design Project, composed of delegates from the major membership organizations, grappled with these issues in the early 1990s, and there continues to be an effort to determine at least minimum criteria to show mediator competency. Another school of thought is that the public will decide who will succeed as mediators, a theory that incompetent mediators will be weeded out by their own failures.

The standards are what exist today for mediators to follow to be ethical in practice. These standards are based on the principles of client-centered mediation, and they offer the best outcomes to clients when followed. What is lacking is a way for clients to expose those who do not adhere to the standards. We hope that the future of mediation practice will expand so that the public will be much more aware of what to expect from a mediator, and can, therefore, discern between good and bad mediation practice.

CHAPTER 9

The Future Impact
of Mediation Practice

I N EXPLAINING how client-centered mediation works, we wanted to go
beyond the dry mechanics of describing a laundry list of mediation
interventions and instead we wanted to set forth the subtleties of new
thinking that are involved in becoming a mediator. We have also not
been reticent about our concern for the future of the field. We believe
there is tremendous potential for mediation to dramatically impact our
society. This impact occurs through mediation's effort to make divorce
more humane, to spare children the harm of their parents' conflict, to
make the workplace more cooperative, and to teach society a new way of
thinking.

This new way of thinking will eventually become the norm. Already,
no less than six states have passed parenting plan legislation in an attempt to reduce custody battles by adopting the thinking of mediators
that focuses on building a future parenting plan instead of determining
custody. The US Postal Service, the largest employer in the United States,
has a policy of mediating all employment disputes. The public is beginning to go to the Internet and look up mediation services instead of seeking lawyer referrals. The ABA is aggressively trying to educate its
members that they must be able to understand and use mediation, because the public is looking for a better way. Some state court systems are
beginning to see a drop in case filings due to the increase of mediation.
Many states will not permit litigants to go on to a final trial unless they

can demonstrate that they have tried mediation or some other alternative dispute-resolution procedure. Children in grade schools are learning mediation skills and school peer-mediation programs are becoming the norm. We are rapidly closing in on the time when working as a peace maker is considered to be an honorable profession. We hope it will continue to grow and become a profession where one can make a reasonable income from the services that are provided. Although mediation fees are not comparable to lawyers' fees, people are much more willing to pay for the services of someone who says, "I am not going decide your controversy. I feel uncomfortable telling you what the law is, and I don't think I am entitled to tell you what is best for you, but you are obviously in a great deal of conflict, and I am willing to help you resolve the conflict. All I ask is that you allow me to help you see new ways of thinking and better ways of listening to each other, and I think I have some skills that may be helpful to you."

FUTURE PREDICTIONS

- Mediation will replace litigation as the favored method used to resolve business and commercial disputes.
- Divorce will no longer have to be a part of the adversarial court system. Although still connected to the state through an administrative process, divorce will be managed and delivered by mediators.
- As more and more couples mediate their divorces, child support payment compliance rates will dramatically increase from the present dismal record of an average of 50 percent compliance.
- Using mediation services, many more divorcing couples will learn to cooperate with each other and share joint parenting responsibilities of their children.
- The words *custody* and *visitation* and their negative connotations will be replaced with the future focus of building parenting plans, which is more useful than trying to determine who will have custody.
- Mediators will band together much like the Century 21 network of realtors. These networks of mediators will provide similar models of mediation at each location.
- As clients become more aware of less restrictive mediation models, such as client-centered or transformative mediation, the more direc-

tive, law-centered versions of mediation practice will become less prevalent.

- Mediators will advocate for and help develop creative spousal or child support payment systems that are more flexible and perceived as less punishing than current collection policies.
- Mediators will assist law enforcement units by working alongside them on cases of abuse with the development of innovative programming and compensation.
- Colleges and universities will expand existing course work on mediation and conflict resolution to offer Masters-level and doctoral programs in these fields.
- Mediation will be the preferred starting point for all difficult conflicts, and other options such as arbitration, litigation, early neutral evaluations, and minitrials will only be considered if mediation fails.
- The term ADR for Alternative Dispute Resolution will no longer be used. It will be replaced by the term ATM for Alternatives To Mediation.
- Ethics codes for attorneys will require them to first exhaust all attempts at mediation before starting litigation.
- The expanded use of restorative justice and sentencing circles will decrease suicide and crime rates.
- Use of mediation will stimulate higher rates of high school graduation through the school peer-mediation programs that help students learn constructive ways to resolve their differences and build their self-esteem.
- The workplace will become safer and more productive through the use of mediation for resolving work-related conflicts. Employees will become more involved in the process, participating in peer mediation groups for departmental issues.
- Effective mediation will significantly reduce medical malpractice litigation, because patients will be heard and satisfied by mediating face to face with those they feel harmed them.
- Medical malpractice awards will be reduced because the transaction cost of the settlements will be significantly reduced through mediation.
- Mediators will be in a position to influence the way our legal system operates.

- Do-it-yourself divorce services will be readily available through the Internet, and even wealthy couples will download sample divorce agreement language and build their own settlement agreements with the help of mediators.
- Research on restorative justice will find that deviant behavior patterns can be significantly changed by having perpetrators of crimes meeting face to face with their victims in mediation sessions.
- Prisoners will be rehabilitated through victim/offender mediation programs, and all the excess prisons built at the turn of the century will be refitted and used for temporary housing.
- Congregations will learn to resolve their internal conflicts through mediation because it is so closely aligned with most religious beliefs.

This list is based upon mediation and conflict-resolution processes that are already in place and beginning to make a difference in the areas where they are applied. All these and more will be realized in the future. As mediation becomes mainstream, people will change the way they think about and address conflict. Values of respect, kindness, assuming the best of others, seeing conflict as an opportunity, and others will be integrated into our culture, and as all the dedicated mediators believe, there will be peace among our people as we have not experienced it before. Are we idealists? No, we are realists, because we have begun to see the power of mediation in all aspects of life.

CONCLUSION

If you are still thinking that this may be a profession for you, pursue it. The practice is uplifting, energizing, and invigorating. Mediators do not burn out. Because mediators are not responsible for others' choices, we just go home each night having done the best we could to help others resolve their differences in as positive, constructive, and healthy a way as possible.

APPENDIX A

Agreement to Mediate

This AGREEMENT TO MEDIATE is signed by the parties and (Mediator), to create and clarify the mediation relationship. The parties desire to mediate all issues that otherwise might be involved in contested litigation. The parties herein agree to abide by the provisions of this Agreement to Mediate. This agreement reflects each party's sincere intention to be fair and equitable during mediation.

In Consideration of the Above:

1) (Mediator) will conduct the mediation and will be compensated at the rate of $\_\_$ per hour for actual mediation sessions. Payment for mediation sessions will be made at the conclusion of each mediation session.
2) (Mediator) has provided the parties with a copy of this Agreement and a description of the fees for mediation services.

AGREEMENT TO BEGIN MEDIATION: All parties must sign this Agreement prior to the commencement of mediation with (Mediator) mediator.

ROLE OF THE MEDIATOR: The Participants understand that the Mediator is an impartial facilitator and is not an attorney for either of them. Although the Mediator may ask questions or express concerns about the parties' agreement, the Mediator will respect the Participants' concepts of fairness and has no responsibility for the fairness or legality of the resolution. The Participants further understand that the Mediator is not serving as an accountant, a child psychologist, or any other substantive expert, and the Participants will not rely on the Mediator for advice about taxes, child development, or other subjects for which they may seek professional expertise. Participants are encouraged to seek whatever professional consultations may be appropriate in their particular circumstances.

CONDUCT OF THE MEDIATION SESSIONS: The mediation process may be conducted in the manner that the Mediator believes will most expeditiously permit full discussion and resolution of the issues. The Mediator will assist the parties in fully discussing and understanding each issue before agreements are made so that both parties arrive at solutions that are fair and equitable to them.

CONCERNS OF THE MEDIATOR: The Mediator may indicate verbally or in writing his or her concerns regarding any final decisions that the parties make when the Mediator is concerned about or does not understand the parties' sense of fairness. The Mediator's comments may appear in the Preliminary and/or Final Memorandum of Agreement.

CONFIDENTIALITY OF MEDIATION SESSIONS: With the exception of limitations noted below, all communications, documents not otherwise discoverable through formal legal processes, and notes made in mediation are confidential and may not be used as evidence for litigation purposes. The Mediator will respect the confidentiality of the participants' communications, and the Participants will not:
a. Subpoena the Mediator, any person assisting the Mediator including neutral experts such as accountants, or any records or documents belonging to or in custody of the Mediator or persons assisting the Mediator; or
b. Attempt to discover or use as evidence in any proceeding any communication or document made in or related to the mediation process.

LIMITATIONS ON CONFIDENTIALITY:
(1) *CHILD ABUSE*: Although Mediators are not mandated by Minnesota Law to report child abuse allegations, the Mediator may encourage self-reporting of any such allegation disclosed during the mediation process, and in circumstances in which the Mediator believes the safety of a child to be in question, the Mediator may report such information to the local Child Protection Agency.
(2) *PHYSICAL SAFETY*: If the Mediator reasonably believes anyone's physical safety is at risk, such as if one party were to make a threat of physical harm or other appropriate circumstances, the Mediator may alert public authorities such as the police.

CONCURRENT LEGAL PROCEDURES: Unless specific exceptions have been agreed to by all parties and the Mediator, while parties are in mediation, the parties will take responsibility for ensuring that all legal processes including filing motions, petitions, discovery or other legal pleadings are suspended until all parties have agreed or been given notice that mediation is terminated either through complete settlement, impasse, or withdrawal from mediation.

CONFLICTS OF INTEREST; WAIVER: The participants and the Mediator have discussed the following relationship(s) which may give rise to a conflict of interest: _____

_____

_____. After having the opportunity to discuss the possible conflict with counsel, by signing this Agreement to Mediate, the participants agree to waive the potential conflict of interest as they do not expect it to interfere with the Mediator's impartiality.

FULL DISCLOSURE: The parties agree that they will fully disclose to the other and to the Mediator all information and writings as requested by the Mediator, including financial statements, income tax returns, etc., and all information requested by the other party if the Mediator finds that such other disclosure is appropriate to the mediation process and may aid the parties in reaching a settlement. At the conclusion of the mediation process, the parties may find that the attorneys will request further verification and disclosure in order to aid their review and implementation of their decisions in mediation and the parties agree that they will provide such information at the request of the other party. Likewise, at the conclusion of mediation, the parties agree that they will sign a verified (notarized) statement declaring that they have fully and truthfully disclosed all information concerning assets, liabilities, and income if so requested by the Mediator or the other party.

PREPARATION OF BUDGETS: The preparation of budgets by each party is an essential part of the mediation process. If either party fails or refuses to prepare a budget adequately reflecting his/her needs, the Mediator shall have the option of suspending mediation of this issue or, at their discretion, declare an impasse.

PARTICIPATION OF CHILDREN AND/OR PERSONS OTHER THAN THE PARTIES: Children of sufficient age or other persons having a direct interest in the mediation may participate in mediation sessions related to their issues with consent of the parties and the Mediator.

PROHIBITION AGAINST TRANSFERS OF PROPERTY, CHANGE OR CANCELLATION OF INSURANCE, OR ANY OTHER ACTION THAT CHANGES THE MARITAL ESTATE: Upon beginning mediation, the parties will not engage in any transactions that materially affect the status quo of the existing marital estate. They agree that transfers or sale of property without the written agreement of both parties and their attorneys is prohibited, except in the usual course of meeting ordinary monthly obligations. Likewise, they agree not to cancel or change health insurance, life insurance, or other benefits while in mediation.

DRAFTING THE MEMORANDUM OF AGREEMENT: No decisions reached in mediation become final and binding until they are approved by the parties' attorneys and implemented through a court order or binding stipulation of the parties and their attorneys.

At the conclusion of the mediation sessions, the Mediator will draft a detailed memorandum setting forth the decisions agreed upon by the parties in mediation. The Memorandum of Agreement will contain background information about the parties and will set forth the factual information relied upon by the parties in reaching settlement. The Memorandum of Agreement will be submitted by each of the parties to their attorney for review and implementation of the decisions as reflected in the Memorandum. Any new or omitted issues raised by the attorneys will be returned to mediation if the parties and their attorneys are unable to efficiently and cooperatively resolve such new or omitted issues.

LEGAL REPRESENTATION: Legal advice and legal representation is not part of mediation and will not be provided by (Mediator). Legal advice is not given in mediation sessions and the parties agree that legal issues created by their decisions reached in mediation will be referred to their attorneys. The parties understand that they are encouraged to retain legal counsel prior to implementing the decisions reached in mediation. The Mediator does not legally represent either of the parties. (Mediator) recommends that the parties retain legal representation at the beginning of the mediation process, but no later than at the conclusion of the mediation process. By doing this, each party will have a better understanding of their legal rights and responsibilities and will less likely be surprised by legal issues or concerns raised by their attorney after thinking that all decisions have been finalized.

Although (Mediator) recommends that each party educate himself or herself about the legal approach to marriage dissolutions, the Mediator will encourage the parties to discuss and negotiate a settlement based on their own standards of fairness and their own decisions about what is best for themselves and their family.

(Mediator) maintains a panel of attorneys who specialize in family law and are familiar with the divorce-mediation process. This list is available to clients upon request. Each party is encouraged to choose and interview an attorney who will respect the work they have completed in mediation and who will provide them with an independent judgment of their decisions.

SCHEDULING OF SESSIONS AND STARTING TIMES: If any party needs to change a scheduled appointment, they are requested to do so *at least* 24 hours in advance. Failure to do this will result in a charge of $_____ for the canceled session. In-session mediation time will be billed commencing with the time that the session is scheduled to begin, unless the delay in starting time is attributable to (Mediator).

FEES: Fees for mediation services include (1) a one-time administrative fee of $_____ for set-up and staff time processing sessions summaries; (2) a professional hourly fee for mediation session time; and (3) the same professional hourly fee for the Mediator's work outside of the mediation sessions, whether for the preparation of the mediated settlement agreement or for discussions with parties, their counsel, or with other persons concerning matters related to the mediation. A detailed fee schedule is given to parties when they begin mediation.

FEE DISAGREEMENTS: Should any disagreements arise between either party and (Mediator) concerning fees or charges, the parties agree that they will use the services of a Mediator to resolve the disagreement (after first trying to resolve it themselves).

INDEPENDENT CONTACT WITH THE MEDIATOR; SAFETY CONCERNS: (Mediator) has a general policy of not caucusing separately with either party unless the Mediator believes it is necessary to do so to avoid possible impasse or to reduce the intensity of the conflict. For this reason, the parties are asked *not* to communicate with their Mediator outside of the working session about any issues of substance associated with a dispute. Procedural questions are permitted. However, parties are encouraged and permitted to discuss with the Mediator, either in sessions or in private, any concerns related to either their physical or emotional safety and well-being as it relates to the mediation process.

If any party feels that separate (private) communications with the Mediator are imperative, they may call their Mediator and present their concern(s) and reason(s) for discussing the matter outside of the scheduled mediation sessions. In general, if communications are necessary between sessions, parties should schedule a short conference call, so that the Mediator may speak with both of them at the same time.

COURT REFERRALS: In the event you have been ordered to mediation by a Court Order, there may be other requirements contained in the Court Order that parties are expected to follow. Special Orders For Protection and other requirements may be in force and will be discussed at the initial consultation. Any other special rules created and adopted by the parties will be contained in the Memorandum of Agreement prepared by the Mediator.

WITHDRAWING FROM MEDIATION: These rules assume that because mediation is voluntary, either person may withdraw from the mediation process at any time. If either party decides to withdraw from the mediation process before final settlement is reached, he or she agrees to return to the mediation table for a short session sufficient to provide an opportunity to clear up misunderstandings, if any, and to assure that all participants are on notice that alternatives such as the court process may be pursued. (A phone call stating you are not attending the next session is not sufficient to comply with this provision.)

RELEASE TO TALK TO THE PARTIES' ATTORNEYS: By their initials here, the parties authorize the Mediator to discuss issues related to the mediation with their attorneys, at the Mediator's discretion. _____   _____

By signing this agreement each party agrees to abide by the provisions within it, both as between themselves and as between the parties and (Mediator). This AGREEMENT TO MEDIATE is signed by the parties and by (Mediator), this _____ day of_____, 20_____.

By_____   _____
Mediator   Party

_____   _____
Party   Party

(Mediator) reserves the right to amend these rules at any time; however, any such amendments will not apply to existing cases in mediation on the date of such amendments.

Adapted from Erickson, S. K. & McKnight, M. S. (1998). *Mediating divorce.* San Francisco: Jossey-Bass Publishers.

APPENDIX B

Mediation Service Fee Schedule

The Initial Consultation: Most clients begin mediation with an initial consultation. This takes about 45 minutes for which there is no charge. The purpose of the consultation is for you to learn about our services. It is also your opportunity to get your questions answered and to get an estimate of necessary services.

MEDIATION FEES: Fees for mediation are charged by the hour. Mediator's fees range from $_____ to $_____ per hour, depending on your mediator. Sessions are usually two hours long. Most divorce cases will need three to five sessions for completion. Most paternity or postdecree mediations take from two to four sessions.

Payment for mediation is due AT THE END OF EACH SESSION and is usually shared by the parties in some way. We accept Visa and Master Card.

The final product of your mediation is a Final Memorandum of Agreement. This Agreement is then taken by you to your attorneys and one of them drafts the Final Judgment and Decree. IN ORDER FOR US TO PROVIDE YOU WITH THIS FINAL AGREEMENT, ALL CHARGES MUST BE PAID IN FULL.

ADMINISTRATIVE FEE: When clients begin mediation an initial fee of $____ is assessed to cover necessary setting and changing of appointments, copying, postage, faxing and a portion of word processing time by (Mediator's) staff.

PHONE CALLS: Calls made to your mediator between sessions will only be accepted if you schedule a time for the call on the mediator's calendar first. Payment for such phone calls to your mediator, conference calls, and any long distance charges will be payable at the next session.

SPECIAL FEES: Some cases require a team of mediators. In those cases, fees are adjusted. If an accountant or other professional provides services in our sessions, they will bill you directly for their fees.

DRAFTING FEES: If your mediator drafts portions of your Memorandum of Agreement outside of the sessions, the fee for such time will be payable at the following session. Any additional fees for drafting will be discussed in advance.

CANCELLATION POLICY: We ask that clients call AT LEAST 24 HOURS IN ADVANCE to cancel an appointment. A $_____ CANCELLATION FEE is assessed for cancellations without this notice.

APPENDIX C

Divorce Mediation Questionnaire

INSTRUCTIONS: Please provide all of the following information to the best of your ability, even though it may duplicate what the other party may provide. *Please use ink to fill out this questionnaire.*

1. Your Full Name: _____ (Maiden Name): _____

   Birth date: _____ Place of Birth: _____

   Street Address: _____ Home Phone: _____

   City: _____ State: _____ County: _____ Zip: _____

   Workplace: _____ Work Address: _____

   City: _____ State: _____ Zip: _____ Phone: _____

   Continuous Residence in this state since: ____ Social Sec. #_____

2. Marriage Date: _____ Place: _____

3. CHILDREN:

   Full Name (First, Middle, and Last):   Birth date: Age: Living With:

   _____   _____   _____   _____

   _____   _____   _____   _____

   _____   _____   _____   _____

   _____   _____   _____   _____

4. Are you and the other party living together? ❑ Yes ❑ No

   If not, please give the date of separation: _____

231

5. Are you employed? ❑ Yes ❑ No Employer: _____ Position: _____

   Employed since: _____ Salary: _____ H.S. Diploma: _____

   College Degrees/Certificates: ___ Major/Year: ____
   Continuous employment since: _____

6. Is your spouse employed? ❑ Yes ❑ No Employer: _____

   Position: _____ Employed Since: _____ Salary: _____

   Educational status: _____ Continuous employment since: _____

7. List all prior marriages. (Include name of prior spouse, and when and where marriage was terminated.) _____

   _____

8. List names and ages of any children from prior marriages and state with whom such children live.

   _____

   _____

   _____

9. Do you have an interest in reconciliation? ❑ Yes ❑ No

10. Is there a dispute involving the children? ❑ Yes ❑ No

11. Have you had marriage or family counseling? ❑ Yes ❑ No

    If yes, with whom? _____

12. Are you presently in therapy or counseling? ❑ Yes ❑ No

    If yes, with whom? _____

13. Attorney's Name: _____ Phone: _____

    Address: _____

14. Are there joint bank accounts to which your spouse has access? ❑Yes ❑ No

15. Does your spouse have credit cards for which you are responsible?
    ❑ Yes ❑ No

    If yes, specify:_____

16. Who referred you to (Mediator)?

    Address: _____

    Do you have any objection to our acknowledging this referral? ❑ Yes ❑ No

17. Date you completed this form: _____

ASSETS AND LIABILITIES: Please list the value of each of the following items of property. If you are unable to obtain the exact present value, estimate what you think the value may be. If any item is located in a state other than that in which you live, indicate where such item is located, and if necessary, give details on a separate sheet. Please indicate items acquired by gift, inheritance, or prior to marriage by marking with a star (*).

Be sure to list the names and account numbers of all of the items, and the legal descriptions of real estate. This information is important in identifying the items, and is necessary for inclusion in your legal papers.

LIST APPROPRIATE INFORMATION AS COMPLETELY AS POSSIBLE

ASSETS:

A. BANK ACCOUNTS:

Bank Name:	Account #:	Balance:	Owner:
_____	_____	_____	_____
_____	_____	_____	_____
_____	_____	_____	_____
_____	_____	_____	_____

B. ACCOUNTS RECEIVABLE, NOTES, LOANS MADE TO OTHERS, ETC.:

Due From:	Balance Due:	Owner:
_____	_____	_____
_____	_____	_____
_____	_____	_____

C. STOCKS AND BONDS:

(List company, # shares, price per share today and total value of stock in owner's column):

Company Name:	Number Shares:	Value/Share	Owner:
_____	_____	_____	_____
_____	_____	_____	_____
_____	_____	_____	_____
_____	_____	_____	_____

D. REAL ESTATE:

Homestead:

Address:_____

Legal Description: _____

Date of Purchase: _____ Purchase Price: _____

Mortgage Company: _____ Account # _____

Amount Owed: _____ Second Mort_____

Appraised Value: _____ Appraised by: _____

Special Information: _____

Other Real Estate:

Address:_____

Legal Description: _____

Date of Purchase: _____ Purchase Price: _____

Mortgage Company: _____ Account # _____

Amount Owed: _____ Second Mort_____

Appraised Value: _____ Appraised by: _____

Special Information: _____

Other Real Estate:

Address:_____

Legal Description: _____

Date of Purchase: _____ Purchase Price: _____

Mortgage Company: _____ Account # _____

Amount Owed: _____ Second Mort_____

Appraised Value: _____ Appraised by: _____

Special Information: _____

E. LIFE INSURANCE:

Company:	**Account #:**	**Face Value:**	**Cash Value:**	**Insured/Beneficiary:**
_____	_____	_____	_____	_____
_____	_____	_____	_____	_____
_____	_____	_____	_____	_____

Where are the policies located? _____

F. BUSINESS INTERESTS:

Please furnish last balance sheet, P & L statement, tax return, buy-sell agreements, etc.:

Name of Business: _____ Location: _____

Owned Since: _____ % Ownership: _____

Appraised By: _____ Appraised Value: _____

Special Information: _____

Name of Business: _____ Location: _____

Owned Since: _____ % Ownership: _____

Appraised By: _____ Appraised Value: _____

Special Information: _____

G. MISCELLANEOUS PROPERTY:

(Patents, trademarks, copyrights, royalties—Please furnish last statement and descriptive booklet):

Description: **Value:**   **Owner:**

_____   _____   _____

_____   _____   _____

H. AUTOMOBILES AND OTHER VEHICLES:

Vehicle Make & Year: _____ NADA Value: _____

Loan With: _____

Acct #: _____ Amount: _____

Vehicle Make & Year: _____ NADA Value: _____

Loan With: _____

Acct #: _____ Amount: _____

Vehicle Make & Year: _____ NADA Value: _____

Loan With: _____

Acct #: _____ Amount: _____

I. **PENSION, PROFIT SHARING, IRA AND OTHER RETIREMENT PLANS:**

Plan Name: Acct. #:   Value: Owner:

_____   _____   _____   _____

_____   _____   _____   _____

_____   _____   _____   _____

_____   _____   _____   _____

_____   _____   _____   _____

J. **PERSONAL PROPERTY, FURNISHINGS, ETC. (Attach lists if necessary):**

Specific Items: Values: Disposition:

_____   _____   _____

_____   _____   _____

_____   _____   _____

_____   _____   _____

K. **INCOME TAX REFUNDS/AMOUNTS DUE:**

                                              Refund Due: Amount Owed:

State: _____ Year: _____   _____   _____

Federal:_____ Year: _____   _____   _____

Special Information: _____

L. **LIABILITIES: (Attach lists if necessary)**

Loans Owed to: Account #:   Amount Due: Whose Account:

_____   _____   _____   _____

_____   _____   _____   _____

_____   _____   _____   _____

Other Debts (Medical, Dental, Charge Accounts, etc.):

_____   _____   _____   _____

_____   _____   _____   _____

_____   _____   _____   _____

MONTHLY BUDGETS:

A. INCOME: (Please supply most recent pay stub.)

How often do you receive paychecks?　　　＿＿＿＿＿＿

Number of exemptions claimed?　　　＿＿＿＿＿＿

Earned Income:

Gross Salary per paycheck:　　　＿＿＿＿＿＿

Federal Tax Deduction:　　　＿＿＿＿＿＿

State Tax Deduction:　　　＿＿＿＿＿＿

FICA Deduction:　　　＿＿＿＿＿＿

Mandatory Pension Deduction:　　　＿＿＿＿＿＿

Medical Insurance Deduction:　　　＿＿＿＿＿＿

Life Insurance Deduction:　　　＿＿＿＿＿＿

Other Deductions:　　　＿＿＿＿＿＿

Net Income per paycheck:　　　＿＿＿＿＿＿

Net Income figured on a monthly basis:　　　＿＿＿＿＿＿

Other Income amortized by month:　　　＿＿＿＿＿＿

Dividend Income:　　　＿＿＿＿＿＿

Interest Income:　　　＿＿＿＿＿＿

Income from Trusts:　　　＿＿＿＿＿＿

Rental Income:　　　＿＿＿＿＿＿

Pension:　　　＿＿＿＿＿＿

Social Security:　　　＿＿＿＿＿＿

Other Income (describe):　　　＿＿＿＿＿＿

Total Monthly Income (Net Pay plus Other Income):　　　＿＿＿＿＿＿

MONTHLY EXPENSES:

ITEM	SELF	CHILDREN
Rent		
Rental Insurance		
Mortgage Payment		
Principle_____		
Interest_____		
R. E. Taxes		
Homeowner's Insurance		
Second Mortgage/Home Equity Line		
Contract for Deed		
Association Fee		
Electricity		
Heat		
Water		
Refuse Disposal		
Telephone		
Cable TV		
Cellular Phone		
Home Maintenance and Repair		
House Cleaning		
Lawn Care		
Snow Removal		
Other Property:		
Contract for Deed/Mortgage		
Insurance and Taxes		
Maintenance		
Utilities		
Food/Groceries		

ITEM	SELF	CHILDREN
Lunches at Work/School		
Eating Out		
Household Supplies		
Clothing		
Dry Cleaning/Laundry		
Medical Insurance		
Uncovered Medical Expenses		
Prescriptions		
Eye Care		
Therapy/Counseling		
Dental Insurance		
Uncovered Dental Costs		
Orthodontia		
Automobile Expenses/Payment		
Gas/Oil		
Maintenance/Repairs		
Auto Insurance		
License		
Parking		
Life/Disability Insurance Premiums		
Recreation/Entertainment		
Vacations/Travel		
Newspapers/Magazines		
Dues/Clubs		
Personal Items/Incidentals		
Hair Care		
Child Care—Day Care		
Babysitting		

ITEM	SELF	CHILDREN
Children's School Expenses		
School tuition		
Books/Supplies		
Activity Fees		
Allowances		
Sports Fees		
Clubs		
Pet Expenses		
Contributions/Religious, Charity		
Gifts		
Other Miscellaneous		
Monthly Debt Reduction		
TOTAL MONTHLY EXPENSES:		
TOTAL MONTHLY NET INCOME:		
SURPLUS/SHORTFALL:		

Adapted from Erickson, S. K. & McKnight, M. S. (1998). *Mediating divorce*. San Francisco: Jossey-Bass Publishers.

Memorandum of Agreement

DATE

Doe, John and Mary Doe

John and Mary have made a decision to live separately and seek a dissolution of their marriage relationship. As a result of that decision, both have agreed to enter into mediation conducted by (Mediator) for the purpose of settling all issues that might otherwise be the subject of contested litigation. Prior to entering mediation, they signed an agreement with each other and with (Mediator).

They understand that mediator does not legally represent either or both of them. Both agree to retain attorneys of their own choice to legally represent them and to provide each of them with an independent judgment about the decisions reached in mediation. They understand that mediated agreements are not final and enforceable until they have been reviewed and approved by each of their attorneys and incorporated in a Stipulation or Marital Termination Agreement executed by both parties and their attorneys and a Judgment and Decree signed by a judge. Mary and John have agreed that if either of their attorneys has a problem with any portion of their mediated agreement, they will attempt to resolve that problem in a cooperative manner through their attorneys or will return to mediation to resolve it.

Mediation was conducted by (Mediator). The following represents their intended decisions reached in mediation after careful review of all facts and options. Both have made a full disclosure to each other of the full nature and extent of their assets, and they wish their attorneys to incorporate the following into a legally binding settlement agreement. Both intend to incorporate this mediation agreement to the fullest extent possible in their legal documents of divorce. However, both understand that there may be some word changes based upon review by their attorneys.

Introduction and Introductory Facts

1. PROCEEDING. The above-named parties intend to commence or have commenced a proceeding for dissolution before County Court.

2. BASIS FOR AGREEMENT. Mary and John consider it to be in their own best interests to agree upon all matters with respect to parenting, the division of property, payment of debt, spousal maintenance, and all other matters at issue between them. They have arrived at agreements through mediation with (Mediator).

3. FULL AND FAIR DISCLOSURE. Mary and John have advised each other as to the extent, nature, and amount of their property, income, and indebtedness, and each is relying on this disclosure in entering into this agreement. This mediated agreement is based upon said full and fair disclosure. Each party represents that they have not withheld from disclosure information, which would materially affect the distribution between them.

4. NAMES AND SOCIAL SECURITY NUMBERS. The true and correct names, addresses, and social security numbers of the parties are as follows:

John Doe
Address
Address
Born: _____, **age** _____
Social Security No. _____

and

Mary Doe
Address
Address
Born: _____, **age** _____
Social Security No. _____

5. PRIOR NAMES.
Mary has been known by the name Mary (Middle) (Maiden) in addition to Mary Doe. John has used no other names.

6. JURISDICTION.
The parties submit themselves to the jurisdiction of the COUNTY County District Court for the purpose of this proceeding. The parties acknowledge that the provisions contained herein may be embodied in a Judgment and Decree entered herein.

7. COUNSEL.
Mary is represented in these proceedings by _____, Esq.; John is represented by _____, Esq.

8. COURT APPROVAL.

Mary and John shall proceed with this dissolution by administrative default and will submit this agreement to the above-referenced Court. If the dissolution is not granted, the terms of this Agreement shall be of no effect, and if this Agreement is not approved by the Court, Mary and John shall be advised and shall be given the opportunity to appear and present argument, witnesses, and evidence. If this Agreement is approved by the Court and the Court grants a dissolution to the parties, the terms of this Agreement shall be made a part of any Decree issued, whether or not each and every portion of this Agreement is literally set forth in the Judgment and Decree.

9. MILITARY SERVICE.

The parties acknowledge that neither party hereto is in the Military Service of the United States of America.

10. CHILDREN; Mary NOT PREGNANT.

There are _____ children as issue of this marriage, namely: _____, born _____, age _____. Mary is not now pregnant.

11. DISSOLUTION OF MARRIAGE.

Because there has been irretrievable breakdown of the marriage relationship, the bonds of matrimony will be dissolved.

12. MARRIAGE AND SEPARATION DATES.

The parties were married on _____ in _____, and separated on _____.

EMPLOYMENT, EDUCATION AND REASONABLE LIVING EXPENSES

13. John. John received a _____, and is employed by _____ as a _____ earning a gross annual income of _____ and a net monthly income of ____. John claims reasonable living expenses for himself and the children in the amount of $_____ per month.

14. Mary. Mary received a _____, and is employed by _____ as a _____ earning a gross annual income of _____ and a net monthly income of ____. Mary claims reasonable living expenses for herself and the children in the amount of $_____ per month.

EXPENSES: During the mediation process, the parties have examined their expenses individually as well as for the children. See attached Appendix A – Monthly Budgets.

AGREEMENTS REGARDING PARENTAL RESPONSIBILITIES

15. JOINT/SOLE LEGAL, JOINT/SOLE PHYSICAL CUSTODY.

The parties agree to share joint legal custody/name John/Mary as sole legal custodian. They (1) agree to share joint physical custody (2) agree to name John/Mary as sole physical custodian of the minor children.

16. PARENTING PLAN AGREEMENT.

John and Mary have _____ minor children of the marriage relationship: _____, born _____, age _____. As parents, they share a concern for the welfare and interest of the children.

They realize they are both very important to their children and they need each of them as an active parent in their lives after divorce. They respect each parent's individual role with the children about the other parent; sending messages to the other parent through the children, and cutting the other parent down is harmful to the children's sense of self and so they each agree not to do these things. They will give the children permission to love, and be proud of, the other parent. The children will be legally and publicly known under the surname (last name) of

_____.

(a) RESIDENTIAL ARRANGEMENTS

John and Mary realize the children's needs are most important to consider as they plan their living arrangements, and also that their needs will change as they grow older. They know the children are individuals and they are sensitive to the children's adjustment during this time of restructuring their family. They recognize that children of all ages adjust to changes better when they know what will be happening to them and what the schedule will be for them to be with each other and with each parent.

Although the children need living arrangements that are predictable, specific, and routine, sometimes there may be exceptions to the normal schedule. John and Mary will consider a request from the other parent for a change in schedule when something unexpected comes up. They will give each other as much advance notice as possible of the need to make changes for special circumstances.

Both parties will from time to time, experiment with different schedules in order to try to find an exchange schedule that does not unduly disrupt the children's daily schedule, but still allows for significant parenting contact by both parties. They will follow an initial time-sharing arrangement as follows:

M=Mom; D=Dad

	MON	TUES	WED	THUR	FRI	SAT	SUN
Week 1							
Week 2							
Week 3							
Week 4							

(b) HOLIDAY SCHEDULE

The parties agree to the following holiday schedule. These holidays will be treated as an exception to the regular weekly schedule of exchanges without the need to have makeup time. The children will spend holidays as follows:

Holiday	Even Numbered Years	Odd Numbered Years
Easter		
Memorial Day		
Fourth of July		
Labor Day		
Thanksgiving (4 days)		
Christmas Eve		
Christmas Day		
Children's Birthdays	According to schedule and the other parent will have some contact as requested by that parent	
Mother's Day	Mom	Mom
Father's Day	Dad	Dad

For summer vacation, they shall have a preliminary discussion about summer plans for the children by February with the final plans being decided upon by May.

If the parties disagree in the future about scheduling changes or have disputes about the holiday schedule, they shall first try to resolve such disagreements on their own, and shall return to mediation should they have difficulties in resolving these new issues on their own.

The future costs of returning to mediation if needed shall be shared equally.

When Mondays are a legal holiday, the children will be with the parent they are normally scheduled to be with.

(c) RELATIONSHIPS IMPORTANT TO THE CHILDREN
They recognize the children will benefit from maintaining ties with grandparents, relatives, and people important to them and they will help the children continue to be with these people from time to time.

(d) ON-DUTY/OFF-DUTY PARENTING
They recognize decision making is an important part of parenting and they agree that the parent the children are with (the on-duty parent) will make decisions about their day-to-day care and control.

They agree to the concept that each of them will provide parenting during the times they are scheduled to care for the children. This means that if the children are ill or either of them have other obligations during the scheduled time with the children, it will be the responsibility of the on-duty parent to make arrangements for the care of the children. The off-duty parent welcomes the on-duty parent to request assistance during their scheduled times with the children, but they both understand that if the off-duty parent is not able to assist the on-duty parent during the scheduled time, it will be the responsibility of the on-duty parent to make alternative arrangements for the children.

(i) Education: Each of them will communicate with the children's schools to remain informed about the children's needs and progress and special events including parent-teacher conferences. They also agree to share information about the children's school progress, behavior, and events with each other. They realize college or technical training is important and they will encourage and support the children's efforts for further education. Major decisions about the children's education will be made by both parents.

(ii) Health Care: In emergencies each parent can consent to emergency medical treatment for the children as needed. Their intent is to take care of the medical emergency first and communicate with the other parent as soon as possible. They each have the right to the children's medical information and records, and they will communicate with each other on major health care for the children, and major decisions about health care will be made by both parents.

(iii) Religion: They will communicate with each other on major religious ceremonies involving the children, and major decisions about religious upbringing will be made by both parents.

(iv) Child Care: If child care is needed by one parent, when practical, they agree to offer the other parent the opportunity to provide this care before seeking someone else to care for the children. Major decisions about child care will be made by both parents.

(e) COMMUNICATION

During separation of more than a week from the children, they will maintain frequent contact with them by phone, (letter, post cards, video or audio tapes). They will also encourage and help the children communicate frequently with the other parent by phone, letter, etc. They agree to give the other parent the address and phone number where the children can be reached anytime they are away from home for more than 24 hours.

(f) SAFETY

They each agree not to compromise the safety of the children. They will not leave the children unattended until they are 12 years old. They agree not to operate a vehicle when under the influence of alcohol or nonprescription drugs when the children are in the vehicle, or use these substances carelessly when the children are in their care.

(g) TRANSPORTATION

They each agree the parent who is receiving the children will pick them up. They will pick up the children's belongings at the same time they pick up the children. Remembering is difficult for children, so John and Mary will cooperate and help the children to remember to take belongings with them, so they will have with them the personal belongings and school supplies they need.

(h) MOVE FROM CURRENT RESIDENCE

If a move from a current residence makes it impossible to continue the schedules in the Plan, John and Mary agree to renegotiate the Parenting Plan Agreement prior to a move. They will focus on how they can still be involved as parents in a way that would meet the needs of the children.

(i) TRANSPORTATION OUT OF STATE

They will not take the children from the State without prior agreement and understanding of the other parent. They will be reasonable when the other parent requests to take the children out of (State) for vacations or travel.

(j) DURATION

John and Mary understand this Plan will be in effect until the court issues a new court order regarding their shared parenting arrangements. They agree any changes to this Plan will be made in writing, dated and signed by each of them. Until such a written change is approved by the Court, they realize agreements made in this Plan will govern any dispute.

As the children grow and their life situation changes, John and Mary agree to be flexible and cooperative, and communicate with each other so they can meet the changing needs of their children. If one parent does not follow a part of this Plan, they understand the other parent's obligations under the Plan are not affected. When John and Mary cannot agree about what a part of this agreement means, or if a significant change (such as a move or remarriage) causes conflict, they will make a good faith effort to resolve their differences through mediation.

FINANCIAL SUPPORT

17. CHILD SUPPORT.

John/Mary agrees to pay child support to Mary/John in the amount of $____ per month according to the percentage required by the State Child Support Guidelines. This amount is ____% of John's/Mary's net monthly income. Child support will continue until each minor child reaches the age of 18 years, enters the Armed Forces of the United States, is emancipated, self-supporting, or deceased, or until each child reaches the age of 20 years if the child is still attending secondary school, or until further Order of the Court.

In the future, they agree to continue to follow the State Child Support Guidelines in computing child support and they agree to include the standard cost of living adjustment clause to be calculated every two years using $____ as the base amount for the calculations.

From the child support payments, Mary will be responsible for payment of all routine expenses of the children such as clothing, food when the children are with Mary, and all other normal costs of the children. John will be responsible for payment of food and other costs associated with the children when they are with him. Should there be extraordinary expenses related to the children that are unusual or extra, they will first meet and agree as to whether to spend the money on behalf of the children and then they will decide upon a method of sharing such extraordinary expenses.

OPTION: In consideration of _____ and the State Child Support Guidelines, John/Mary will pay Mary/John $_____ per month as child support.

Deviation from Child Support Guidelines: (No exchange of Child Support):

John and Mary have agreed to an arrangement for sharing the costs of raising their children that calls for itemizing all expenses related to the children and sharing these costs on a pro rata basis according to their incomes. (Each will contribute toward the children's expenses by calculating the percentage their own income is in relation to their combined incomes.)

18. CHILD CARE COSTS.
John/Mary will pay _____ to John/Mary for child care costs.

19. CHILD SUPPORT COLLECTIONS.
Option 1: Child support will be collected by the County at a rate of _____ each pay period. Option 2: Mary/John waives her/his right to have child support collected through the Minnesota Department of Health and Human Services, and Petitioner shall make child support payments directly to Mary/John. If, at any time, Petitioner's child support payments become sixty (60) days overdue, Mary/John shall have the right to petition the Department of Health and Social Services for child support collection services.

20. DEPENDENCY EXEMPTIONS.
John/Mary shall claim the exemption for _____, and John/Mary shall claim the exemption for _____.

OPTION: When one child may no longer be claimed as an exemption by either party, John/Mary shall claim the remaining exemption during the even years, and John/Mary shall claim the exemption during the odd years. The parties each agree to execute IRS Form 8332, Release of Claim to Exemption for Child of Divorced or Separated Parents, in accordance with present and future Internal Revenue Code provisions and/or corollary state income tax forms, as required to fully implement the foregoing agreement. If either party fails or refuses to execute IRS Form 8332 and there is no valid reason for their failure to execute the form, then the party not in compliance shall be obligated to reimburse the other party for any additional taxes, penalties, accountant fees or attorneys' fees incurred, if any, by the party entitled to the exemption under this section.

21. SPOUSAL MAINTENANCE.
John/Mary shall pay spousal maintenance to Mary/John in the amount of $_____ for a period of _____ months beginning _____.

OPTION: Regardless of whether Mary/John remarries, payments shall be made _____.

OPTION: (With the exception of these payments), each party waives all claims to past, present, or future spousal maintenance, the possibility of any spousal maintenance, or modification of the waiver of spousal maintenance. Except as provided herein, no spousal maintenance shall be awarded from one party to the other, and each party hereby waives and is forever barred from receiving spousal maintenance from the other.

By presently waiving their right to receive or modify maintenance other than as provided above, the parties intend to divest the Court of jurisdiction regarding any future spousal maintenance, including the right to award spousal maintenance or to modify spousal maintenance, pursuant to (State Statute). This waiver of future spousal maintenance is given in consideration of the mutual waiver, the assets awarded to each party, and all other agreements made herein. Before agreeing to the waiver of modification of spousal maintenance, each party has made full disclosure of assets and liabilities, asset values, and income. Both parties are in good health and are capable of supporting themselves; both are currently employed. The parties believe the provisions of this agreement to be fair and equitable.

22. OPTION: WAIVER OF COUNTY COLLECTIONS.
Mary/John waives her/his right to have the County collect child support and/or spousal maintenance on her/his behalf. John/Mary shall pay spousal maintenance directly to her/him.

HEALTH EXPENSES

23. Health Insurance and Uninsured Health-related Expenses for the Children
John/Mary currently maintains health insurance for the parties and the children through his/her employment under Policy. She/He will continue to be responsible for providing and paying for health insurance coverage for each child until neither parent has a child support obligation for that child.

OPTION: The parties have agreed to share equally in any uncovered health-related expense for the children. Before arranging for any elective uncovered health-related procedures, the parties will agree on the procedure before assuming the other will participate in the costs of the procedure.

24. Health Insurance for Spouse Through COBRA and State Statute
John/Mary currently receives health insurance through John/Mary's policy. He/She intends to establish a policy under (State Statute) and 26 U.S.C. ' 162(k) (COBRA). _____ will be responsible for the premiums.

OPTION: Each spouse will be responsible for his or her health insurance and uncovered health-related expenses.

LIFE INSURANCE

25. LIFE INSURANCE.

As and for security for spousal maintenance and child support, John/Mary shall name Mary/John as primary beneficiary on his/her existing life insurance policies and shall maintain those or other life insurance providing a death benefit to Mary/John in the amount of at least____ until the child is ____years of age. As and for security for child support, Mary/John shall name John/Mary as primary beneficiary on her existing life insurance policies for a total benefit amount of at least ____or shall secure and maintain other life insurance with an equal benefit until the youngest child is ____ years of age. Otherwise, the parties are free to name other beneficiaries on any new life insurance policies as they choose.

PROPERTY DIVISION

26. FINAL DIVISION.

The following is a full, final, complete, and equitable property division. Each party is to be awarded the property described below.

Non-Marital Property

27. NON-MARITAL PROPERTY.

Mary claims the following nonmarital property:

John claims the following nonmarital property: Neither Mary nor John claim any nonmarital property.

28. PROPERTY IDENTIFICATION AND DIVISION.

The following is a complete listing of property as disclosed in mediation by John and Mary. Unless otherwise indicated, the date of valuation is _____. Starred (*) items indicate nonmarital items.

29. BANK ACCOUNTS.

Name of Bank	Type of Account/#	Balance	Owner

30. NOTES AND ACCOUNTS RECEIVABLE.

Description	Value	Owner

31. STOCKS AND BONDS.

Description	Value	Owner

32. HOMESTEAD.

	Property Value	Owner

First Mortgage

John and Mary are joint owners of the homestead at _____, which was purchased in _____ for _____. The legal description is:

Legal description here

A first mortgage is held by _____ with a current balance of _____. Present fair market value is approximately _____ as determined by _____. Without considering selling costs, the net equity of their house is approximately _____.

John/Mary shall have all right, title, interest, and equity in and to the above-described homestead of the parties subject to the mortgage in favor of ____ and subject to a lien in favor of Mary/John in the amount of _____, to be satisfied upon the sale of the house or the minor child's eighteenth birthday, whichever is sooner. John/Mary shall be solely responsible for any capital gains taxes that may apply in the event that he/she chooses to sell the homestead.

Within sixty (60) days from the entry of the Judgment and Decree, Mary/John shall provide John/Mary with an executed Quit Claim Deed releasing her interest in the homestead. If Mary/John fails or refuses to do so, the filing of a certified copy of the Judgment and Decree with the County Recorder will be sufficient to transfer title to said real estate to John/Mary.

John/Mary will hold Mary/John harmless from any claim from any source with respect to the homestead, including, but not limited to, the mortgage note. John/Mary shall apply for refinancing to remove Mary/John's name from the mortgage. If the Mortgagee will not agree to remove Mary/John's name from the mortgage, then in the future, John/Mary shall inform Mary/John if he ever becomes more than six (6) months in arrears on the mortgage or fails to keep the property insured for an amount equal to or greater than the mortgage balance. In either case, Mary/John shall have the right to have the property listed for sale and have it sold to protect her interest, with all proceeds payable first to retire the underlying mortgage, the costs of sale paid, any costs incurred by Mary/John incident thereto, and the balance of the proceeds paid to John/Mary.

33. OTHER REAL PROPERTY.

34. LIFE INSURANCE.

Company	Face Value	Cash Value	Owner/Insured

35. AUTOMOBILES.

Vehicle Make & Model   N.A.D.A. Value less outstanding loan   Owner

36. PENSION, PROFIT SHARING, AND IRA ACCOUNTS.

Description   Value   Owner

Option: Items _____ will be awarded to John, and items _____ will be awarded to Mary.

Option: John and Mary will divide the retirement assets as follows:

37. MISCELLANEOUS HOUSEHOLD GOODS & OTHER PERSONAL PROPERTY.

Option: John and Mary have agreed to the following distribution of their household goods and personal property:

Item   Value   Owner

Option: Other than as specifically exempted herein, John and Mary each shall have all right, title, interest, and equity, free and clear of any claim on the part of the other, in and to household goods, furnishings, jewelry, tools and all other tangible personal property in his or her possession as of _____.

38. LIABILITIES.

Both agree that all debts and obligations incurred in their own name since the date of separation will be the responsibility of the person incurring the debt and, other than the below listed liabilities, there are no other unpaid debts and obligations of the marriage.

Description   Debt Owner

SUMMARY OF PROPERTY DIVISION

Narrative about distribution of property and discussion of why this is fair to each of them.

   See attached Property Distribution Summary.

39. REMAINING TAX CONSEQUENCES OF THE SETTLEMENT.
They will consult with their accountant or attorney about the remaining tax effects of this agreement, particularly the liability that each of them have now and in the future for taxes as a result of the manner in which they are dividing the homestead. In addition, both will cooperate in correcting any errors or requests for information about previous year's tax filings.

MISCELLANEOUS PROVISIONS

40. NAME CHANGE.
Mary will/will not change her legal name to _____ as part of the dissolution proceedings.

41. DISPUTE RESOLUTION.
Any claim or controversy arising under this Agreement which cannot be resolved by and between the parties through direct communication and without mediation, shall promptly be submitted to mediation, and in any case, no motion shall be filed in court unless the parties have first made an attempt at good faith negotiation through mediation.

a. **Definition of Mediation.** Mediation is a voluntary process entered into by the parties. In this process the parties continue direct communication, but with the assistance of a neutral person—a mediator—who has no authority to require any concession or agreement. A good faith effort shall be made to resolve any claim or controversy arising between the parties.

b. **Selection of a Mediator.** The mediator shall be agreed upon by the parties, and if the parties cannot agree, then upon Petition to the court, the court shall appoint a mediator, or the parties shall obtain a list of five qualified persons and then alternately strike names.

c. **Duties and Responsibilities of Mediator.** The mediator shall have the duty and responsibility to assist the parties in resolving all issues submitted for mediation.

d. **Payment of Costs.** Both parties shall share the mediator's fees and disbursements equally unless they mutually agree otherwise. The mediator shall provide the parties with his or her fee and disbursement schedule in advance of mediation.

e. **Exhaustion of Remedies.** The parties shall make a good faith effort to resolve their differences through mediation, and in the case of parenting disputes, through mediation and arbitration, before either party may apply to the court for relief.

42. LEGAL DOCUMENT DRAFTING.
John's/Mary's attorney will draft the legal documents including a Marital Termination Agreement, Findings of Fact, Conclusions of Law and Judgment and Decree, all necessary QDROs, and any other document that may be required. John/Mary will pay attorney's fees for drafting.

43. ATTORNEY'S FEES AND COSTS.

Option: Mary/John and John/Mary will split 50-50 the attorney's fees for drafting the Petition, Marital Termination Agreement, and Judgment and Decree, but otherwise are each responsible for paying his or her own attorney's fees, costs, and disbursements incurred in this proceeding.

44. EXECUTION AND EXCHANGE OF DOCUMENTS.

Each party hereto shall hereafter upon any reasonable request made by the other party execute and deliver to the requesting party such assignment and other documents as may be necessary and required to fully effectuate each and all of the provisions contained herein; and in this connection, the party entitled to, and/or requesting, such assignments or other documents shall pay for any expenses incurred in the preparation hereof and shall also pay any and all recording and filing fees and all other attendant expenses.

45. RELEASE.

Subject to all foregoing provisions and subject to full compliance therewith, each of the parties in all respects, manners, and things releases and fully discharges the other from any liability, claim or obligation of any kind or character, whether arising out of the marriage relationship or otherwise. The agreements contained in the final Marital Termination Agreement shall be deemed a full, final, and complete settlement between the parties.

Adapted from Erickson, S. K. & McKnight, M. S. (1998). *Mediating divorce.* San Francisco: Jossey-Bass Publishers.

Academy of Family Mediators

Standards of Practice for the Family and Divorce Mediators

I. Preamble

Mediation is a family-centered conflict resolution process in which an impartial third party assists the parties to negotiate a consensual and informed settlement. In mediation, whether private or public, decision-making authority rests with the parties. The role of the mediator includes reducing the obstacles to communication, maximizing the exploration of alternatives, and addressing the needs of those it is agreed are involved or affected.

Mediation is based on principles of problem solving that focus on the needs and interests of the participants, fairness, privacy, self-determination, and the best interest of all family members.

These standards are intended to assist and guide public, private, voluntary, and mandatory mediation. It is understood that the manner of implementation and mediator adherence to these standards may be influenced by local law or court rule.

II. Initiating the Process

    A. **Definition and Description of Mediation.** The mediator shall define mediation and describe the differences and similarities between mediation and other procedures for dispute resolution. In defining the process, the mediator shall delineate it from therapy counseling, custody evaluation, arbitration, and advocacy.

    B. **Identification of Issues.** The mediation shall elicit sufficient information from the participants so that they can mutually define and agree on the issues to be resolved in mediation.

C. **Appropriateness of Mediation.** The mediator shall help the participants evaluate the benefits, risks, and costs of mediation and the alternatives available to them.

D. **Mediator's Duty of Disclosure**
   1. *Biases.* The mediator shall disclose to the participants any biases or strong views relating to the issues to be mediated.
   2. *Training and experience.* The mediator's education, training, and experience to mediate the issues should be accurately described to the participants.

III. Procedures

The mediator shall reach an understanding with the participants regarding the procedures to be followed in mediation. This includes but is not limited to the practice as to separate meetings between a participant and the mediator, confidentiality, use of legal services, the involvement of additional parties, and conditions under which mediation may be terminated.

A. **Mutual Duties and Responsibilities.** The mediator and the participants shall agree upon the duties and responsibilities that each is accepting in the mediation process. This may be a written or verbal agreement.

IV. Impartiality and Neutrality

A. **Impartiality.** The mediator is obligated to maintain impartiality toward all participants. Impartiality means freedom from favoritism or bias, either in word or action. Impartiality implies a commitment to aid all participants, as opposed to a single individual, in reaching a mutually satisfactory agreement. Impartiality means that a mediator will not play an adversarial role.

The mediator has a responsibility to maintain impartiality while raising questions for the parties to consider as to the fairness, equity, and feasibility of proposed options for settlement.

B. **Neutrality.** Neutrality refers to the relationship that the mediator has with the disputing parties. If the mediator feels, or any one of the participants states, that the mediator's background or personal experiences would prejudice the mediator's performance, the mediator should withdraw from mediation unless all agree to proceed.

C. **Prior Relationships.** A mediator's actual or perceived impartiality may be compromised by social or professional relationships with one of the participants at any point in time. The mediator shall not proceed if previous legal or counseling services have been provided to one of the participants. If such services have been provided to both participants, mediation shall not proceed unless the prior relationship has been discussed, the role of the mediator made distinct from the earlier relationship, and the participants given the opportunity to freely choose to proceed.

D. Relationship to Participants. The mediator should be aware that post-mediation professional or social relationships may compromise the mediator's continued availability as a neutral third party.

E. Conflict of Interest. A mediator should disclose any circumstance to the participants that might cause a conflict of interest.

V. Costs and Fees

A. Explanation of Fees. The mediator shall explain the fees to be charged for mediation and any related costs and shall agree with the participants on how the fees will be shared and the manner of payment.

B. Reasonable Fees. When setting fees, the mediator shall ensure that they are explicit, fair, reasonable, and commensurate with the service to be performed. Unearned fees should be promptly returned to the clients

C. Contingent Fees. It is inappropriate for a mediator to charge contingent fees or to base fees on the outcome of mediation.

D. Referrals and Commissions. No commissions, rebates, or similar forms of remuneration shall be given or received for referral of clients for mediation services.

VI. Confidentiality and Exchange of Information

A. Confidentiality. Confidentiality relates to the full and open disclosure necessary for the mediation process. A mediator shall foster confidentiality of the process.

B. Limits of Confidentiality. The mediator shall inform the parties at the initial meeting of limitations on confidentiality, such as statutorily or judicially mandated reporting

C. Appearing in Court. The mediator shall inform the parties of circumstances under which mediators may be compelled to testify in court.

D. Consequences of Disclosure of Facts Between Parties. The mediator shall discuss with the participants the potential consequences of their disclosure of facts to each other during the mediation process.

E. Release of Information. The mediator shall obtain the consent of the participants prior to releasing information to others. The mediator shall maintain confidentiality and render anonymous all identifying information when materials are used for research or training purposes.

F. Caucus. The mediator shall discuss policy regarding confidentiality for individual caucuses. In the event that a mediator, on consent of the participants, speaks privately with any person not represented in mediation, including children, the mediator shall define how information received will be used.

G. Storage and Disposal of Records. The mediator shall maintain confidentiality in the storage and disposal of records.

H. Full Disclosure. The mediator shall require disclosure of all relevant information in the mediation process, as would reasonably occur in the judicial discovery process.

VII. Self-Determination

A. **Responsibilities of the Participants and the Mediator.** The primary responsibility for the resolution of a dispute rests with the participants. The mediator's obligation is to assist the disputants in reaching an informed and voluntary settlement. At no time shall a mediator coerce a participant into agreement or make a substantive decision for any participant.

B. **Responsibility to Third Parties.** The mediator has a responsibility to promote the participants' consideration of the interests of children and other persons affected by the agreement. The mediator also has a duty to assist parents to examine, apart from their own desires, the separate and individual needs of such people. The participants shall be encouraged to seek outside professional consultation when appropriate or when they are otherwise unable to agree on the needs of any individual affected by the agreement.

VIII. Professional Advice

A. **Independent Advice and Information.** The mediator shall encourage and assist the participants to obtain independent expert information and advice when such information is needed to reach an informed agreement or to protect the rights of a participant.

B. **Providing Information.** A mediator shall give information only in those areas where qualified by training or experience.

C. **Independent Legal Counsel.** When the mediation may affect the legal rights or obligations, the mediator shall advise the participants to seek independent legal counsel prior to resolving the issues and in conjunction with formalizing an agreement.

IX. Parties' Ability to Negotiate

The mediator shall ensure that each participant has had an opportunity to understand the implications and ramifications of available options. In the event a participant needs either additional information or assistance in order for the negotiations to proceed in a fair and orderly manner or for an agreement to be reached, the mediator shall refer the individual to appropriate resources.

A. **Procedural Factors.** The mediator has a duty to ensure balanced negotiations and should not permit manipulative or intimidating negotiation techniques.

B. **Psychological Factors.** The mediator shall explore whether the participants are capable of participating in informed negotiations. The mediator may postpone mediation and refer the parties to appropriate resources if necessary.

X. Concluding Mediation

A. **Full Agreement.** The mediator shall discuss with the participants the process for formalization and implementation of the agreement.

B. **Partial Agreement.** When the participants reach a partial agreement, the mediator shall discuss with them procedures available to resolve the remaining issues. The mediator shall inform the participants of their right to withdraw from mediation at any time and for my reason.

C. **Termination by Participants.** The mediator shall inform the participants of their right to withdraw from mediation at any time and for any reason

D. **Termination by the Mediator.** If the mediator believes that participants are unable or unwilling to participate meaningfully in the process or that a reasonable agreement is unlikely, the mediator may suspend or terminate mediation and should encourage the parties to seek appropriate professional help.

E. **Impasse.** If the participants reach a final impasse, the mediator should not prolong unproductive discussions that would result in emotional and monetary costs to the participants.

XI. Training and Education

A. **Training.** A mediator shall acquire substantive knowledge and procedural skill in the specialized area of practice. This may include but is not limited to family and human development, family law, divorce procedures, family finances, community resources, the mediation process, and professional ethics.

B. **Continuing Education.** A mediator shall participate in continuing education and be personally responsible for ongoing professional growth. A mediator is encouraged to join with other mediators and members of related professions to promote mutual professional development.

XII. Advertising

A mediator shall make only accurate statements about the mediation process, its costs and benefits, and the mediator's qualifications.

XIII. Relationship with Other Professionals

A. **The Responsibility of the Mediator Toward Other Mediators/Relationship with Other Mediators.** A mediator should not mediate any dispute that is being mediated by another mediator without first endeavoring to consult with the person or persons conducting the mediation.

B. **Co-mediation.** In those situations where more than one mediator is participating in a particular case, each mediator has a responsibility to keep the others informed of developments essential to a cooperative effort.

C. **Relationships with Other Professionals.** A mediator should respect the complementary relationship between mediation and legal, mental health, and other social services and should promote cooperation with other professionals.

XIV. Advancement of Mediation
A. **Mediation Service.** A mediator is encouraged to provide some mediation service in the community for a nominal or no fee.
B. **Promotion of Mediation.** A mediator shall promote the advancement of mediation by encouraging and participating in research, publishing, or other forms of professional and public education.

References

Anderson, J. F. & Bingham, L. (1997, October). Upstream effects from mediation of workplace disputes: Some preliminary evidence from USPS. *Labor Law Journal.*

Bush, R. A. B. & Folger, J. P. (1994). *The promise of mediation.* San Francisco: Jossey-Bass Publishers.

Crum, T. F. (1987). *The magic of conflict: Turning a life of work into a work of art.* New York: Simon & Schuster.

Deutsch, M. (1973). *The resolution of conflict: Constructive and destructive processes.* New Haven: Yale University Press.

Ellis, D. & Stuckless, M. (1996). *Mediating and negotiating marital conflict.* San Francisco: Sage.

Erickson, S. K. (1988). Chapter 6. In J. Folberg & A. Milne (Eds.), *Divorce mediation: Theory and practice.* New York: Guilford Press.

Erickson, S. K. & Erickson, M. S. (1988). *Family mediation casebook: Theory and practice.* New York: Taylor & Francis.

Erickson, S. K. & McKnight, M. S. (1998). *Mediating divorce.* San Francisco: Jossey-Bass Publishers.

Etheridge, J. P. & Dooley, L. (1994). *Coming to the table: A guide to mediation in Georgia.* New York: American Lawyer Media, LP.

Folberg, J. & Milne, A. (Eds.). (1988). *Divorce mediation: Theory and practice.* New York: Guilford Press.

Lederach, J. P. (1995). *Preparing for peace: Conflict transformation across cultures.* Syracuse, NY: Syracuse University Press.

McGuire, T. J. (1999, September 12). Starting today, we embrace our competitor. *Minneapolis Star Tribune*, p. A27.

Slaikeu, K. A. & Hasson, R. H. (1998) *Controlling the costs of conflict: How to design a system for your organization*. San Francisco: Jossey-Bass.

Stockwell v. Stockwell, 775 Pacific 2nd 611 (Idaho 1989).

Ury, W. L., Brett, J. M. & Goldberg, S. B. (1988). *Getting disputes resolved: Designing systems to cut the costs of conflict*. San Francisco: Jossey-Bass.

US Postal Service (June 1998). *Mediating postal disputes*. Publication 102.

Wallerstein, J. S. & Kelly, J. B. (1980). *Surviving the breakup: How children and parents cope with divorce*. New York: Basic Books.

Resources

Ahrons, C. & Rodgers, R.H. (1987). *Divorced families*. New York: W. W. Norton.

Ahrons, C. (1994). *The good divorce*. New York: Harper Collins.

Auerbach, J. S. (1983). *Justice without law? Resolving disputes without lawyers*. New York: Oxford University Press.

Brown, E. M. (1999). *Affairs: A guide to working through the repercussions of infidelity*. San Francisco: Jossey-Bass.

Bolton, R. (1979). *People skills: How to assert yourself, listen to others and resolve conflicts*. New York: Simon & Schuster.

Bunker, B. B. & Rubin, J. Z. (1995). *Conflict, cooperation and justice: essays inspired by the work of Morton Deutsch*. San Francisco: Jossey-Bass.

Bush, R. A. B. (1989). Mediation and adjudication, dispute resolution and ideology: An imaginary conversation. *University of San Diego School of Law, 3*.

Cohen, A. R. (1964). *Attitude change and social influence*. New York: Basic Books.

Dunlop, J. T. & Zack, A. M. (1997). *Mediation and arbitration of employment disputes*. San Francisco: Jossey-Bass.

Emery, R. E. & Jackson, J. A. (1989). The Charlottesville mediation project: Mediated and litigated child custody disputes. *Mediation Quarterly*, Summer.

Erickson, S. K. & McKnight-Erickson, M. S. (1992). *The children's book: A guide to separate parenting*. West Concord, MN: CPI Publishing.

Erickson, S. K. (1984). A practicing mediator answers the questions most often asked about divorce mediation. *Mediation Quarterly, 3.*

Fisher, R. & Ury, W. (1981). *Getting to yes: Negotiating agreement without giving in.* New York: Penguin Books.

Folberg, J. (1984). *Joint custody and shared parenting.* The Bureau of National Affairs, Inc. and the Association of Family and Conciliation Courts.

Folberg, J. & Taylor, A. (1984). *Mediation: A comprehensive guide to resolving conflicts without litigation.* San Francisco: Jossey-Bass.

Garrity, C. B. & Baris, M. A. (1994). *Caught in the middle: Protecting the children of high-conflict divorce.* San Francisco: Jossey-Bass.

Gold, L. (1992). *Between love and hate: A guide to civilized divorce.* New York: Plenum Press.

Hasson, R. H. & Slaikeu, K. A. (1998) *Controlling the costs of conflict: How to design a system for your organization.* San Francisco: Jossey-Bass.

Heen, S., Patton, B. & Stone, D. (1999). *Difficult conversations: How to discuss what matters most.* San Francisco: Jossey-Bass.

Johnston, J. R. & Campbell, L. E. G. (1988). *Impasses of divorce.* New York: Free Press.

Kaslow, F. W. (1988). The psychological dimension of divorce mediation. In J. Folberg & A. Milne (Eds.) *Divorce mediation: Theory and practice.* New York: Guilford Press.

Kaslow, F. W. & Schwartz, L. L. (1987). *Dynamics of divorce: A life cycle perspective (Frontiers in couples and family therapy).* New York: Brunner/ Mazel.

Kaslow, F. W. & Schwartz, L. L. (1997). *Painful partings: Divorce and its aftermath.* New York: Wiley.

Kelly, J. B. (1989). Mediated and adversarial divorce: Respondents' perceptions of their processes and outcomes. *Mediation Quarterly,* Summer.

Kelly, J. B. (1990, December). Final report, mediated and adversarial divorce resolution processes: An analysis of post divorce outcomes. Prepared for the Fund for Research in Dispute Resolution.

Kressel, K. (1997). *The process of divorce: Helping couples negotiate themselves.* Northyale, NJ: Jason Aronson.

Kressel, K., Pruitt, D. G. & Associates. *Mediation research.* San Francisco: Jossey-Bass.

Miller, S. & Miller, P. A. (1997). *Core communication: Skills and processes.* Littleton, CO: Interpersonal Communication Programs.

Mnookin, R. H. & Maccoby, E. E. (1992). *Dividing the child: Social and legal dilemmas of custody.* Cambridge, MA: Harvard University Press.

Neuman, G. M. & Romanowski, P. (1998). *Helping your kids cope with divorce: The sandcastles way.* New York: Random House.

Neumann, D. (1996). *Choosing a divorce mediator.* New York: Henry Holt.

Olson, W. K. (1991). *The litigation explosion.* New York: Dutton.

Parsons, R. J. (1991). *The mediator role in social work practice.* Social Work 36(6). pp. 483-487.

Phillips, B. A. (1994). *Finding common ground: A field guide to mediation.* Halfway, OR: Hells Canyon Publishing.

Ricci, I. (1980). *Mom's house, Dad's house: Making shared custody work.* New York: Macmillan.

Rubin, J. Z. & Brown, B. R. (1975). *The social psychology of bargaining and negotiation.* New York: Academic Press.

Saposnek, Donald T. (1998). *Mediating child custody disputes* (rev. ed.). San Francisco: Jossey-Bass.

Slaikeu, K. A., Pearson, J. & Thoennes, N. (1988). Divorce mediation behaviors: A descriptive system and analysis. In J. Folberg & A. Milne (Eds.) *Divorce mediation: Theory and practice.* New York: Guilford Press.

Slater, A., Shaw, J. A. & Duquesnel, J. (1992, April). Client satisfaction survey: A consumer evaluation of mediation and investigative services. *Family and conciliation courts review.*

Stone, D., Patton, B., Heen, S. & Fisher, R. (1999). *Difficult conversations.* New York: Penguin Books.

Ury, W. (1991). *Getting past no: Negotiating with difficult people.* New York: Bantam Books.

Ury, W. (1999). *Getting to peace.* New York: Penguin Books.

Weiner-Davis, M. (1992). *Divorce busting.* New York: Summit Books.

Yankelovich, D. (1999). *The magic of dialogue: Transforming conflict into cooperation.* New York: Simon & Schuster.

Index

CPSIA information can be obtained at www.ICGtesting.com
Printed in the USA
LVOW040947170911

246676LV00002B/1/A